D0881164

AN ILLUSION OF
HARMONY

AN ILLUSION OF HARMONY

Science and Religion in
ISLAM

TANER EDIS

Prometheus Books

59 John Glenn Drive
Amherst, New York 14228-2197

Published 2007 by Prometheus Books

Inquiries should be addressed to
Prometheus Books
59 John Glenn Drive
Amherst, New York 14228–2197
VOICE: 716–691–0133, ext. 207
FAX: 716–564–2711
WWW.PROMETHEUSBOOKS.COM

11 10 09 08 07   5 4 3 2 1

Library of Congress Cataloging-in-Publication Data

Edis, Taner, 1967–
    An illusion of harmony : science and religion in Islam / by Taner Edis.
        p. cm.
    ISBN 978–1–59102–449–1 (alk. paper)
    1. Islam and science. 2. Islam and reason. I. Title.
    BP190.5.S3E35 2007
    297.2'65—dc22
                                                        2006032642

Printed in the United States of America on acid-free paper

CONTENTS

Chapter 6. A Liberal Faith?   201

Chapter 7. Science at Arm's Length   239

PREFACE

While working as a physicist, I have also long been interested in questions about religion, philosophy, and the nature of science. I have especially been fascinated with those beliefs at the fringes of science, such as creationism, UFOs, and psychic powers. My perspective on such matters has also been shaped by the fact that I grew up in Turkey, and have now spent about half my life in Turkey and half in the United States. Ever since the early 1990s, when I discovered a small book defending creationism back in Turkey, I have been observing the varieties of pseudoscientific ideas in the Islamic world, trying to make sense of them in terms of the many ways Muslims have responded to modern science. So it was perhaps inevitable that I should write a book on Islam and science.

Islam and science, however, is a very broad topic, and doing it justice required that I approach the subject from the perspectives of many disciplines. Hence I have taken as much advice as I could from a group of very helpful readers who previewed and commented on the text as it developed. I owe many thanks to Mustafa Akyol, Amy Sue Bix, Ömer Gökcümen, Mike Huben, Ahmet T. Karamustafa, Zaheer Alam Kidvai, Ergi Deniz Özsoy, Brad Smith, Barend Vlaardingerbroek, John Wilkins, and Mohamed Chams Eddine Zaougui. I would also like to thank Pervez Hoodbhoy for his encouragement, and Steven L. Mitchell, editor in chief of Prometheus Books, for his patience with me as I went half a year beyond my deadline.

I have tried to make the book accessible to readers with no extensive knowledge about Islam; I have especially tried to clarify those Turkish approaches to Islam that are my main focus. One useful bit of advice to that end was that I should include a glossary of Muslim religious terms. I have minimized my use of such terminology, but I provide a list here so readers do not have go back in search of where I first introduce a term.

> *Fitra*: Created nature, particularly referring to humans. It generally has a positive moral connotation.

> *Hadith*: A report of a saying by the prophet Muhammad or his Companions. This term is also used to describe a body of collected reports considered sound by Muslim scholars. These reports serve as a kind of secondary scripture. Orthodox Muslims believe a handful of hadith to contain the direct words of God, as the Quran is supposed to do, but most reports are anecdotes of early Islamic practices that are supposed to set down the ideal examples that the faithful should follow.

> *Ijtihad*: Independent legal reasoning based on the sacred sources (hadith or the Quran). It usually contrasts with *imitation*—legal reasoning that closely follows settled precedent.

> *Madrasa*: Classical Muslim educational institution, devoted especially to training religious scholars.

> *Nizam*: Order. Often used to refer to the divinely imposed order of the universe.

> *Sharia*: Islamic law. Used narrowly, sharia means a recognized body of legal rulings and religious practices. More broadly, it can stand for the whole legal and ritual framework of traditional Islam.

Shiite: The minority branch of Islam, claiming the allegiance of about 10 percent of Muslims worldwide. Shiites are the majority in Iran and Iraq.

Sufism: A term standing for a variety of mystical and ascetic currents within Islam. Although some forms of Sufism emphasize a mystical experience of divine love to the extent of downplaying the importance of the sharia, most Sufi orders are more orthodox.

Sunni: The majority branch of Islam, to which about 90 percent of Muslims belong. Orthodoxy (and orthopraxy) in Islam is largely defined by common Sunni practice. Though there are doctrinal differences between Shiite and Sunni Islam, few are relevant where science is concerned.

Tawhid: The doctrine of the unity and uniqueness of God. Tawhid is also often understood to imply the unity of nature under the sovereignty of God.

Ulama: The traditional class of religious scholars learned in Islamic law. The ulama are, in effect, the Muslim clergy. Their role, however, is not equivalent to a Christian priesthood—the role of the ulama is much more like that of rabbis in Orthodox Judaism.

Umma: The worldwide community of Muslims. Like "the Church" or "the body of Christ" in Christianity, its precise boundaries can be hazy. Nevertheless, it is a central concept in Islamic political thought.

The spellings of these terms vary widely in the literature; I have kept them as simple as possible.

Also, since I use many Turkish names, a brief guide to pronouncing the letters in the Turkish alphabet should be useful. Ö and ü are like the same letters in German; English does not have precise equivalents. The undotted *i*—ı—is like the *e* in *water*. C always sounds like a *j*. Ç is as the *ch* in *chip*. A ğ lengthens the preceding vowel. And ş sounds like the *sh* in *shower*.

All translations from Turkish are my own. I have tried to reproduce the originals as best as I can, including peculiarities in phrasing and grammatical errors in some cases.

CHAPTER 1

TO SEEK KNOWLEDGE IN CHINA

A RELIGION OF REASON

"Seek knowledge even if it is in China." This saying, attributed to the prophet Muhammad, is known to millions of Muslims all over the world. I first encountered it during my early schooling in 1970s Turkey; I remember a teacher citing it to encourage us to work hard at absorbing the content of our textbooks. My classmates and I were usually more interested in playing outside than in schoolwork, so we must have needed a reminder that "our religion" honored learning, especially in scientific and technological areas.

I, for one, was certainly fascinated by science. I did not care much about religion, though—as a child of a secularist Turkish father and a nonreligious American mother, religion was not a significant part of my life as I grew up. My interest in science was nourished by my numerous encyclopedias and children's science books, not by any sacred literature. We lived in a westernized area of the secular Republic of Turkey, and the public schools were not heavy-handed about Islam. It was understood that about 99 percent of Turkish citizens were Muslims, whether observant or not, but religion rarely intruded into classrooms. The echoes of Islam that we heard usually served the worldly purpose of trying to modernize Turkey. I constantly got the impression that Islam (or at least the Islam the authorities wanted) was supposed to be a rational religion, with no theological obscurantism. In particular, Islam supported science; many people even suggested that Islam was fundamentally a scientific religion. It enjoined believers to seek knowledge, even if it required a trip to China.

Few intelligent students believe everything they hear in school, and I was not entirely impressed with the claim that Islam was a religion of reason. Almost everyone around me believed in supernatural beings and events, but all that struck me as little different than fairy tales. The notion that any book, let alone the Quran, was infallible, miraculous, and sacred seemed strange. And I could never see much reason behind the idea of a God. Still, although it was obvious from early on that I was to remain an incorrigible skeptic, some of the constant insistence that Islam was a uniquely rational religion must have had an effect. I entered my college years convinced that Islam had lagged behind when compared to the political and scientific progress derived from the European Enlightenment. But even as I hoped Islam would progress to become just a cultural coloration fading into the background of a fully modern Turkey, I also thought it was somehow more reasonable than other religions. Didn't Islam at least make more sense than the outlandish fantasies that Christians had to accept? I did not know much about either Islam or Christianity—certainly little about the more sophisticated intellectual traditions they both harbored. But I thought that even if Islam was not scientific, then at least it was a more suitable precursor to the science-based Enlightenment rationalism I had come to identify with.

The jumble of impressions I had about Islam were not all consistent with one another. After all, looking at Turkey, it was easy to perceive poverty and backwardness all around. I grew up in an academic family, in middle-class surroundings, with some of the most thoroughly westernized areas of Istanbul as my neighborhoods. Outside of that small and unrepresentative sample, however, Turkey was simply backward. Our economy was weak and dependent on the industrialized West. Culturally, it seemed Turks did not produce much of note. We looked toward Western examples for ideas about how to do everything. Proper art, clothing, government, civilized behavior, technology—the West was home to all. Turks also had stereotypes of Western Europeans as emotionally cold, exploitative people, but we all knew they had made the modern world. And we wanted, desperately, to be modern.

While worrying about development and hoping that Turkey would once again gain respect in the world, it was hard not to notice that the more intense Muslim religiosity flourished in the poorer, more backward parts of Turkish society. On one hand, there were the orthodox followers of Islamic law, the sharia. Secularists such as I worried about their influence. Constantly caricatured in the secular press as bearded men in medieval dress followed by four veiled wives, the orthodox, we thought, threatened to drag us back to the Middle Ages and to impose their ossified understanding of religion on us all. Never mind developing scientifically, we would not even continue to enjoy basic freedoms if the fans of Islamic law were to have their way. On the other hand, much of popular religion, though much less rigid, was if anything even more superstitious. How, when so many people continued to pray for the intercession of saints or attempted to heal disease by making magic charms out of Quranic inscriptions, could the country catch up with a rapidly advancing Western world where everything depended on science and technology?

My early views about Islam and science were certainly naive, not much more than an intensified version of the conventional wisdom in Turkish secularist circles. In any event, I pursued science in my studies. I have ended up as a physicist who works in the United States, briefly visits Turkey every now and then, and indulges a fascination with questions about science and religion. And now, I find myself thinking more specifically about Islam again.

MUSLIM SCIENCE AS IDEAL AND REALITY

Pronouncements about Islam being a rational, scientific religion are not a peculiarity of 1970s Turkey. All countries with majority

Muslim populations face a similar challenge of catching up to the West. For centuries, it has been clear that the Europeans gained an advantage over the lands of Islam because they became able to develop increasingly powerful technologies. Industrial and military production, which appeared to be linked with powerful scientific capabilities, was the key. If Muslims were not to be colonized and relegated to a second-class civilization, they somehow had to appropriate science without losing their cultural identity. Many Muslims sought to help this process along by portraying Islam as a scientific religion. Even in the nineteenth century, the anticolonial thinker and activist Jamal al-Din al-Afghani insisted that "the Islamic religion is the closest of religions to science and knowledge, and there is no incompatibility between science and knowledge and the foundation of the Islamic faith."[1] More recently, Sayyid Abul A'la Maududi, a leading Islamist thinker who has been very influential in South Asia, said of the prophet Muhammad that

> it was he who, in place of baseless speculation, led human beings to the path of rational understanding and sound reasoning on the basis of observation, experiment, and research. It was he who clearly defined the limits and functions of sense-perception, reason, and intuition. It was he who brought about a *rapprochement* between the spiritual and the material values. It was he who harmonized Faith with Knowledge and Action. It was he who created the scientific spirit with the power of religion and who evolved true religiosity on the basis of the scientific spirit.[2]

Muslims in Western countries also present Islam as a uniquely rational religion with a powerful intellectual attraction. Jane I. Smith claims that "Anglo Americans choose to convert to Islam for a variety of reasons. Some find the intellectual appeal of a great civilization of scholarly, scientific, and cultural achievements a refreshing antidote to the often anti-intellectual and secularist climate of the contemporary West."[3]

Most devout Muslims worry about the relative poverty and lack of power of Muslim peoples. With the exception of some extreme traditionalists and mystics, almost all think that technological development is imperative in order to improve their lot. And so, whether liberal modernists or fundamentalists, Muslims assert that Islam and science not only coexist in complete harmony but that Islam and science mutually support each other. It is unfortunate that in the area of science, the West has leapt ahead of the community of Muslims, the *umma*. In fact, many say that Europeans only built upon the heritage of Muslim science at the peak of Islamic civilization, while Muslims fell away from the purity of their religion and allowed themselves to stagnate. Still, for now, it is clear that science and technology have to be imported. There is widespread agreement that technical knowledge is a singularly acceptable aspect of the modern West that can be transplanted without harming the integrity of Muslim culture. Indeed, not a few Muslims think that a more Islamic version of science can do even better than Western science. After all, although Western science does very well in investigating material reality, Islam gives a true picture of spiritual realities; therefore, it must achieve a more accurate representation of reality as a whole.[4]

In the popular literature, praise of the superior harmony between Islam and science can become quite extravagant. Maududi guarantees success to the Muslim scientist, since such a scientist begins with the knowledge that there is no god but the Muslim's God. "In every field of inquiry—may it be that of physics, chemistry, astronomy, geology, biology, zoology, economics, politics, sociology, or humanities, you will find that the deeper you probe, the clearer become the indications of the truth of *La ilaha illallah* [no god but God], in every field of knowledge and inquiry." Without this realization, "the universe becomes meaningless and the vistas of progress get blurred and confused."[5] Like many others, Maududi emphasizes the ethical aspect of the superiority of science done by Muslims:

> The man who knows God with all His attributes knows the beginning as well as the ultimate end of reality. He can never be led astray, for his first step is on the right path. . . . In philosophy he will ponder over the secrets of the universe, and will try to fathom the mysteries of nature, but, unlike an unbelieving philosopher, he will not lose his way in the maze of doubt and scepticism. . . . In science, he will endeavour to know the laws of nature, uncover the hidden treasures of earth and direct all the hitherto unknown forces of mind and matter—all for the betterment of humanity. . . . At every stage of his inquiry his God-consciousness will save him from making evil and destructive uses of science and scientific

method. He will never conceive himself claiming to be the con-
queror of nature, arrogating to himself the godly and sovereign
powers and nourishing the ambition of subverting the world, sub-
duing the human race and establishing his supremacy over all and
sundry by means fair and foul. Such an attitude of revolt and defi-
ance can never be entertained by a Muslim scientist—only a *Kafir*
[infidel] scientist can fall a prey to such illusions and by submit-
ting to them expose the entire human race to dangers of total
destruction and annihilation.[6]

Running into hyperbole in popular religious writings is hardly a
surprise. But similar themes of rationality, harmony, and moral
superiority surface in the writings of more sophisticated Muslim
thinkers as well. Fazlur Rahman, for example, is a leading modernist
who tries to persuade Muslims to interpret their religion anew in the
light of what he claims are the main themes of the Quran. One of
these themes is that the Quran sets a very high value on knowledge.
He interprets verse 20 Ta Ha 114, "Exalted is God, the true ruler. Do
not rush with the Recital before its revelation to you is concluded;
but say 'My Lord, increase me in knowledge'"[7] in the context of his
view that the more knowledge one has, the more one is capable of
faith. Other verses, such as 30 Ar-Rum 7, "They know the superficials
of the life of the world, but they are heedless of the hereafter" are
more naturally and traditionally interpreted to mean that it is *religious* rather than worldly knowledge that the Quran demands. Still,
Fazlur Rahman presents a possible interpretation available for Muslims who want to put more emphasis on science and reason.[8] He is
not the only respected scholar who argues in this fashion.

Part of the reason for such a common emphasis on the rationality and science-friendliness of Islam is, again, the almost universal
desire of Muslims to catch up with the modern world. Islam is not
the only belief system that gets pressed into serving this aim; secular
nationalism works much the same way. My early education included
a lot more sayings of Kemal Atatürk, founder of the Turkish
Republic, than words attributed to Muhammad. Many of these
praised the intellectual capabilities and glorious past of the Turkish
nation. We were taught in school that practically all the famous
Muslim philosophers of medieval times—described by a word that
could mean scientist as well as philosopher—were ethnically

Turkish. None of this was entirely true, but the authorities must have thought that an ideology of modernization had to include confidence-building myths.

All this talk about the inherent rationality and scientific orientation of Islam or of the nation, however, runs up against the obvious reality that Muslim countries lag far behind in this regard. To ordinary Muslims, this is clearest in their encounters with technology. Turkey, for example, used to import just about any product that was highly technological. Today, Turkey is a significant manufacturer of automobiles, appliances, and household electronics. But this is an artifact of multinational corporations seeking cheap labor. Turkish workers assemble the parts, but the engineers who design the finished product are based in Europe.

In terms of productivity in science and applied science, the Muslim world is in a pitiful condition, as confirmed by United Nations reports.[9] Muslims are quite aware of the problem. For example, prominent Egyptian Islamists urge their compatriots to do more of the critical work needed for development, observing that compared to Arabs, on a per capita basis, Israel has ten times the number of scientists, thirty times the money to spend on research and development, and seventy times the number of scientific publications.[10]

Almost all Muslim countries suffer from a brain drain, where students leave for Western countries to complete science and engineering doctorates, often not returning because the conditions for research and intellectual life are so much more favorable in the West. A large number of my college classmates from Turkey are now scattered around Europe, North America, and Australia. I have always had a foot both in the United States and in Turkey, but when it came to deciding where I might do better as a physicist, there was no contest. Working in a Turkish university would mean having to deal with no end of headaches American academics do not have to face. And so, not surprisingly, Turkish universities have very low scientific productivity. In the natural sciences, Turkish academics produce about one internationally available scientific paper per academic personnel every ten years; in social science the figure is much lower.[11] I do not often come across Turkish or Muslim names on papers I read; when I do, their institutional affiliation is almost always somewhere in the Western world.

So the Muslim world's contributions to science today are nearly negligible, despite the popularity of the belief that there is a pre-established harmony between science and Islam. Optimists might think Muslims are merely poised for a scientific resurgence, or would be if they could finally shake free of Western colonialist influences. But much Muslim thinking about science, though superficially supportive of science, provides no encouragement that any resurgence is on its way. Popular Muslim literature provides an amazing sampling of fringe-scientific and outright weird beliefs. The coexistence of enthusiastically protechnology attitudes and wildly pseudoscientific ideas is not unique to contemporary Islam; conservative Christian culture in the United States is very similar in this regard. Followers of alternative spiritualities in Western countries endorse a wide range of popular paranormal beliefs, from astrology to psychic healing. Nevertheless, the Muslim world can compete with the best in the West with its variety and popularity of scientifically rejected notions. Many of these have a specifically Islamic flavor.

Consider Fethullah Gülen, a prominent religious leader from Turkey. He was well known for backing relatively liberal Islamic schools in the Turkic republics of Central Asia, and in the 1990s he became very influential in Turkey as a cleric who was close to major political figures—the Billy Graham of Turkey. Internationally, he became known as a moderate promoting tolerance between different religions. More recently, he has had to live in exile in the United States, after accusations that members of his religious order were infiltrating the Turkish government and the fiercely secularist Turkish military. His writings include much of the standard talk about the rationality, modernity, and science-positiveness of Islam. Gülen, however, is also committed to the orthodox belief in invisible spirits known as jinn. Belief in jinn has an ancient pedigree in the Middle East, and it has spread to other Muslim regions, usually by adapting local beliefs about spirits. The Quran affirms the existence of jinn, speaks of them repeatedly, and gives them a significant place in the Quranic conception of the world. So, modernizing believers such as Gülen have to reconcile jinn with science. He says that

> although science does not yet accept the existence of invisible
> beings and restricts itself to the material world, we think it is worth

considering the possibility that evil spirits play some part in such mental illnesses as schizophrenia. We constantly hear of cases that those who suffer from mental illness, epilepsy, or even cancer recover by reciting certain prayers. Such cases are serious and significant, and should not be denied or dismissed by attributing them to suggestion or auto-suggestion. When science finally accepts the existence of the metaphysical realm and the influence of metaphysical forces, its practitioners will be able to remove many obstructions and to make far greater advances and fewer mistakes.[12]

Moreover, Islam can help us use jinn, apparently. Based on a number of Quranic verses (21 Al-Anbiya 82; 34 Saba 12, 13; 27 An-Naml 36–44) that refer to a story of how Solomon was helped by jinn in constructing the Temple and in instantly bringing the Queen of Sheba from Yemen to Jerusalem, Gülen says that "these verses suggest that a day will come when mankind are able to use them [jinn] in many jobs, especially in communication. It is quite probable that they will also be employed in security affairs; mining and metal work, and even in space studies and historical researches. Since Jinn can live about one thousand years, they may be useful in establishing historical facts."[13]

Amazingly, the "science" produced in some universities can be just as bad as that practiced by religious leaders. Physicist Pervez Hoodbhoy documents the sorry state of science and science education in the Muslim world, especially in his native Pakistan. A particular lowlight is a "Scientific Miracles Conference" at which science and engineering professors try to explain Muhammad's ascension to heaven through relativistic time dilation, make graphs plotting the quantity of divine reward versus the number of people in the praying congregation, or speculate that the origins of jinn are in methane gas and other saturated hydrocarbons.[14] These are not isolated incidents; the Muslim world appears to be well supplied with physicists who claim that they can calculate the speed of light based on Quranic verses and with engineers who do bizarre mathematical calculations to show that the Quran is a miracle. Today, most of these are easily available on the Internet. Critics such as Hoodbhoy can only react with disgust and suggest that the Muslim world is in dire need of genuine skeptical rationalism and real scientific thinking.

In such conditions, the widespread conviction of perfect harmony between Islam and science begins to look like an illusion. Perhaps harmony is an ideal, a hope for the future. But the reality today is so far removed that the ideal itself inspires skepticism.

A HOST OF QUESTIONS

Clearly, Muslim scientific performance and common Muslim attitudes concerning science do not match the widespread conviction that Islam is a perfectly rational, scientific religion. This raises a host of questions. Why, for example, did modern science arise not in the Muslim world but in Europe, if the fundamentals of Islam were always so scientific? Why, after more than a century of trying to catch up, do Muslim countries continue to lag in scientific and technological capabilities—indeed, why has modernization remained partial at best? Inescapably, questions concerning the role of religion follow. Have Muslim cultures stagnated because of deviations from the original spirit of revelation, or is there something about Islam itself that has to be overcome? How much are Western colonialism and global capitalism responsible for setting back Muslim development? What kind of institutional and social changes do Muslims need if they want to establish a thriving scientific community? Is the problem about science and Islam mainly a problem of poor countries not having the resources for a very expensive enterprise, rather than anything specifically about Islam? What, in the end, must be done?

The questions keep coming and threaten to become overwhelming. I will not address them all. Public intellectual life in Muslim countries, fairly dismal to begin with, is made worse by the conversation continually revolving around diagnoses of deep ills and plans for political fixes of some kind. So I will not prescribe solutions with any great degree of confidence. My roots are in Turkish secularism, which tried to impose a version of the European Enlightenment on a deeply pious peasant population. But I cannot claim any unqualified success for this approach. I do not see much that is promising among other alternatives, but I cannot say much more.

With some of the questions about Islam and science, I find myself at a loss. For example, what is the role of external influences such as colonialism and simple poverty in keeping science hobbled in Muslim lands? What about social factors, such as widespread corruption, which do not have an obvious connection to religion?

No doubt lack of resources is a large part of the story. Modern science is long past the stage where important discoveries can be made without expensive equipment and institutional support. Erdal İnönü, a Turkish physicist, examined the Turkish world rankings in scientific publications, and noted that while Turkey came in forty-fifth in per capita publications in 1999, it was forty-seventh in per capita income. At the same time, the United States enjoyed the world's highest per capita income but came in only fifteenth in the per capita scientific productivity rankings.[15] Clearly, poverty has a lot to do with the Muslim lag in science, although oil-rich Arab countries have not been able to translate their wealth into intellectual contributions.

Social and cultural factors are also important. For example, one reason most Turkish universities suffer from a lack of quality is that many of them are shells recently created for political purposes rather than established intellectual institutions. A new university in the provinces means government investment, students, and a revival of local trade, so voters love having a new university. Political parties oblige, not only creating schools that fail at higher education but also harming established universities in order to staff the ill-conceived new institutions.[16] Rampant corruption in the public sphere of all Muslim countries does not help either. Constant favoritism, political meddling, and diversion of public resources for private gain makes it difficult to sustain institutions devoted to proper scientific practice.

Sorting out the influence of such social factors is, unfortunately, extraordinarily difficult. After all, we must also ask how much religion contributes to social features that inhibit science. Devout Muslims are proud of the extent to which religion shapes their societies, expecting that God-consciousness should penetrate all aspects of life. Consider corruption. As anthropologist Lawrence Rosen notes, in the Middle East, corruption is conceived of as "the failure to share with those with whom one has forged ties of dependence any largesse that comes one's way. . . . corruption can be seen as interfering with 'the game,' as getting in the way of the formation of negotiated ties of interdependency by which society is held together."[17] This is quite different from corruption as understood in the context of the impersonal standards upheld by modern Western societies and institutions—much that looks like illegitimate favoritism is just what is expected in the Middle East. Rosen points out that complaints about corruption have increased with modernization, as modernization has led to the fraying of personal ties and the older relationship-based way of life. This comes as no surprise to anyone familiar with the history of modernization in Muslim lands. By today's standards, the administration of the Ottoman Empire was thoroughly corrupt, even at the peak of its power, and reformers in the disintegrating empire and the later Republic of Turkey tried hard to establish more impersonal, merit-based structures. But according to traditional norms, the Ottoman model does not look so exceptionally corrupt. A more personal, relationship-based approach is deeply ingrained in traditional Islamic society and Islamic law. Moving toward more impersonal public relationships often leads to an increase in the perception of corruption. So if social factors such as corruption contribute to inhibiting science, these factors are themselves hopelessly entangled with religion.

Questions concerning colonialism, whether in the age of European empires or today's neocolonialism, are similarly entangled with questions about religious culture. Certainly, colonial domination and rapaciousness do not help. But it is hard to say that Muslim countries have used the resources they have been able to command in order to encourage science. Oil-rich Arab states, for example, have established shiny new universities and imported faculty, only to find out that an intellectual tradition cannot be created overnight—their scientific capacity remains as unimpressive as their militaries equipped with very expensive hardware that they cannot properly use. And Saudi Arabia funds some of the worst Islamic-flavored pseudoscience in circulation. In any case, even many political Islamists who strongly oppose Western influence realize that underdevelopment is not just a colonial imposition. There is always the question of why once strong Muslim countries found themselves in an overwhelmingly weak position against Western empire builders. It is true that colonialism has much to answer for—an uncomfortable amount of Western wealth originates in various forms of plunder—but explaining Muslim problems as being due to colonialism is itself part of the irritating habit of putting Western actions at the center of everything.

So I will set such questions aside, touching on them at most indirectly. I will concentrate instead on a narrower set of questions concerning current Muslim thinking about science and religion. After all, the debate over the relationship between science and religion has always been interesting. In these times of global religious resurgence, the topic seems as important as ever. Discussions of science and religion that Western readers encounter, however, are most often framed in a Christian context. And in the Muslim world, serious literature on science and religion usually shares this Christian emphasis, often resulting in an argument that friction between science and religion is an artifact of the authoritarian church structure of medieval Christianity.[18] Therefore, many say, Islam need not suffer from any conflict with science—provided that some of the materialist philosophy grafted onto science in the secularized West is identified and removed. In reality, relations are not quite that smooth. Still, Islam is a religion that is similar to Christianity but also distinct enough in history and emphasis that comparing how the two have responded to the challenge of modern science can be very illuminating. Muslims have produced an extensive literature on science and religion that proposes various ways to accommodate science intellectually and institutionally. Most Muslim responses parallel intellectual options that Christians also have taken, but there are also significant differences. Exploring these should help us better understand the interaction between modern science and all the Abrahamic religions.

Muslim views about science include detailed reflections by influential thinkers. I will not, however, concentrate just on debates between intellectuals—weird but popular ideas, pseudoscientific apologetics, and simplistic conceptions of science promoted by modernizing religious movements are just as important. Religion is not an elite academic activity; religious creativity is never the province of intellectuals alone. Serious science will always be practiced within an elite, and ordinary citizens of advanced Western countries typically have no deep understanding of science. Nevertheless, local scientific communities are not isolated from their surrounding cultures, and popular attitudes about science and religion do affect the health of a scientific enterprise.

Critically examining current Muslim ideas about science and

religion will, I hope, also tell us a few things about the particular difficulties the Muslim world is facing with regard to science. After all,
where supernatural and metaphysical claims are concerned, science-
based challenges to Christianity and Islam are very similar. But
many forms of Christianity have gone much further in accommodating science. So, another interesting question is whether
responding to science in the manner of liberal Christianity is a
viable option for Muslims today.

WHICH ISLAM?

Before going further, I would like to make clear where I stand on
Islam, and what exactly I mean by Islam in the first place.

First, I am not a Muslim in any religious sense. I appreciate
Muslim culture and civilization, and since I grew up in Turkey, this is
inevitably part of who I am. But I am very skeptical that there is a God,
I do not believe Muhammad had any supernatural connections, and I
think of the Quran as an interesting ancient religious text. In fact, I am
a bit of a physics chauvinist—I think that according to the best of our
current knowledge, our world is an entirely natural, physical place that
does not depend on any supernatural powers. I have argued this else-
where,[19] and my concerns in this book are different. But my naturalism definitely colors how I look at science and Islam.

Perhaps the most obvious effect of my naturalistic perspective is
that I am quick to emphasize areas where modern science and traditional Islam come into conflict. Still, I will not tell a story where science, identified with perfect rationality, clashes with the blind faith
of Muslims. The relationship of Islam and science is considerably
more complicated. In any case, I am not satisfied with how many
writers approach possible interactions between science and religion.
Templeton Prize winner Ian Barbour, for example, discusses four
broad models of how science and religion can relate to one another:
conflict, independence, dialogue, and integration.[20] Skeptics are naturally inclined toward a conflict view, and devout Muslims mainly
prefer to seek integration. But Barbour's scheme oversimplifies. Neither science nor religion are just bodies of fact claims and methods
of seeking knowledge. Both are powerful social institutions as well.

From a naturalistic perspective, a theistic description of the world is fundamentally mistaken. If the naturalistic tendency of modern science is correct, we can expect science and almost all varieties of Islam to produce diverging views on questions involving supernatural beings, souls, or revealed knowledge. So I will emphasize such conflicts in order to highlight the serious differences between modern science and important Islamic beliefs—they are not superficial misunderstandings. But differing views do not determine how science and religion will relate to one another as social institutions. For science in the lands of Islam, a very important question is how to negotiate peaceful relations while the potential for intellectual disagreement is ever-present.

Second, Islam is too diverse to single out any view as *the* Islamic position. For Muslims, today especially is a time of religious creativity. Believers experiment with new ways to be faithful even while they present their innovations as a reaffirmation of essentials. Many thinkers, traditionalists and political Islamists in particular, like to speak for "true Islam." They do not, however, agree on what true Islam is, and I do not think there is any such thing. I will not try to define a set of essentials of Islam and work out their consequences for science—that would misrepresent the current state of Islam.

Some scholars who identify themselves as "anti-orientalist" dispute that Islam is a single coherent entity, portraying it as a grab-bag of "discourses."[21] I agree that *Islam* can be an impossibly broad term, serving as little more than a symbol for all that is good and proper as seen by someone identifying themselves as a Muslim. I have friends who believe they are good Muslims, though they disregard all of the traditional observances and know very little about the content of the sacred sources for orthodox Islam. Turkish popular Islam is, in general, diverse and inconsistent. For example, many Turks enjoy their alcohol, though this is strictly prohibited according to Islamic law. But these same people are almost always very careful not to eat any pork, which is also forbidden. Being Muslim means believing in a God, having a vague sense that the Quran is holy, and being a good person (since morality, most Muslims believe, is impossible without religion). What other content they give "Islam" varies. Nevertheless, I do not want to overstate this diversity, and I will certainly avoid the postmodern jargon and ideological preoccupations of too many anti-orientalists. Almost all believers, when asked to explain what their religion is about, fall back on talking about the Quran and hadith (tradition) collections. Moreover, however imperfectly, their views of what the sacred sources say echo traditional ideas. The widely affirmed form of orthodox Sunni Islam is a good first approximation—not an idealized "true Islam," but still a good starting point. Similarly, we can legitimately identify streams of Muslim thought labeled as fundamentalist or modernist. Diversity should not distract us from a certain overall stability and coherence in Islam, and particularly in Islamic literature.

So I need to strike a balance. I will not, in particular, portray Islam as if it were a set of doctrines proceeding from sources that are considered holy. Believers are liable to think this way; a major attraction of a religion like Islam is the notion that there are fixed points of moral and factual truth available through well-known sources of divine revelation. Many critics of Islam, however, also take the view that an essence of Islam is to be found in the sacred sources. Robert Spencer, for example, refers to 5 Al Maidah 64, "The Jews say the hand of God is bound. *Their* hands are bound, and they are accursed, by what they say . . . ," and interprets it as an objection to Jewish and Christian notions of a created universe that operates according to laws. Islam, apparently, does not accept a rational, orderly universe, and hence is antagonistic to science.[22]

Spencer is mistaken. 5 Al Maidah 64 has nothing to do with an orderly universe—it is about a dispute with Jews over taking action to prevent some very vaguely described immoral acts. Yes, medieval Muslim theologians and philosophers were very concerned to preserve God's complete freedom and omnipotence, to the extent of denying that causal patterns had any independent integrity aside from God's will. They looked for proof-texts in the sacred sources, including 5 Al Maidah 64, which they could interpret in a way that supported their views. And this emphasis might—it is hard to be certain—have contributed to religious distrust of an approach that treated nature as a more independent system. It is a gross misrepresentation, however, to suggest that one particular medieval interpretation is what naturally proceeds out of the Quran and inhibits scientific development. Especially today, other approaches are easily available to Muslims.

Indeed, *availability* is the key. Consider another example, the debate over what *jihad* means. In the Western world today, Islam is most often discussed in the context of terrorism, immigration, and the prospects for democracy. And Islam has a reputation as a religion of holy war, enjoining believers to be ready to fight and conquer the infidel. Critics of Islam point to the history of expansion by Muslim empires and the numerous verses of the Quran that urge believers to fight against and kill infidels.[23] Indeed, Muslim history is full of holy wars from its earliest days, and it is clear that the sacred sources are quite aggressive in promoting war against nonbelievers.[24] Muslim dynasties such as the Ottomans derived political legitimacy by pointing to their zeal in carrying out jihad against the infidel.

Nevertheless, war against infidels does not exhaust the possible meanings of jihad. Many jurists of classical Islam took jihad to be a means of establishing an Islamic state, the main purpose of which was the effective propagation of the faith. As Fazlur Rahman points out, in a contemporary version of such an interpretation, "What was spread by the sword was not the religion of Islam, but the *political domain* of Islam, so that Islam could work to produce the order on the earth that the Qur'an seeks."[25] Naturally, this is hardly a modern, liberal political doctrine. But some Muslims go further and observe that jihad's primary meaning is "struggle" and that in classical Islam, the greater jihad was considered to be a struggle to discipline one's self. Furthermore, they argue that jihad as holy war should be seen as primarily defensive, or that the doctrine of jihad is a version of just-war theory.[26] Many would add that today the aggressive form of jihad is inappropriate, as Muslims are free to peacefully propagate their faith.

In that case, what is the real meaning of jihad? We might seek a solution in history, looking for the earliest Muslim uses of the word. After all, the beginning of Muslim history, at the formation of the Islamic Empire, was a time of war and rapid expansion in which jihad was understood very aggressively indeed. Later, with the empire established and stable, and religious scholars consolidating their influence, it would hardly be surprising if the meaning of religious struggle shifted in emphasis to include less warlike pursuits. Yet even if it were clear that the original meaning of *jihad* was "war against the infidel," this would hardly be very relevant. After all, religion is never a pristine revelation that can only be transmitted properly or corrupted along the way. Islam was not created by Muhammad—it was also the work of jurists in the classical period; even today, Islam is continually a work in progress. Establishing an original meaning, even if possible, would not necessarily tell us what is available to Muslims today.

So, today both violent jihadis and peaceful Muslims lay claim to the true understanding of the duty of jihad. Both draw on legitimate strands of Muslim doctrine and tradition that are available to them; both reinterpret and remake their religion to adapt to their circumstances. The ulama (traditional Muslim scholars) try to give authoritative interpretations, but they commonly disagree and even resort to calling rivals un-Islamic. This is nothing new—it is part of the way Islam has always worked, even in periods of relative stability. There is no way to decide who is right, and no need to do so unless we accept the myth of a pristine revelation or essence of Islam that we must recover.

Concentrating on what is available to Muslims does not mean anything goes. Clearly, not every interpretation of Islam is equally compelling; availability is historically constrained. Traditional, orthodox Islam is still the Islamic center of gravity. But now we can ask more relevant questions about what is available today and what is not.

Consider, once again, the saying that one should seek knowledge even if it is in China. According to orthodox Muslim standards, this turns out to be a weakly attested hadith, one unsuitable to base rulings on. Indeed, it is easy to imagine a saying such as this gaining currency in the cities of the early Islamic Empire, when the religious scholars and hadith collectors were consolidating their influence. It is a saying that validates the authority of the scholars, since that authority is derived from their religious knowledge. So, in all likelihood, seeking knowledge in China is not a tradition that went back to the earliest times, and it had more to do with specifically religious knowledge than scientific pursuits.

Nevertheless, as it is understood today, the popularity of "seek knowledge in China" indicates some openness to science. Not every aspect of modern science is equally available to Muslims—most Muslims readily assimilate technology but resist Darwinian evolution. Modern science has become entirely independent of spiritual beliefs, describing the world in purely naturalistic terms, and this makes devout Muslims suspicious. As with jihad, we must ask what views of science are available to Muslims, what views seem strongest, and what common themes might exist in a diversity of interpretations. What we find is not a single Muslim position but a complicated landscape of interlocking and clashing views concerning science and reason. I hope to explore some of this landscape, and ask to what extent Muslims will seek knowledge, even if it disturbs their faith.

NOTES

1. Jamal al-Din Afghani, "Lecture on Teaching and Learning," quoted in Roxanne L. Euben, *Enemy in the Mirror: Islamic Fundamentalism and the Limits of Modern Rationalism* (Princeton, NJ: Princeton University Press, 1999), p. 196.

2. Sayyid Abul A'la Maududi, *Towards Understanding Islam*, trans. and ed. Khurshid Ahmad (Indianapolis, IN: Islamic Teaching Center, 1977), p. 53.

3. Jane I. Smith, *Islam in America* (New York: Columbia University Press, 1999), p. 65.

4. Mevlüt Uyanık, *Bilginin İslamileştirilmesi ve Çağdaş İslam Düşüncesi* (Ankara, Turkey: Ankara Okulu Yayınları, 2001), pp. 104–105.

5. Maududi, *Towards Understanding Islam*, p. 73.

6. Ibid., pp. 10–11.

7. For the Quran, I use the translation by Thomas Cleary, *The Qur'an: A New Translation* (Chicago: Starlatch Press, 2004).

8. Fazlur Rahman, *Islam and Modernity* (Chicago: University of Chicago Press, 1982).

9. UN Arab Human Development Reports, 2002 and 2003. Though these concentrate on Arab countries, their conclusions about science ring true for the Islamic world as a whole. See also the special feature on Islam and Science on the online version of *Nature*, November 2, 2006, at http://www.nature.com/news/islam (accessed December 2, 2006).

10. Fahmy Huwaidy, cited in Raymond William Baker, *Islam without Fear: Egypt and the New Islamists* (Cambridge, MA: Harvard University Press, 2003), p. 153.

11. Mete Kaynar and İsmet Parlak, *Her İle Bir Üniversite: Türkiye'de Yüksek Öğretim Sisteminin Çöküşü* (Ankara, Turkey: Paragraf Yayınevi, 2005).

12. M. Fethullah Gülen, *Essentials of the Islamic Faith* (Fairfax, VA: Fountain, 2000), pp. 86–87.

13. M. Fethullah Gülen, "Can We Employ E.T. (Jinns) in Different Jobs?" http://www.pearls.org/index.php/content/view/921/56/ (accessed December 2, 2006). Some versions I have found attribute this article to Said Nursi, founder of the movement of which Gülen leads a branch.

14. Pervez Hoodbhoy, *Islam and Science: Religious Orthodoxy and the Battle for Rationality* (London: Zed Books, 1991), pp. 142–47.

15. Erdal İnönü, *Üçyüz Yıllık Gecikme: Tarih, Kültür, Bilim ve Siyaset Üzerine Konuşmalar* (İstanbul, Turkey: Büke Yayınları, 2002), pp. 112–14.

16. Kaynar and Parlak, *Her İle Bir Üniversite.*

17. Lawrence Rosen, *The Culture of Islam: Changing Aspects of Contemporary Muslim Life* (Chicago: University of Chicago Press, 2002), p. 13.

18. Adil Şahin, *İslam ve Sosyoloji Açısından İlim ve Din Bütünlüğü* (İstanbul, Turkey: Bilge Yayıncılık, 2001), pp. 177–82. Mehmet S. Aydın, *İslâmın Evrenselliği* (İstanbul, Turkey: Ufuk Kitapları, 2000), p. 86.

19. Taner Edis, *The Ghost in the Universe: God in Light of Modern Science* (Amherst, NY: Prometheus Books, 2002); Taner Edis, *Science and Nonbelief* (Westport, CT: Greenwood Press, 2006).

20. Ian G. Barbour, *When Science Meets Religion: Enemies, Strangers, or Partners?* (New York: HarperSanFrancisco, 2000).

21. Bobby S. Sayyid, *A Fundamental Fear: Eurocentrism and the Emergence of Islamism* (London: Zed Books, 1997).

22. Robert Spencer, *Islam Unveiled: Disturbing Questions about the World's Fastest-Growing Faith* (San Francisco: Encounter, 2002), p. 126.

23. Ibn Warraq, *Why I Am Not a Muslim* (Amherst, NY: Prometheus Books, 1995), pp. 217–18.

24. Rudolph Peters, *Jihad in Classical and Modern Islam* (Princeton, NJ: Markus Wiener, 1996); Reuven Firestone, *Jihad: The Origin of Holy War in Islam* (New York: Oxford University Press, 1999).

25. Fazlur Rahman, *Major Themes of the Qur'an*, 2nd ed. (Minneapolis, MN: Bibliotheca Islamica, 1994), p. 63.

26. Reza Aslan, *No God but God: The Origins, Evolution, and Future of Islam* (New York: Random House, 2005), pp. 84–88. See also Ingmar Karlsson, *Din, Terör ve Hoşgörü* (İstanbul, Turkey: Homer Kitabevi, 2005), chap. 7.

CHAPTER 2

A USABLE PAST

THE GOLDEN AGE

In 1911 Mehmet Akif, the famous Turkish poet, published his first book. A devout Muslim, Mehmet Akif was deeply disturbed by the slow collapse of the Ottoman Empire and the inability of Muslims to compete with the European powers. He could not help but exclaim:

> O God, who has been disciplining us for so long
> O God, who oppresses the world of Islam, makes it cry out
> We who have believed in your divine promise
> We who have called on you for more than a thousand three
>   hundred years
> We who when humanity was worshiping many gods
> Overthrew that great blasphemy, ended it forever
> We who in one move ended baseless fears
> Who brought the True God to the temples

We who made the world know your name
If we have seen your reward, O Lord, it is now enough
What pain, what suffering have you not made us endure
Every moment of life is a day of punishment for us[1]

If Muslims today lag in science and technology, and suffer economically and militarily because of this, an immediate question is
how Muslims fell so far behind in the first place. The question is particularly important to Muslims who, like Mehmet Akif, feel pride in
the past glories of their civilization and are painfully aware of how
once things were different. Just a few centuries ago, Western Europeans were outlying barbarians whom Muslims did not even consider
culturally interesting. After all, Muslim lands were richer, Muslim
cities more populous, Muslim libraries extensive beyond anything
European scholars could dream of. Muslim armies kept conquering
new lands, making the True Faith available to the populations that
came under their protection. For many centuries, the lands of Islam
enjoyed a more advanced civilization, and, for all their fear of Muslim
expansion, many a Western Christian traveler had to agree.

Muslims had a particular advantage in matters of knowledge and
scholarship. Christianity had taken over the Roman Empire, but as
the empire disintegrated, Western Christendom's institutional structure for education and scholarship had also collapsed outside of the
monasteries. Western Europe lost most of its knowledge of the philosophy and science of pagan antiquity. Islam, in contrast, made
better use of pagan intellectual resources when it formed its own
empire. Muslim elites appropriated knowledge from different
sources, from Greek philosophy to Indian mathematics. Muslims
preserved and extended the science of antiquity. And so when
Western Europeans sought to recover what they had lost, some of
their first sources were Arabic translations and commentaries on
Greek philosophy, medicine, and science.

Many Muslims today think something must have gone wrong,
something that made Islam lose its intellectual edge. The favorite
explanation for stagnation seems to be that Muslims allowed themselves to forget the progressive, rational side of the earlier, more vigorous faith of their forebears. For example, medieval Muslim jurists
declared that "the gates of *ijtihad* were closed"—that community

consensus on interpreting the sacred sources had been established and individual reasoning could no longer reopen settled questions. Henceforth, close adherence to precedent, together with the mystical piety of Sufi orders, would characterize Islam. If this is the case, the first step toward advancing in science again must be to readmit that reason has a role in Islam.

Some liberally inclined Muslim intellectuals go even further. Looking back at the Muslim past, they notice the Mutazila, members of an early theological school that drew on the Greek philosophical tradition and put rationality at the center of their view of religion. Fatima Mernissi, for example, laments that what she describes as the open, rational, humanist spirit of Mutazilite Islam lost out to ancient equivalents of political fundamentalists. Indeed, she says the Mutazila were scientists:

> The Mu'tazila intellectuals were not only philosophers, mathe-maticians, engineers, doctors, and astronomers; they were also Sufis, who found in religious texts everything they needed to bol-ster the idea of the thinking, responsible individual. It must be remembered that in the beginning scientific investigation was nec-essarily linked to the flowering of mystical reflection, in that the best homage one could render to God was the good use of one's mind. The tension in the early modern period between the Church and scientific investigators, so well represented by Galileo's fate, does not exist in Islam in normal times.[2]

According to Mernissi, when the Mutazila and their intellectual descendants lost influence, Muslim science suffered as well.

Others, including many who are more skeptical about the claim that there is no tension between science and religion in Islam, also consider the Mutazila an example of rationalism indigenous to Islam. It seems that from about the ninth to the twelfth century, Islam enjoyed an intellectual golden age, a flowering of science and rationalist philosophy. But after the Mutazila lost influence and as philosophy came under suspicion, orthodox and mystical religiosity alike stifled reason in the lands of Islam.

Al-Ghazali, one of the greatest Muslim theologians of all time, figures prominently in this version of the story. An accomplished tra-ditional scholar, he suffered a personal crisis in 1095 that he eventu-

ally resolved by taking a mystical Sufi path while remaining uncom-
promisingly orthodox. He then wrote books aiming to renew the
vigor of the Muslim religious sciences and penned a famous attack
on the Greek philosophical tradition. Many defenders of reason in
Islam argue that after al-Ghazali rejuvenated Sunni orthodoxy,
Muslim intellectual life became more rigid. The mainstream ulama
had always been cool toward the "foreign sciences" such as philosophy and mathematics, and al-Ghazali's condemnation of them carried the day. In an increasingly theocratic environment, independent
reasoning became more difficult, leading to intellectual stagnation.[3]
When European science began to take off, education and intellectual
life in Muslim lands were completely dominated by orthodox
scholars and Sufi saints, neither of whom encouraged attention to
knowledge that did not have any explicit religious purpose.

According to this story of a golden age, the Mutazila and the
philosophers represented Muslim rationality, which was then submerged in an era of overbearing orthodoxy. The actual history is
more complicated. Nevertheless, the idea of a golden age has much
appeal. It tells today's Muslims that they are heirs to a great civilization that encouraged intellectual development. And this greatness
had an authentically Muslim source: the devout use of reason that
opened the world up to Muslim philosophers and scientists, producing the basic ideas that Europeans would later borrow and use to
such devastating effect. The moral of the story is that today's Muslims should reclaim their heritage; reason and science are not, after
all, alien notions that must be imported from the West.

So the story of a golden age strongly affects how Muslims view
science. For Muslim modernists and even secularists, it suggests a
way forward inspired by a usable past. Fundamentalists are less
enthusiastic, since their ideal past is their vision of the time of the
Prophet and his Companions. Still, even fundamentalists have to
react to the idea of a golden age of reason, if only by presenting an
alternative heritage and a different view of rationality. In that case, it
is worth looking more closely at Muslim history to see how Muslim
concepts of science and rationality have changed. A picture of a glorious past can spur redoubled efforts to catch up with the modern
world. But it can also obscure what is new and different about
modern science.

REASON AND SCIENCE IN CLASSICAL ISLAM

The earliest phase of Islam, when Arabs were first conquering the territories of their empire, did not produce many profound reflections on science. Nevertheless, the new religion did emphasize a particular view of knowledge. As with early Christianity, Islam found its first support among people who were strongly attracted to the egalitarian ideal promised by a revealed Abrahamic faith. In both cases, a commitment to justice and suspicion of elites led to a conception of knowledge that limited the scope of rational criticism. Instead of being subjected to human authorities, believers of all social backgrounds would submit to the One God; as a modern Islamist slogan goes, being slaves of God is the one way to avoid being slaves to men. Conservative Muslims demand obedience, but this is obedience to a revealed, morally egalitarian authority.

Modern intellectuals are rarely enthusiastic about claims of transcendent authority. Priests and other official interpreters of revelation can easily become oppressive authorities; reason, being available to all, could lead to a more egalitarian politics. Fatima Mernissi, for example, argues that "by introducing reason into the political theater, the Mu'tazila forced Islam to imagine new relationships between ruler and ruled, giving all the faithful an active part to play alongside the palace."[4] In practice, however, relying on reason can just as easily have elitist consequences. Reason, after all, is *not* available to all equally. Critical thought is a difficult skill, needing much training and background knowledge, and scientific reasoning especially is not a simple extension of common sense. So it is no accident that popular religion has almost always included a suspicion of intellectual elites; in Islam, scholars who emphasized personal piety and revealed truth have always had a strong popular constituency.

So, popular Islamic conceptions of knowledge developed along egalitarian lines. The religious leadership of the community fell to the ulama, the class of scholars and teachers who specialized in collecting and transmitting reports about the Prophet and his Companions. They would interpret these hadith and apply them to immediate practical problems of the community of believers. The ulama were not a remote elite: their status derived from religious merit recognized by each other and by the community at large. And so the concept of knowledge in Islam was shaped on the model of transmitting hadith. Muslims were not entirely uncritical about the hadith; traditions could be misreported. What was reliable, however, was determined by the degree of personal trust one could put in the transmitters. Knowledge took on a narrative, personal quality—"What is real is what has happened, and this we know from the mouths of our pious forefathers."[5] Truth was not to be tested according to abstract, impersonal criteria. Indeed, the whole system of education in Muslim societies would come to share this personal quality, as the main way to recognize reliability and competence was to ask whether the testimony of devout, morally upright persons could back up knowledge claims.[6]

A personal, narrative view of knowledge is much more accessible to nonelites, relying not on abstract, impersonal reasoning but on judgments of character and trust that are much closer to the skills of everyday life. And so it became a solidly entrenched part of the Islamic worldview, among the public as well as its religious leaders. Other aspects of a revelation-centered, egalitarian view also served to downplay critical reasoning. For example, devout Muslims even today typically associate doubt with an immobilizing uncertainty, even unbelief, while they require true knowledge to be certain, free of doubt.[7] The Quran, in 10 Yunus 36, says that "conjecture is of no avail against truth," and Muslim civilization developed to locate certain truth in the testimony of pious persons.

None of this is unique to Islam. In Christendom as well, philosophy and science have been elite activities that regularly generate religious distrust. Many a Protestant fundamentalist today will still insist that modern science is not trustworthy about the age of the earth. Since no one witnessed what supposedly happened geological ages ago, secular science produces mere conjecture, not to be compared to the divine testimony in the Bible.[8] In the lands of Islam, however, a more expansive view of reason never overcame the impediment of popular mistrust.

Still, popular opinion is not all-powerful. After their initial conquests, Muslim Arabs found themselves a small religious minority in charge of a large empire. To administer the empire, they drew on the imperial expertise they found in the Byzantine and Persian lands they had overrun. Together with non-Muslim administrative and legal traditions, Muslim rulers also drew on other practical knowledge that the subject peoples had to offer. Additionally, Muslims with intellectual inclinations found themselves surrounded by representatives of sophisticated religious rivals. Syrian Christian thinkers, for example, had absorbed much from the philosophy of antiquity into their theologies. They responded to the claims of Islam by philosophical criticism, while also observing that the Quran seemed a disorganized, hardly coherent work. Muslims drew confidence from the divine favor shown their religion by the enormous success of their conquests, but they also had to enter theological debates with their counterparts in rival monotheistic religions.

Both the demands of empire and the close interaction with non-Islamic thinkers led some Muslims to affirm and reimpose elite forms of knowledge. Immediately after the Arab conquests, communities such as the Nestorian Christians became involved in translating a multitude of ancient texts into Arabic, particularly anything that promised practical value such as medicine or astrology. The urban centers continued to maintain much of the high culture of antiquity; Muslim rulers supported an intellectual elite that included Christian, Jewish, and other thinkers together with Muslim scholars.

The Mutazila emerged from among this elite, and they imposed the concerns of Greek rationalism upon Islam. Reason was, in fact, fundamental for the Mutazila, as expressed by Abd al-Jabbar:

> **1. If it is asked:** What is the first duty that God imposes upon you? *Say to him*: Speculative reasoning which leads to knowledge of God, because he is not known intuitively nor by the senses. Thus, He must be known by reflection and speculation. . . .

> **3. Then if it is asked:** Why did speculative reasoning become the first of the duties? *Say to him*: Because the rest of the stipulates of revelation concerning what [we should] say and do are no good until after there is knowledge of God.[9]

Naturally, this approach conflicted with pure faith in the Quran or mystical illumination as the first source of divine knowledge. The Greek philosophical tradition also demanded certainty, but this was found in pure rational demonstrations, as in mathematics. Combining Muslim and Greek approaches, the Mutazila naturally made speculative reasoning fundamental to the faith. The popular religious leaders disagreed.

The Mutazila took both the Muslim insistence on the unity and uniqueness of God and Greek philosophical monotheism very seriously, which also brought them into conflict with popular beliefs. For example, they were disturbed by Quranic anthropomorphisms such as references to God's hands or eyes, and they declared that this must be figurative language. After all, actual hands or eyes would make God too similar to his creatures. Most ulama preferred to read the text literally, even if no one could understand exactly what the anthropomorphisms were all about. The Mutazila argued against the miracles attributed to Sufi saints and other important religious leaders, restricting the ability to perform miracles to a select few prophets such as Moses, Jesus, and Muhammad. In contrast, popular religion was full of miracles. The Mutazila insisted that God must be just, and that humans must be fully responsible for their own actions if they are to merit eternal punishment in hell. Most orthodox theologians emphasized divine omnipotence instead, making God the only true cause of everything. And most notoriously, the Mutazila insisted that the Quran had been created by God, while the ulama and their allies said that the Quran was uncreated and eternal.

Debates over such matters as whether the Quran was created or eternal may seem obscure and strange today, much like fourth-century Christian controversies over whether God and Christ were of a similar substance or of the same substance. But in both the Christian and Muslim cases, theological minutiae were linked to serious political divides. Although there was consensus on many questions, such as the Quran being the direct word of God, it was not clear who would get to interpret Islam for the community. The traditionalist ulama were one possibility; they were disorganized but enjoyed popular support. The Mutazila found favor from the caliph, the commander of the faithful, and looked for support among imperial elites.

Indeed, Mutazila doctrines such as the created Quran received official endorsement, to the extent that one of the best-remembered inquisitions in Muslim history, from 835 to 848, was set up to coerce scholars to affirm Mutazila doctrines.[10] The Mutazila exercise of reason was far from being liberal and tolerant. Indeed, Mutazilism had a strong streak of arrogant elitism: some Mutazila went so far as to declare that the Muslim masses were actually unbelievers since they could not appreciate the true path to God through demonstrative reasoning. The common people, many thought, should not even be allowed to discuss theological matters.

Traditionalist scholars resisted the imperial impositions and won all the more respect from ordinary believers for demonstrating superior moral character. Some historians see the inquisition as a final attempt to impose caliphal authority over religion;[11] whatever the political struggles the inquisition expressed, it is clear that the traditionalist, populist party emerged victorious. Among conservative Muslims, the Mutazila experience is still remembered as a cautionary tale of the dangers of letting reason precede faith in the sacred sources.

Even as Mutazilism declined, however, interest in elite thinking did not vanish. Instead, philosophy and science became better integrated into the developing classical Muslim conception of knowledge. At its peak, this was a very attractive view, promising to unite all knowledge under a single conceptual scheme centered on God. The centerpiece of the classical view was revelation, and the personalistic view of knowledge popular among the ulama and ordinary Muslims came together with the metaphysical speculation beloved by intellectuals. As Seyyed Hossein Nasr describes it,

> The Muslim intellectual saw revelation as the primary source of knowledge, not only as the means to learn the laws of morality concerned with the active life. He was also aware of the possibility of man purifying himself until the 'eye of the heart' ('ayn al-qalb), residing at the centre of his being, would open and enable him to gain direct vision of the supernal realities. Finally, he accepted the power of reason to know, but this reason was always attached to and derived sustenance from revelation on the one hand, and intellectual intuition [in a Platonic, mystical sense] on the other. The few in the Islamic world who would cut this cord of reliance and declare the independence of reason from both revelation and intuition were never accepted into the mainstream of Islamic thought.[12]

Revealed truth came first. As with the scientists of antiquity whose work they continued, medieval Muslims loved to make lists. And they classified knowledge as well, giving the greatest prestige to the "religious sciences" such as Quranic interpretation, hadith collection and criticism, jurisprudence, theology, Arabic grammar, the interpretation of dreams, and so forth. All knowledge was unified—all of this was "science"—but mathematics, medicine, physics, astrology, logic, and the likes were considered "foreign sciences." Alternatively, they were called "rational sciences" as opposed to "transmitted sciences." Eventually the ulama were trained in madrasas supported by the state and by charitable foundations, and their education emphasized the politically important areas of Islamic law and religious knowledge. Practical sciences such as medicine also found steady support. Instruction in philosophy, however, was a more individual affair, transmitted from scholars who took a personal interest to those pupils who were intellectually attracted to philosophy. Muslim philosophers typically made a living as religious scholars; their interest in the foreign sciences was an extension of their revelation-centered outlook.

This classical framework of knowledge deeply affected how Muslims thought of nature. It would be misleading to say that religious concerns shaped all aspects of intellectual life in Muslim lands or that Muslims were impeded in their curiosity. Nevertheless, ambitious thinkers interested in an overall picture of nature kept coming back to the classical, God-centered framework. Ultimately, understanding nature required grasping the relationship between the created and the creator. The most true, the most useful knowledge was knowledge of God and God's purposes in nature, which would help direct Muslims in the right path.[13] Even the foreign sciences were not merely useful—at their best, they also could serve religion. The Greek medical tradition and the writings of Galen, for example, provided support for the argument from design that showed the existence of God. The parts of the human body worked together in unison for the benefit of the whole, which obviously meant that there had to be a beneficent designer who determined this harmonious order.[14]

Moreover, the foreign sciences regularly raised suspicions among the ulama. After all, the foreign sciences had preceded the Islamic revelation and it was not always clear how they should fit into a revelation-centered framework. Al-Ghazali's attack on philosophy attracts the most attention, as it had long-lasting effects and is a philosophically informed, sophisticated critique in its own right.

Still, orthodox worries about non-Islamic knowledge did not originate with al-Ghazali and they continued long after. Many ulama declared philosophy to be religiously prohibited. Mostly, they picked and chose from among the foreign sciences according to whether they served Islamic purposes. Even as late as around 1700, mainstream thinkers such as Muhammad ibn Abi Bakr al-Marashi followed al-Ghazali in affirming the importance of logic, saying, "The fact that logic is related to philosophy does not necessitate its condemnation, as not all branches of philosophy are prohibited. The prohibited parts of philosophy are just those that concern physics and metaphysics; [mathematical] calculation, though it is also part of philosophy, is not prohibited."[15]

One reason Muslim views of philosophy and its attendant sciences became cooler is that the political circumstances, and indeed the nature of religious scholarship itself, changed over time. The classical Islamic view of knowledge came to include what could be easily absorbed and made useful from the heritage of antiquity— there was little controversy over the obviously practical sciences; the disputes were mainly over speculative philosophy. By the time the institutions of the Sunni ulama such as the madrasa crystallized into their long-established forms, starting in twelfth-century Iran,[16] Islam was no longer an empire learning from its predecessors but a politically fragmented community. Muslims were not a minority anymore; the majority of the populations in the conquered lands had converted. And the ulama were not just guardians of religious knowledge and popular morality but leaders who had to keep the community together in times of severe political instability. The scholars' mutual recognition of religious knowledge became not just the basis for conservative religious authority but a significant source of social order. In such a context, while the religious sciences remained vital, the foreign sciences were more secondary.

None of this, however, means that classical Islam stood against reason. It is more accurate to say that Muslim thinkers took the Greek philosophical concept of reason they inherited and remade it into a form more suited for a revelation-based civilization. The classical Islamic view of knowledge was quite robust. It allowed for considerable intellectual activity, including speculative metaphysics, as long as revelation retained its central position. Indeed, orthodox

Muslim thinkers could be very enthusiastic about reason, provided reason was exercised within its proper limits. Even the most fundamentalist thinkers did not demand blind obedience to the ulama; they acknowledged that the faithful must use reason to understand and apply the sacred sources.

Indeed, while orthodox Muslims may have rejected much of Greek philosophy, they affirmed and made extensive use of reason in developing their theology. The Asharite school, which has had a strong and continuing influence on mainstream Muslim thought, including that of al-Ghazali, suggested that reason was a critical component of acknowledging the truth of Islam:

> Al-Ash'ari suggested that people are led gradually to recognize the authority of the teaching of Islam. There is a rational order of the progress of faith which starts with the acknowledgement of the contingency of the world and its creatures, moves to the impotence of the world with respect to God, the true prophethood of Muhammad and the consequent veracity of his message. In this model the veracity of the Prophet and the validity of his claims and authority are established by signs and miracles which *follow* the conclusive arguments and demonstrations of the first two stages.[17]

Such a process still seems reasonable to modern Muslims, certainly more so than defining rationality through the tradition of Greek philosophy. Miracles, for example, would be perfectly legitimate as evidence for a supernatural reality. Among the Mutazila and other followers of the Greek tradition, many were tempted to deny miracles and to argue that reason was sufficient in matters of morality. The conclusion that revelation was therefore optional became hard to avoid. Such a position naturally invites religious opposition. Moreover, in modern terms, it is hard to see this conflict as greatly significant. The orthodox declared certainty in revelation, while the philosophers sought certainty in a particular style of armchair reasoning—neither approach was that close to a modern scientific skepticism that thrives on tentative conclusions.

While philosophy remained under suspicion of impiety, many of its attendant sciences flourished long after the peak of Muslim philosophy. Muslim rulers supported astronomers in order to obtain the best astrological advice. The utility of medicine was hard to deny. Around the eleventh to the thirteenth centuries, Muslim scientists such as al-Tusi, Ibn Al-Haytham, and Ibn Al-Nafis were doing their best work in fields such as astronomy, medicine, pharmacology, mathematics, optics, and more. In a way, the conflict with philosophy set Muslim science free; as long as science was integrated into the classical Islamic view of knowledge and served distinctly Islamic purposes, its value was recognized.

The relative decline of Muslim science set in around the fifteenth century and later, when the Mutazila were a distant memory and long after al-Ghazali's views triumphed over the philosophers.[18] Even calling it a decline is largely a matter of hindsight and comparison with the explosive growth in modern European science. Many historians have thought that among later Muslims, the level of innovation and interest in science dropped, and scholarship became largely devoted to transmitting established knowledge.[19] But even if so, this is an indication of stability: a sign of the social success of the classical Muslim view of knowledge. Within the religious sciences, legal scholars continued to compare different cases, make analogies, and extend rulings to new and even hypothetical cases. Those of the foreign sciences that were integrated into classical Islam worked well for Muslim purposes, and without the possibility of a radically new way of looking at nature, soon tinkering around the edges was all that was socially necessary. Islam was intellectually confident and culturally self-sufficient; until recently, it faced the challenges of political and economic instability rather than external threats.

Culturally, the classical Islamic view of knowledge and reason worked very well. It was this very success that would make the later encounter with modern conceptions of knowledge so traumatic.

MEDIEVAL SCIENCE

The Muslim mainstream downplayed philosophy and domesticated reason. Even so, there has never been a single form of Islam accepted by all. Even Mutazila ideas never wholly disappeared. The Shiite branch of Islam has given individual reasoning a higher profile in religious matters; developed Shii theology is in many respects a revived Mutazilism.[20] Shiite Iran is still one of the most intellectually interesting parts of the Muslim world. This has not, however, led to a level of critical thinking about religion and science that is comparable to what has become routine in Western academic circles. Rationalist influences do not necessarily mean much; in Shiite Islam rationalism has not amounted to more than a refusal to be bound by a Sunni-style scholarly consensus when referring to the sacred sources. When liberal Muslims praise the Mutazila, they engage in mythmaking, trying to claim a past usable for today's purposes. But if the Shiite example is anything to go by, a Mutazila revival would do little to advance science in Muslim lands. The myth of the Mutazila works only so far as it remains vague and historically inaccurate.

An alternative is to re-embrace the classical Islamic view of knowledge, including reason as the servant of revelation. Seyyed Hossein Nasr, for example, argues that the mistakes of both secularism and the sterile puritanism of much modern fundamentalism is due to a departure from this rich intellectual heritage. He proposes to once again subordinate science to a medieval Muslim metaphysics. No doubt this would be religiously and culturally very appealing—not a few Muslims look back with longing to the days when Muslim intellectuals were confident that the classical Islamic view was correct. Unfortunately, the classical view was just what remained static while Europe underwent the scientific revolution. A serious, historically informed restoration of the classical Islamic view of knowledge, placing revelation and the religious sciences at the center of intellectual life, would be disastrous for science in Muslim lands. As with nostalgia about the Mutazila, exaltation of the classical view can only work as a nonspecific myth that supports modern agendas.

Myths concerning the golden age of philosophy, the Mutazila, or the medieval Muslim picture of reality do more than oversimplify history. These myths generate diagnoses and prescriptions for what ails Muslims; they are at least partly intended to suggest courses of action for those who, like the poet Mehmet Akif, feel that modern Muslim history is one of constant humiliation. They look for aspects of the glorious past that can be used to revive Muslim science and technology. And the main problem with such myths is that they obscure the radical differences between modern and medieval science. Medieval Muslims may have enjoyed the most advanced knowledge about nature in their time, but they did *not* do science in the modern sense.

The most noticeable difference is, naturally, how religion pervades the medieval Muslim conception of reality. This was not just a matter of giving religious knowledge higher prestige; other areas of knowledge were never independent of religion to begin with. Concepts like God, divine purpose, design, and morality were integral to the whole enterprise of acquiring and interpreting knowledge, whether it was in medicine or astronomy.

A good way to appreciate how thoroughly religion was entangled with all knowledge is to look at some of the more controversial ideas in classical Muslim intellectual life. After all, these mark out what some Muslim thinkers thought could be done differently. Consider, first, the mystical metaphysics concerning the "unity of Being," promoted by Sufis such as Ibn al-Arabi. This came dangerously close to pantheism for orthodox tastes. Indeed, Sufi-style metaphysics has always been controversial in Muslim theology, considered by some to be the most profound insights into the nature of God and his creation, and dire heresy by others. Muslim discussions of such issues had, however, little direct connection with natural science—nothing in the debate turned on issues involving physical reality. If anything, the controversy illustrates how physical reality was of little significance compared to the really important spiritual matters.

Another example is the status of occult sciences such as astrology and alchemy among the foreign sciences inherited by Muslims. These were legitimate parts of Muslim science, though astrology occasionally attracted theological objections beyond general condemnation of the foreign sciences. These objections, however, were part of the discomfort that a few orthodox ulama had with predicting the future and thereby presuming to know what is to be determined by the unconstrained divine will.[21] In practice, astrology flourished—it was considered to be useful. Whether done by court astrologers, religious scholars, or local diviners who gave advice on when best to set sail, astrology remained part of Muslim life. Muslim astronomers, like their medieval Christian counterparts, routinely engaged in astrology.

Again, as with Sufi metaphysics, astrology is not important as an example of mainstream belief but as a marker for the limits of

Muslim imagination. A conventionally orthodox scholar might have been horrified by the language some Sufis used about God, and he may have doubted the Islamic credentials of astrology, but these ideas were not alien. They could fit comfortably into a picture of reality conceived of in top-down, God-centered terms. The mystical illuminations of Sufi metaphysicians could deepen the classical Muslim view of knowledge, especially if domesticated so as to acknowledge the importance of Islamic law. If reality was fundamentally a spiritual and moral order, the occult conception of a living, intelligence-pervaded universe could make good sense. The appropriate way of investigating reality could well be to purify oneself and enter into an appropriate relationship with the living universe—as astrologers and alchemists claimed to do. Such alternatives were viable options within the classical Muslim view of knowledge and reality, though their influence on the mainstream varied.

For science, the significance of such spirit-centered conceptions of reality was largely in what methods of investigation seemed plausible. It is a modern myth that there is a "scientific method"—something involving hypothesis testing through controlled experiments—that is a universally applicable way of getting reliable knowledge. The best ways of obtaining knowledge depend on what sort of reality we inhabit. If we did in fact live in a world as the occult tradition imagined it, if life and spirit pervaded the universe, understanding the world would indeed require a spiritual journey. Rather than breaking objects apart and setting up mechanical experiments, the occult investigator would do better by getting in tune with the harmonies of nature and grasping the living wholeness that drives it all. Many Muslim thinkers were drawn toward such a view. In contrast, modern conceptions of a physical nature that is independent of anthropocentric spiritual and moral concerns, that operates according to impersonal laws, that can be investigated by setting up systematic reality tests, were hardly even on the periphery of the Muslim imagination.

This is not to say that examples of Muslim thinking about nature that are similar to modern science do not exist. The notion of physical experiments and, more rarely, physical theory in the modern sense, occasionally appears. Ibn al-Haytham's work on optics and the human eye, for example, relies on systematic experiments and some practical applications and was a useful if secondary part of the intellectual culture, but its connection to technical innovation was limited.[24] There is, however, another critical difference between modern and medieval science: the role of theory.

Ancient and medieval science has very little true theory. It produces lists, classifications, collections of "facts." The facts it collects like stamps are not integrated into conceptual schemes comparable to Newtonian physics or evolutionary biology. The models of medieval science are bestiaries and encyclopedic collections of odd or useful facts. Even fantastic notions such as snakes with human heads were accepted as long as someone could be said to have testified to their reality. Muslims viewed science as an assemblage of true facts, which were perhaps systematized but not explained within an overall theoretical scheme. And as true facts, the facts of the sciences were not subject to innovation and improvement. There was no shortage of abstract reasoning, but this invariably went into elaborate but vague metaphysical schemes such as variations on Neoplatonic cosmologies and mystical doctrines. The science that made contact with physical reality operated at the level of common-sense folk theories; it could not challenge or greatly contribute to entrenched conceptions of reality. And without proper theories, even systematic experiments could do little but produce extra facts to add to the lists.

In a way, medieval Muslim science suffered from both too much and too little pragmatism. It was too practical, demanding useful knowledge rather than theoretical explanation. And it was too impractical, emphasizing what was culturally and religiously useful rather than what was technologically innovative.

We may wonder again if things would have been any different if the philosophical tradition had found a warmer welcome in Islam. It is hard to say for certain, but there is room for doubt. After all, reason in the Greek philosophical tradition had a different thrust than scientific reasoning as we understand it today. With hindsight, heirs of the European Enlightenment like to look back and single out the more naturalistic and empirically oriented aspects of Greek philosophy. This, however, is as misleading as portraying medieval science as a less developed version of modern science. After all, Hellenistic philosophy, Neoplatonism, and the scientifically barren cen-

includes efforts toward a mathematical formulation of optical pr:
ciples. His work, and those of some others who did optics in t
thirteenth century, is recognizable by physicists today as a precur:
of physical science as we now understand it.[22] Greek astronomy a
its Muslim sequel was also a developed field well on its way
becoming a true science. Emphasizing such examples, howev
gives a distorted picture. Seeing medieval science as a less advanc
stage of today's science requires selective attention: looking
exquisitely crafted astronomical instruments while downplayi
their astrological purposes, picking out sensible diagnoses a
hygiene advice while ignoring the immense amount of weirdness
medicine. Medicine, as one of the most important sciences, is a go
example. Looking at medieval texts—even at texts that were in t
up to the end of the Ottoman Empire[23]—we find no end of c
courses about the spiritual nature of man reflected in the bo
metaphysical ramblings about the perfect man derived from v
sions of Neoplatonic philosophy, folk remedies, miscellanec
superstition, Greek humor theory, astrology, evil spirits, and mc
Most physicians practiced bloodletting, denied contagion of disea
and presented plagues as divine punishments. Medieval medic:
did perfect the occasional useful technique, and urban Muslims (
build some impressive hospital complexes and managed put
health decently enough—especially compared to the barbarians
Europe. And it is perhaps no small thing that medicine as an int
lectual discipline existed at all. Nevertheless, only a select portion
Muslim medicine is celebrated today; the overall context
medieval medical thought is often ignored.

There are other important differences between medieval a
modern science. Scientists today depend on the systematic use
controlled experiments. A few Muslim thinkers came close to dev
oping a modern concept of experiment, but their work, at t
periphery of the larger Muslim intellectual community as was
often the case, never put down roots. Natural science today is clos
tied to technological progress, which is the main reason Muslims i
impressed by science. But even though Muslim cultures have ty
cally emphasized useful knowledge rather than knowledge for t
sake of curiosity, when compared with modern science, Muslim s
ence was technologically not very productive. Muslim science h

turies of Byzantine mystical theology that preceded the Islamic era have more plausible claims to be the natural outcome of Greek philosophy. Emphasizing reason leads to a desire for coherence in religious doctrines and a distaste for popular excesses of pious emotion and magical thinking, but not necessarily anything like modern science. Greek rationalism very often conceived of reason as a kind of supernatural illumination providing certain knowledge of higher realms of truth. This Platonic, mystical view of reason predominated among Muslim philosophers—how would it have helped science if they had won over the ulama? If al-Ghazali and similar thinkers had lived in obscurity and never denounced the philosophers for impiety, it seems a higher dose of rationalism would still have led to something much like the classical Islamic conception of reality. Science, it seems safe to say, would very likely have remained a stamp-collecting enterprise, and spiritually attractive superstitions would have continued to fill the medical texts.

Consider some of the classical Islamic philosophical positions that are often blamed for inhibiting the development of science. Toward the top of the list is the Muslim distrust of natural law and causality, a preference for letting everything in nature directly depend on an omnipotent God. Indeed, to preserve omnipotence and divine freedom, many Muslim philosophers and orthodox thinkers alike were drawn toward varieties of occasionalism, in which God creates the world anew and decides the motion of its constituent atoms in each moment. Al-Ghazali famously took this to the limit of an almost Humean skepticism about cause and effect. He correctly pointed out that there was no necessary, certain connection between a cause, such as fire, and an effect, such as a piece of cotton burning up. What happened was up to the divine will, which could always go otherwise. Hence philosophical reasoning based on causes and other such alleged necessities of reason could not be trusted.

Al-Ghazali had good reason to object to philosophers, especially those who took the metaphysics of causality and necessity to such lengths as to confine God to willing the possible to exist, with practically no choice as to the options available.[25] Still, from a modern point of view that does not demand as much certainty, both al-Ghazali and the philosophers' concerns seem misguided. Presumably an al-Ghazali–style distrust of causality could inhibit scientific investigation into natural laws and causes. But even then, strictly following al-Ghazali's views was not the only orthodox option available. Some medieval Muslim thinkers found a compromise solution: they argued, as Remzi Demir describes, that "God is capable of changing the course of nature and moving it in this or that direction, but since he has no cause to change the natural order he determined in the beginning—and the existence of such a cause would mean limiting divine omnipotence anyway—he does not make such a change and keeps the natural order as he created."[26] Demir also points out that this is a reasonable solution to the Muslim dilemma about reconciling divine omnipotence and a natural order, but observes that this view failed to gain much currency.

Clearly it was difficult to break out of the mold of the medieval view of reality. Neither the philosophical nor the religious elements in this view had any intrinsic tendency toward modern science. Yes, with hindsight and selective attention again, we can pick out habits of thought that impeded the development of science and we can also see some alternatives that were not taken. But none of this means Muslim thinkers made any mistake, or took a wrong turn. They developed a perfectly sensible, eminently satisfactory philosophical framework for a religious civilization. No one could have anticipated that some of the alternative approaches they failed to emphasize could have led to a new, much more powerful way of understanding nature.

It would have taken some fortuitous historical accidents for all the modern sciencelike elements of medieval Muslim thought to fall into place: systematic experiments becoming more widespread, objections to occult thinking having a stronger effect, a moderate occasionalism allowing for natural predictability, and so on. It did not happen, and that was mainly bad luck. Going on a quest for a usable past is, in the end, not helpful. More Mutazilism, more philosophy, a renewed commitment to medieval metaphysics—none of these can be the centerpiece of an effort to improve Muslim science today. Modern science is simply too different; Muslims cannot adapt to it in medieval terms.

WHAT ABOUT THE WEST?

Muslims search their medieval past to discover what went wrong, and they also look at the example of the Christian West to see how modern science and technology arose. After all, the medieval Christian conception of knowledge and reality was remarkably similar to that of the Muslims. Their basic notions of revelation were very close—they just did not accept each other's revelations as fully authentic. Medieval Catholics also organized knowledge around *scientia*, revealed truth. Their approach to science, as a kind of stamp-collecting activity, was comparable as well. So how did Western Christian intellectual culture, by all appearances an inferior cousin of classical Islam, end up giving rise to modern science?

Muslims looking at European history often find a mirror for their own preoccupations. Seyyed Hossein Nasr laments the fact that Christians ended up capitulating to secular trends and gave up on *scientia*.[27] Those who focus on the suppression of philosophy as the source of Muslim stagnation see European science as a direct outgrowth of the rediscovery of Greek philosophy in the West—ironically, a rediscovery in which translations from Muslim sources were instrumental. Others see the story of how European science struggled to become independent of religion as another opportunity to attack secularism. Western science and secularism, they say, embody a critique applicable to the ecclesiastical institutions of Catholic Christianity. Islam does not need a secularized science, as Islam recognizes no clerical authority that can impede scientific inquiry.[28]

Historians of science also ask why science emerged from Christendom rather than from the more advanced lands of Islam. This is an open question, and different historians emphasize different aspects of a complicated process. But it appears that historical accidents play a large role. A number of features of Western European intellectual life converged to create circumstances that allowed modern science, when it arose, to break the medieval mold.[29] Christians did not intend this, nor were they on an inevitable path of intellectual progress culminating in the scientific revolution. But they allowed science to emerge from within their own religion-centered intellectual life, and failed to keep control of it.

With the usual selective hindsight, we can see that some intellectual trends in medieval Christianity favored science. For example, there was less of an attraction to occasionalism. Many philosophers within the church adopted a reading of Plato's *Timaeus* that portrayed nature as a rational, orderly system. This need not have automatically favored a scientific attitude; after all, Platonism could just as easily have focused attention on nature as a divine design, leading to an emphasis on questions about divine purpose. In fact, Platonism is very naturally directed toward religious ends, encouraging philosophers to intuit the true realities behind mere physical shadows. But in twelfth-century Europe, which was developing more contacts with the outside world and enjoying a spurt of economic growth, *Timaeus* fed into a climate of enthusiasm about human reason. The rational orderliness of nature came to support ideas about making a clearer distinction between the natural and spiritual-supernatural realms.[30] In the East, Platonic rationalism took its more natural course of mystical theology; in the West, for a while, it served as scaffolding for what would end up as a very non-Platonic turn of thought.

Perhaps even more important are some institutional features of intellectual life. In Western Christendom, unlike in Islam, law was not at the top of the intellectual hierarchy. Legal reasoning could thereby gain some autonomy from religious concerns, later serving as a model for the independence of science.[31] Then there is the ethos of secrecy concerning the foreign sciences that prevailed in Muslim lands. The classical model of education formally presented the religious sciences in madrasas, while the foreign or rational sciences depended on individual master-apprentice relationships.[32] In Christendom, sophisticated ideas may not have reached the common people, but they were reasonably freely discussed in monasteries. Such features of Christian intellectual life helped prepare the groundwork, so that when the power of the church was challenged, when European economies started their transition to capitalism, science had an opportunity to consolidate its independence as an institution.

Another perspective on the development of science in Europe comes from looking at the occult and mystical spiritual traditions. In Muslim lands, the main alternatives to orthodox, law-centered Islam were varieties of Sufism. There was often tension between the Sufis and the ulama, especially since the Sufi reliance on direct intuition of divine reality had the potential of endorsing unorthodox views. This was typically resolved, however, as long as Sufi orders submitted to the discipline of Islamic law. The orders acquired an important social role, and the more emotional, mystical practices of Sufism came to be seen as complementary to the revealed texts and laws.

Sufi beliefs did not encourage a scientific attitude. After the twelfth century, the Sufi orders became full of the typical magical practices that accompany mysticism, from numerology and letter-magic to dream interpretation and astrology. Popular religion, heavily influenced by Sufism, perceived supernatural power everywhere; popular Sufism and folk supernaturalism were indistinguishable. Even for the educated, an occult view of reality steeped in Sufi concepts was compelling. The divine intuition that was the basis of spiritual knowledge was granted only to a select few masters. Their disciples had to absorb their teachings unquestioningly, undergoing a lifetime of arduous mystical training with hopes of eventually being granted illumination themselves. Ordinary reason and worldly knowledge could, in fact, be barriers to enlightenment, to direct contact with the divine. Madrasas trained ulama by rigidly transmitting established interpretations of the sacred sources, and the Sufi orders trained disciples to absorb the wisdom of their masters. And there were no other significant educational institutions. The result was an intellectual climate that did not greatly encourage critical inquiry into nature.

So, for all its periodic conflicts with orthodox legalism, Sufism did not create a prominent alternative. Politically, most Sufi orders were either quietist or they engaged in conservative social activism that underlined their orthodox credentials. Their institutions became integral, even comfortable parts of premodern Islamic society.

In Europe, mystical and occult beliefs exhibited some of the same antirational, quietist tendencies. But again, as an interesting historical accident, the occult ended up playing a different role. In Renaissance Italy, as the educated elite rediscovered ancient philosophy, occult sciences such as astrology also enjoyed a revival. But instead of being absorbed into the established structure, occult ideas became part of a more individualist spiritual alternative to the medieval Church. The Renaissance brought forth the more irredeemably pagan aspects of classical thought, and the occult took on a much more anti-establishment color.

At the beginnings of modern science in Europe, it was hard to separate religious, occult, and scientific ways of thinking. Isaac Newton spent more time on biblical prophecy and alchemy than on physics. There was a period of fluidity and shifting alliances between institutions and intellectual attitudes associated with orthodox religion, the occult or natural magic tradition, and what would become natural science. But in the beginning, the more serious rival to the church was individualist, occult spirituality. For a while, an occult picture of the world, independent of established religion and textual revelation, presented an attractive alternative for some of Europe's educated elites.

Such developments spurred the rise of mechanistic thinking. The mechanical philosophers sharply separated the natural and supernatural realms, letting nature operate according to mechanical laws. Supernatural acts, such as miracles, became more than just spectacular demonstrations of power—they were violations of nature's law. Some of the most thorough mechanists, such as René Descartes, adopted a dualism according to which animals were only mechanical automatons and humans were distinguished by a supernatural soul not bound by physical laws. By granting nature autonomy, mechanistic thinking prepared the ground for independent scientific investigation of natural laws. But at the time, a large attraction of mechanistic philosophy was how it excluded the occult. Natural philosophers would make pronouncements on a dead, mindless nature working according to iron laws, while the established church would remain the authority on the higher spiritual realities. Astrologers and alchemists, who envisioned a world where the natural gradually shaded into the supernatural, where the universe itself was in large part alive and spiritual, would be out of a legitimate job.

Today, mechanistic philosophy and Cartesian dualism look like stages on the way to a fuller naturalism and the complete autonomy of science. The emerging scientific community continued to expand its intellectual territory, realizing the worst fears of the theological critics of "mechanick theism," that natural science was making gains at the expense of a religious view of the world.[33] Yet it is interesting to note that in this case, the opportunity for science to flourish was in part due to the challenge that orthodox religion faced from occult spirituality. And even after it submerged again, occult thinking in the West periodically resurfaced. Often, as with Mesmerism after the Enlightenment or psychical research since the nineteenth century, the occult tradition generated attempts to form an alternative science. In Muslim lands, the three-way competition between occult, orthodox, and scientific views did not develop the same way.

So what can the European experience tell Muslims? Not, presumably, that they can benefit from a fiercer occult current in their intellectual life. If there is any moral to the story, it is that modern science is new and different, that it has significant discontinuities with medieval thinking of all sorts. Europeans stumbled upon modern science by a series of accidents; it was not an inevitable outgrowth of their particular religious culture.[34] They got lucky. So instead of reclaiming past glories, Muslims can think of claiming a part in a scientific enterprise open to all comers. Indeed, after Muslims realized the power of European science and technology, these were the questions: how to attain this new power, and how to use it for Muslim ends.

WESTERNIZATION BEGINS

For centuries, Muslim armies continued to expand the territory of Islam. After the initial Arab conquests, conquered peoples such as the Turks took over the task of fighting for the faith. India came under Muslim rule; through Sufi activity and the influence of Muslim traders, much of Indonesia and Malaysia became Muslim. Conversions in North Africa continued apace. And though the Arab kingdoms of Spain and Sicily were retaken by European Catholic states, the Ottomans took Constantinople in 1453, making it their capital. The Ottoman Empire pushed ever farther into the Balkans, into Eastern Europe.

Even at the peak of Muslim success, Europeans had an edge in some military technologies. They were barbarians, but Muslims appreciated their weaponry. The Ottomans used cannons built by renegade Europeans to batter the walls of Constantinople. But Muslims enjoyed an advantage in other respects. For example, they perfected the social technology of slave-soldiers. The Yeniçeri (janissaries), the formidable fighting force of the Ottomans, consisted of children levied from the Christian population, converted to Islam, and brought up to serve as the sultan's military slaves. By and large, Muslims did as well and often better than the Europeans on the battlefield. Borrowing weaponry was about the extent of what they required of European knowledge.

By the seventeenth century, the conquests were over, and the wars with Christendom had ground down to a stalemate. Europe was undergoing the scientific revolution, exploring new continents and exploiting new colonies, and rapidly changing in culture, religion, and economics. Meanwhile, few in the Muslim world paid attention to events in the lands of the infidels. This was especially true for science. Galileo and Copernicus came and went, but as Bernard Lewis observes,

> until the late eighteenth century, only one medical book was translated into a Middle Eastern language—a sixteenth-century treatise on syphilis, presented to Sultan Mehmed IV in Turkish [in] 1655. Both the choice and the date are significant. This disease, reputedly of American origin, had come to the Islamic world from Europe and is indeed still known in Arabic, Persian, Turkish and other languages as "the Frankish disease." Obviously, it seemed both appropriate and legitimate to adopt a Frankish remedy for a Frankish disease. Apart from that, the Renaissance, the Reformation, the technological revolution passed virtually unnoticed in the lands of Islam, where they were still inclined to dismiss the denizens of the lands beyond the Western frontier as benighted barbarians, much inferior even to the more sophisticated Asian infidels to the east.[35]

In 1683 the Ottomans besieged Vienna for the second time and were soundly defeated. Turkish historians today look at 1683 as a turning point, as the beginning of the long collapse of the empire. Economically, the empire suffered from a lack of war spoils and the loss of control over trade routes as Europeans found other ways to conduct their business. After Vienna, the Ottomans suffered a string of further ignominious defeats at the hands of the Austrians, Russians, and the nationalist movements of the Balkan Christian peoples. Gradually, Muslims were being thrown out of Europe, and they would have been ejected even quicker if the Ottomans had not been able to play the European Great Powers against one another. After two and a half centuries of military defeat and Balkan Muslims tending to come out on the losing side of ethnic-cleansing campaigns,[36] the First World War finished off the Ottomans. Istanbul, the capital, turned into a city of Balkan refugees, with ruin and poverty all around its ancient monuments. The Anatolian heartland was in even worse shape.

Meanwhile, Europeans had been taking over the rule of Muslim North Africa and penetrating the Arab heartlands. India had become a British possession. Iran was at the mercy of the Russians and the British. The whole Muslim world looked like it was being overrun by Europeans. Mehmet Akif was not the only poet who felt as if God himself had turned against his people, that a whole civilization was burning down around him.

When it first became obvious that the defeats in the Balkans were serious, Ottomans began to admire European military organization and training as well as weapons technology. Some thinkers began to realize that there was an intellectual aspect to Muslim backwardness that went beyond inferior administrative methods. In 1656 the Ottoman scholar Katib Çelebi tried to persuade his readers that Muslims needed to pay more attention to the foreign or rational sciences. It was once necessary to prohibit these, since

> in the first days of Islam, the Companions of the Prophet, or those Muslims who first adopted the faith, embraced the Book and Tradition they obtained from the Prophet Muhammad. They did not think it was permissible to devote attention to the other sciences until the fundamental laws of Islam had thoroughly taken root among the common people. Perhaps they were very strict in prohibiting the sciences; the Caliph Umar had thousands of volumes of books burnt after conquering Egypt and Alexandria; because if this was not done, the populace would not have preserved God's Book and the Prophet's Tradition and paid attention to the sciences instead, and therefore the laws of Islam would not have been established and taken root to the degree that they have by now.

Now, however, things were different, and the old prohibition no longer had a rationale. Katib Çelebi went on to urge Muslims to recognize how useful geometry, astronomy, and geography were, and to

once again think for themselves rather than blindly imitate preceding generations.[37] The rhetoric of urging reform, embracing
useful knowledge, and avoiding imitation became standard among
Ottoman intellectuals who wanted to arrest the decline of the
empire. It was not greatly effective.

The religious establishment was divided about change. In 1580
the chief religious scholar, known as the Şeyhülislam, ordered an
observatory destroyed three years after it was built. The first Muslim-
operated Ottoman printing press did not appear until 1727, after
the Şeyhülislam was finally persuaded it was permissible and then
only for printing nonreligious books. It was set up by İbrahim Müteferrika, a Hungarian Protestant who was captured in war and converted to Islam. The press printed only seventeen books and was
never economically viable.

Change was, however, inescapable. It began, naturally, with the
military—abolishing old systems like the Yeniçeri troops and eventually reorganizing the military around a European model under the
supervision of European advisers. The empire kept losing territory,
and Ottoman thinkers continued to assert a need for reform and
also a rededication to religion and a purification of morals. The
more radical reformers enjoyed periodic victories, which inevitably
modernized—westernized—important institutions. A landmark
example is the Reform Rescript of 1839. It started by announcing
impeccably conservative sentiments:

> As known, since the virtuous judgments of the Quran and the
> sharia rules had been obeyed completely, ever since the founda-
> tion of our state, the strength of our country and our subjects' wel-
> fare and happiness was at its peak. But in the last 150 years, as
> sharia and imperial rules were not obeyed due to the disorders
> pursuing each other and some other reasons, former power and
> welfare turned into weakness and poverty. It is absolutely impos-
> sible for a country not ruled by the sharia rules to survive.[38]

It then announced some modest reforms concerning the rule of
law—state law, not Islamic law. Most importantly, under pressure
from European powers, it made a move toward equality of citizens:
"All Muslim or non-Muslim subjects shall benefit from these rights."
For both political and religious reasons, this was controversial.

Non-Muslim minorities, particularly Christians, had always managed Ottoman relationships with Europe, and by the nineteenth century many had attained positions of privilege or wealth due to trade or diplomatic work. This sometimes led to resentment among Muslims. Moreover, where Christians were a local majority, nationalistic movements of secession were carving the empire apart. Some Ottoman officials and intellectuals exposed to the West had hoped to transform the empire into a multiethnic state similar to the Austro-Hungarian Empire, in which all citizens were supposed to owe allegiance to the Ottoman dynasty regardless of creed or ethnicity. The nationalism of Christians made these hopes unrealistic, so Ottoman elites increasingly tried to fashion an ideology of pan-Islamism that could hold the remainder of the empire together. Most of the ulama kept their traditional distance from imperial politics, intervening only when they thought the essential prescriptions of religion were at stake. They typically enjoyed the support of the common people. Indeed, westernization often meant a new variety of corruption. As the new elites eroded the power of more established classes like the ulama, they also disrupted traditional institutions that had worked reasonably well and allowed some measure of liberty for the peasants.[39]

Throughout the slow process of modernization, science was as much an import from Europe as was military strategy. Muslims had no other option; Europe was too far advanced. Borrowing knowledge had a religious justification, based on the principle that it was permissible to imitate the infidels in order to better fight against them. But while this justification authorized seeking knowledge, it also restricted it to a desire to acquire knowledge when there were immediate practical reasons. Muslims were not moved to produce new knowledge; they imported science from the West like they once imported weaponry. And always, the transfer of knowledge raised concerns about maintaining religious and cultural purity. İbrahim Müteferrika, the Hungarian convert, argued that Europeans had developed their rational science because their inferior religion did so little to help them solve practical problems. Thus, they ended up developing superior military and other technologies. In practical knowledge, Muslims were not as advanced, and it was legitimate to borrow the infidels' knowledge to use against them. In religious knowledge, however, Muslims were supreme.[40]

So in the nineteenth century, as modernization proceeded, many European works of science and philosophy began to be translated. As could be expected, the emphasis was on works that promised immediate practical utility. But the options broadened. Modernizers formed new educational institutions along Western lines, which immediately became more popular among elites than the traditional madrasas. Some intellectuals began to think a deeper borrowing from the West was necessary to save the empire, or even Islamic civilization itself.

MODERNISM

Many Muslim thinkers, in and outside the Ottoman Empire, found it impossible not to be impressed with European modernity—even when they strongly opposed the imperialism that had forced Muslims to pay attention to the modern world. Jamal al-Din al-Afghani, who traveled Islamic lands in the second half of the nineteenth century agitating for reform, was one of the first inspirations for modernism. Al-Afghani insisted that Islam was the most rational of religions and that there was no religious barrier to studying the modern sciences. He represented a different possibility for Islam: not the medieval system of the ulama, but a streamlined, modernized faith capable of carrying Islam back to glory. His position attracted many intellectuals who had been exposed to westernizing currents, but critics distrusted his conception of Islam. Indeed, al-Afghani's views of Islam turned it into more of a quasi-nationalistic ideology of resistance to colonialism than the kind of full-blooded religion that could claim the allegiance of conservatives.[41]

At about the same time, Sayyid Ahmad Khan identified with a similar position. He admired Western administration and knowledge and was loyal to the British Empire to the extent of being knighted. In 1875 he established the Muslim Anglo-Oriental College, the precursor to Aligarh Muslim University, in Aligarh, India. In his writings, he even appeared to put science ahead of revelation. Most supernatural and magical beliefs, he thought, were false, indeed condemned by the Quran. His willingness to reinterpret the sacred sources figuratively whenever they disagreed with science invited opposition; conservative Muslims today still cite Ahmad Khan as an example of going too far in accommodating Western rationalism. Certainly, though Ahmad Khan was widely influential and his activism and institution building is even credited with reviving Indian Islam, few Muslims found his implicit relegation of revelation to secondary status palatable.[42]

Most modernism, however, was never so radical. Many Muslims realized that the premodern social order was making change too difficult. Parts of modernity were welcome. The modernists tapped into the tradition of *ihya*—calls to reform and rebuild institutions so as to reassert the eternal truths of faith in new conditions. They produced a cultural defense and apologetics for a retooled Islam in order to block both Western colonialists and local westernizers. Muslim modernists have not perceived themselves as putting a distance between religion and society or religion and science.[43] Modernists have helped Muslims to move beyond tradition and begin to discuss the possibility of different interpretations of the faith. Nonetheless, the term *modernist* can be misleading—unlike liberal Christianity in the nineteenth century, the modernist current in Islam is not a force that fully cooperates in or even drives social modernization. Instead, it is an impulse to adapt to the external pressures of modernity.

Consider Muhammad Abduh, Egyptian reformer and well-known modernist of around the turn of the nineteenth century. Abduh sought to revive a Muslim rationalism akin to that of the Mutazila; he insisted that Muslim education had to be modernized and that it should have room for the rational sciences including those recently developed in Europe. He came into conflict with the established ulama, insisted that the gates of *ijtihad* needed to be kept open, and hoped that Islam could be purified of medieval innovations and popular superstitions in light of the sacred sources. Abduh argued that nothing in the Quran conflicted with modern science; as Ahmad Khan did, he often resorted to a metaphorical interpretation of miracle stories.[44] Yet Abduh had an equally strong conservative streak: the main object of his relative openness to reason was to defend as much as possible of a traditional view of religion, which was never really open to criticism. Looking for a usable past, Abduh declared Islam that was "the first religion to address human reason, prompting it to examine the entire universe, and giving it free rein to delve into its innermost secrets as far as it is able. It did not impose any conditions upon reason other than that of maintaining the faith."[45] Still, even Abduh ran into conservative opposition.

Modernists encouraged science and affirmed its place in education, but they had a superficial understanding of science.[46] They treated science as a symbol of rationality and insisted that Islam was the most rational religion. Science and religion were not just compatible but mutually supportive; Abduh echoed conservative Christians by saying, "God has sent down two books: one created, which is nature, and one revealed, which is the Quran."[47] Naturally there had to be complete harmony between the two. Science was fine as a catalog of God's creation, as a basis for technology, and as a tool to achieve prosperity. As a result, modernists supported modern education, provided students were also properly rooted in Islam. But their approach to science rarely reached beyond the common Muslim view of taking what is useful from the West while taking care to avoid religious contamination.[48] In the poem where he lamented the sorry state of Muslims, Mehmet Akif also urged them to

Take the science of the West, take its technology
Keep working hard as fast as you can
Because it is not possible to live without these anymore
Because science and technology have no nationality;
. . .
To overtake all the ages of progress
Let the essence of your own spirit be your guide[49]

There is little in such a concern for borrowing useful knowledge and preserving the culture that encourages Muslims to join Westerners in creating new knowledge. This is understandable; when responding to the immediate trauma of poverty and humiliation, Muslims were trying to inspire and spur the *umma* to action. Intellectual life was clearly one of the areas that urgently needed jumpstarting; deeper reflections on the nature of modern science and technology were not to the point. Muslims needed to absorb what they could as fast as possible, while making sure that it was always a distinctly Islamic culture that they were improving. And so Muslim intellectuals were very interested in finding models for progress.

Models outside the West would serve especially well. Mehmet Akif, like so many other Muslims, pointed to Japan as a successful example of selective westernization—the Japanese, Muslims thought, had adapted Western technology and had become a military power while remaining an Asian culture in all essentials. Their knowledge of Japan was as superficial as their view of European science, but again, that was not important. Japan demonstrated the possibility of competing with the West without losing one's religious soul.

Modernist themes and rhetorical devices remain a significant part of the Muslim intellectual landscape today. In part, this is because for all the changes that have come to the Muslim world in the last 150 years, Muslims still occupy a similar position of inferiority in military and economic power, and in scientific and technological capability. It would appear that the modernist style continues to work well for cultural defense and for raising hopes of revival. Finding religious revival in the Muslim world today is not difficult; the scientific revival has not arrived.

MILITARY SECULARISM

The Ottoman military was the institution that confronted Western power most directly. They had to adapt, and quickly. So, the military copied what was successful. They took on Western weapons, organization, and training, even a Western style of uniforms. The first challenge to the intellectual and educational dominance of the ulama came from the military training academies. The graduates of military engineering, officer, and medical schools became a powerful constituency for change. This new class of military-based intellectuals were used to seeing knowledge and science in more Western terms, and they were prepared to impose reform on their society.[50]

In the twentieth century, militaries in Muslim lands found themselves unopposed in their bid to become the social vanguard. Even after defeats against colonial powers, militaries remained the most stable modern institutions. And as the Ottoman Empire collapsed after the First World War, the remnants of the Turkish military, under a Western-oriented leadership, fought one of the first successful anticolonial wars. They emerged from the war with the power to implement their prescriptions. The new Republic of Turkey was much smaller, reeling from continual wars, and an economic shambles. Nevertheless, the military intellectuals were firmly in control, and they pressed a radical agenda of wholesale change.

The Turkish Revolution of the 1920s and 1930s attempted to bring a devastated, conservative, peasant society into the modern world within decades. Kemal Atatürk, the hero of the war of independence and the first president of the republic, was much influenced by French culture and attempted to cast Turkey into the mold of a modern, secular European country. The revolutionaries abolished the sultanate and the by-now-symbolic office of the caliphate. They continually downplayed the role of Islam in lawmaking and soon removed "the religion of the state is Islam" from the constitution. They westernized the calendar, weights and measures, and even passed and enforced a law prohibiting Muslim-style dress, replacing the fez and the turban with the European hat. Nationalism was to be the guiding ideology of the country, not Islam. They shut down the Sufi orders, prohibiting many forms of devotion. They switched from the Arabic to the Latin alphabet and embarked on a campaign to purify the Turkish language by getting rid of the heavy Arabic and Persian influence that had turned the Ottoman court language into an unwieldy hybrid. The list goes on—the Kemalist revolutionaries imposed a full-blown cultural revolution on Turkey.

Mehmet Akif and other devout intellectuals were appalled; indeed, Mehmet Akif found one of his poems of religious nationalism adopted as the words to the Turkish national anthem, yet he soon left for exile in Egypt. But the Kemalists had their way. The ulama, Sufi orders, bazaar merchants, and other centers of power in traditional society were exhausted and disorganized; they could offer little but passive resistance and the occasional futile rebellion. The remains of the Ottoman bureaucratic and military elite stood behind the program of forced westernization. So the Kemalists held on to the state and even enjoyed some success. Although facing popular resentment, many of the reforms took root. Republican Turkey began to slowly build up its economy, even paying off Ottoman debts to the West. In the 1930s, it seemed that Turkey was on its way to become a modern European state, with reasonably efficient institutions and a secular nationalist ideology.

The Muslim countries that achieved independence after the Second World War took notice of the Kemalist model. Although they never tried to be as secular as the Turkish revolutionaries, military intellectuals in the Muslim world took advantage of opportunities to gain power. Muslims had usually been ruled by centralized empires, and modernization gave new impetus to the authoritarian aspects of Muslim political culture. A centralized bureaucratic apparatus, modern communications and police forces, and the weakening of intermediate local layers of authority, all gave the state immense power in society.[51] Reformers and Muslim restorationists alike therefore sought control over the state.

Kemalist Turkey certainly fit this authoritarian pattern. Nevertheless, it would be misleading to think that Kemalists were strictly opposed to religion, or that their reform program amounted to blind imitation of the West. Kemalists ultimately wanted Islam to take on a role similar to that of Christianity in modern Europe. They wanted religion to become a matter of private conscience. The influence of Islam, they thought, should legitimately be felt in the realm of culture and morals. Personal relationships with God, in the form of private religious devotion and community observance of worship and rituals, were, again, perfectly legitimate expressions of Islam. Religion could be misused, however, if it entered politics or attempted to become an all-encompassing system regulating all aspects of life. The public sphere belonged to secular ways of handling the affairs of this world.

The problem, as the Kemalists saw it, was that religion had regularly been misused. The worst offenders were the ulama, who had become a dead hand on society, and the Sufis, who had drowned the straightforward, rational religion of Islam under an ocean of superstition. Religion had to be reformed, and there was no clean way of doing this. Conservative resistance had to be broken—for the good of the nation, even for the good of Islam. Otherwise, in a world dominated by often hostile Western powers, there would soon be nothing left to save.

The Kemalist view of science followed its approach of westernizing all worldly matters. If Turks joined modern European culture in its public aspects, they would also do science like Europeans. Many Kemalists believed that there was but one way of being civilized in the modern world, and that was the European way. They did not just borrow knowledge and a Western form of education, but also clothes, daily habits, even music. To this day, appreciation of Western classical music marks out the truly westernized Turk. In matters of science, Kemalists insisted that science and technology could not forever be imported—it was important to become able to produce new knowledge. Otherwise, the nation would remain subordinate, dependent on those Western powers that were able to produce original scientific research.[52] And scientific creativity did not take place in a vacuum. Turks needed to absorb the whole cultural background that drove continual technical innovation. After a century of Ottoman failure to import technology and social techniques without compromising Muslim culture, the military and bureaucratic elites decided that the worlds of science and traditional Islam did not go together. So the Kemalist solution to Muslim scientific backwardness was to westernize and let local science operate according to Western ways.

Republican reforms included modernizing universities according to a German model and sending students abroad. This resulted in a number of scientists who returned to train the next generation of Turkish academics. But as with most of the ambitions of the Turkish Revolution, successes were partial and ambiguous. Republican ideals were compelling to many intellectuals, but implementing them led to no end of compromises and contradictions. The military secularists constructed an authoritarian, state-centered ideology in the name of liberating individuals from the ulama and the medieval community. They wanted to save the nation by forcing religion to retreat to a private sphere, but the peoples they wanted to forge into a nation largely defined themselves through religion.

So although Kemalists promoted a privatized religion as an ideal, in practice the necessity of taming Islam came to the fore. Moreover, Islam was inseparable from Turkish nationalism, and therefore religion could be used as an instrument of the state to promote goals such as national unity. And so the secular Republic of Turkey formed a powerful Directorate of Religious Affairs to control and fund Sunni religious institutions. The state-employed clergy were supposed to legitimate the Turkish state, to promote modernization, even to support the secularity of the state as part of the true interpretation of Islam. Moreover, the military secularists strenuously opposed folk and Sufi Islam in a manner much like orthodox Sunni revivalists. For example, the practice of worshiping at tombs of saints and hoping for supernatural favors was condemned by the traditionalist ulama, Islamists, and secularists alike. The republican ruling elites were strongly influenced by the urban Sunni tradition and saw folk Islam as a degeneration of Islam by means of superstitious accretions. Although republican secularism greatly reduced the power of the ulama, the ulama's Sufi rivals suffered even worse, and so Sunni orthodoxy was left in a better position to claim the allegiance of the devout.[53]

Indeed, many themes of the earlier Muslim modernism reemerged in secularist thought. For example, Şemsettin Günaltay was a prominent revolutionary-era politician who later became prime minister between 1949 and 1950. He pointed out that the peasants did not understand educated discourse, and so they trusted their local ulama implicitly. This meant that modernizers needed to take control of the religious apparatus, to change the peasantry by reforming their religious leaders. He also claimed that Sufism, though a positive spiritual force at first, had become corrupted and an obstacle to progress. Günaltay argued for the republican agenda, not, however, as someone hostile to religion but as an observant Muslim who saw reform as a purification and renewal of the faith.[54] He fused Islamic modernism with republican secularism, so that while Islamic law was the divine path to development and happiness, this became very like the Enlightenment notion that people should live according to nature's laws. Günaltay proclaimed, like most Muslim thinkers, that societies only succeed as long as they are properly religious. Since premodern Muslim societies had failed, the reason had to be a departure from true religion. So some Muslim modernists such as Günaltay were able to think of secularism as a much-needed return to religious purity.

By the 1950s, the revolution had run out of steam. After a transition to multiparty democracy, a more conservative leadership took power. Although the conservatives did not question the fundamental principles of the republic, they were not averse to satisfying popular demands by allowing Islam a larger symbolic role. This could serve to reconcile the people to the state, allowing modernization to take root.[55] But it also encouraged the quest for a more Islamic flavor of modernity. For example, conservative governments (which have usually been in power since 1950) oversaw the bifurcation of the education system into ordinary secular schools and religious schools. The religious schools were originally set up to train the state-employed clergy, but they vastly expanded beyond that need and became alternative educational establishments.

Conservative populism, in the end, fed into a gradual re-Islamization of public culture in Turkey. Although conservative governments encouraged religion, the Islamic revival mainly bubbled up from below, as segments of society other than the old military and bureaucratic elites gained power and asserted their cultural identity. Turkish scientific institutions continued to look toward the West for a model of doing science, and scientists remained a secularist constituency. But secularism itself became subject to debate as never before. And today, at the beginning of the twenty-first century, it appears that the political moment of military secularism has passed.

In the 1930s, many Muslims were still impressed with Turkey's defeat of European colonial powers to gain independence. Many Indian Muslims were disappointed with the Turks for abolishing the caliphate, and most religious conservatives naturally saw the Turkish revolution as an abomination. Still, others perceived Turkey as a progressive force. Muhammad Iqbal, the great Urdu poet, praised the Turkish separation of religion and state, republican government, and even proposals such as requiring the call to prayer to be made in Turkish rather than Arabic.[56] And eventually, some other Muslim states, notably Tunisia, had experiences with milder forms of secularism. Today, however, Turkish modernization is no longer seen as a reawakening of *ijtihad* and evidence of the vitality of Islam but as a failed experiment—Turkey, Islamists say, became an American client-state that repressed Islam but failed to reach secular goals. The quasi-secular authoritarian governments in other Muslim countries suffer from an even worse reputation. In the past few decades, the political initiative has passed to Islamist movements that represent a different kind of hope to achieve a Muslim modernity.

THE ISLAMISTS

Puritan revivalist movements are not new in Muslim history. For example, the Wahhabis in eighteenth-century Arabia tried to reform the faith by returning to Islam as they imagined it was at the beginning—getting rid of Sufism, the practice of venerating saints at their tombs, and anything else they thought was an innovation. These innovations had become traditional, so the Wahhabis and their intellectual forebears also attacked blind adherence to tradition. Muslims were to be guided solely by the sacred sources as understood by the first generation of believers. The Ottomans, who ruled the Hijaz when Wahhabism first emerged, considered the Wahhabis to be desert fanatics who wanted to abolish too much of Islamic civilization. Although the Ottomans tried to crush the movement, Wahhabism continues to thrive today, as the established faith in oil-rich Saudi Arabia. And through Saudi financing, the Wahhabi style of Islam has become influential, finding passionate converts and provoking reactions similar to that of the Ottomans.

So fundamentalism, in the sense of a political reformist movement that proposes to purify Islam by going back to the sacred sources, is not just a recent phenomenon. With the encroachments of European modernity, however, fundamentalism found a wider constituency. And in doing so, fundamentalism became political Islam: it took on the character of both a reaction against modernization and a search for an alternative, authentically Islamic form of modernity.[57]

Indeed, Islamist politics are hard to understand outside the context of rapid, usually state-imposed modernization. This modernization succeeded, but only partly. Denizens of the urban centers of Turkey today participate in the McDonald's and Hollywood blockbusters form of consumer culture. They dress in jeans and T-shirts and jackets; the contents of their refrigerators and their homes have much more in common with urban material culture across the globe than what was common to the Middle East just a century ago. This superficial modernity is not confined to Turkey; as Olivier Roy observes, even with the insistence on a modest dress code, "The Tehran of the mullahs has a very American look"—it has little to do with the dress or way of life of a premodern Iranian town.[58]

construct alternative structures of religious authority—an engineer without a traditional education in the religious sciences can just as easily lead a group studying the Quran. And since fundamentalists assume that the holy texts have to speak to current needs, they often find the traditional scholarship of the ulama irrelevant.[63] Nevertheless, in matters of doctrine they do not usually deviate far from the interpretations established by the ulama.

With all this religious change, Islamists also stray from the classical Muslim view of knowledge. As with fundamentalists of all religions, Muslim fundamentalists live in a world of modern technology and modern economic transactions; many of them do quite well in areas such as applied science. Indeed, the prevalence of engineers especially among the leadership of Islamists has often been noticed. Islamists are often very positive about technology; they certainly use the latest communication technologies to support their networks. They derive prestige from their technological and financial competence: they can plausibly say that they have mastered the sources of power in the modern world and that they can help lead Muslims out of the wilderness. This is not an entirely new development—the technology-positive attitudes of Islamists draw on the long-standing Muslim tendency to emphasize useful knowledge while downplaying theoretical understanding: "it remains true that many fundamentalists, especially in what might be called the middle management leadership of the movements, have obtained degrees in engineering, in medical technology, or in other technical scientific disciplines. By contrast, one finds few fundamentalists trained in astrophysics or other branches of science that are less empirical and more speculative and theoretical in orientation."[64]

Most modern Muslims equate science with practical technological knowledge, and so they have little trouble claiming that their view of the world is completely consonant with modern science. Consider Sayyid Qutb, one of the most influential Muslim fundamentalist thinkers of the twentieth century. Qutb states that Muslims have a collective obligation, as part of their vicegerency for God on Earth, to further the practical sciences; that science has its roots in Islam rather than the West; that science does not challenge anything in religion, provided that it confines its attentions to immediate empirically verifiable matters. However, modern science has

become arrogant; Western science harbors philosophical speculation disguised as concrete fact. In fact, Qutb is very much against
philosophy, even medieval philosophy, as a perversion of human
reason that puts itself before revelation. Reason, Qutb argues, has to
be strictly submitted to revelation—to the extent that the intuitive
personal understanding of revelation takes precedence over all.[65]
Because thinkers such as Qutb remain positive about applied science, their ambivalence about Western science and their antitheoret-
ical attitudes do not attract as much attention. Fundamentalists sincerely think of themselves as supporting science while endorsing
views that would cripple scientific practice.

Islamist approaches to science are particularly important because
versions of political Islam have captured the imagination of large
numbers of Muslims around the world. This has not necessarily translated into political success: the most revolutionary forms of fundamentalism have been frustrated outside of Iran and a few peripheral
locations such as Afghanistan. In many cases, the most uncompromising forms of political Islam have receded to a sullen "neofunda-
mentalism" that does little but continually demand that Muslims
should live their lives according to the sharia.[66] But even without
clear-cut success, Islamists have deeply influenced mainstream politics
in all Muslim lands. While the top-down version of Islamic revolution
that proposed to take over the state in order to impose a puritan Islam
on the population has failed, movements of cultural re-Islamization
from below have been much more successful.[67]

Today, political Islam continues to set the agenda in Muslim
countries, in the form of a conservative populism that has toned
down its anti-imperialist rhetoric and aims toward becoming full
players in the global economy. Islamically inspired political parties,
such as the AKP that governs Turkey today, present themselves as
mainstream conservatives that favor intuitive ways of knowing and
historically rooted religious cultures over the dry, antihuman mech-
anization of modern rationalism. Their intellectuals proclaim that
their movement embodies a critique of the European Enlightenment and its inherent violence, especially seen in the French model
of secularism that was copied by military secularists in Muslim
lands.[68] Islam in politics is here to stay, and in many places the real
competition is between rival visions of how Islam should shape the

life of the nation, rather than between older varieties of fundamentalism and secularism.

So today many different visions of religion and intellectual life compete. There are old-fashioned ulama who give rulings according to time-honored ways, except that they post their decisions on Web sites and take questions by e-mail. There are Sufi movements adapting to the modern urban landscape, and strict religious orders that try to construct a purely Islamic bubble for their members to live in. There are jihadis devoted to violence, and modernists who want to grant worldly institutions more autonomy under the umbrella of a religious civilization. All have views on science, whether it is a superficial claim of compatibility with religion, an insistence on keeping all corrupting Western influences away, or an ambition to reconstruct science along an Islamic pattern. But not all options concerning science are equally available. The medieval Islamic conception of knowledge has receded, but it continues to influence Muslim desires to see the divine unity in all aspects of life and to make science harmonious with a religious perception of reality. Muslim thought continues to be populist, oriented toward community, and centered on revelation. And the Western model continues to meet with ambivalence. On the one hand, it is an illustration of worldly success, and academic scientific institutions in Muslim lands continue to maintain a secular, westernized outlook. On the other hand, Muslim thinkers also see the West as an example to avoid—letting science become too independent can only support secularism. And few today want such an outcome.

NOTES

1. Mehmet Akif Ersoy, from *Safahat* book 5, quoted in Erdoğan Aydın, *İslamiyet ve Bilim* (İstanbul, Turkey: Cumhuriyet Kitapları, 2001), p. 61. My translation does not preserve the original's poetic quality.

2. Fatima Mernissi, *Islam and Democracy: Fear of the Modern World*, trans. Mary Jo Lakeland (Reading, MA: Addison-Wesley, 1992), p. 34.

3. Pervez Hoodbhoy, *Islam and Science: Religious Orthodoxy and the Battle for Rationality* (London: Zed Books, 1991), chap. 9.

4. Mernissi, *Islam and Democracy*, pp. 32–33.

5. Anthony Black, *The History of Islamic Political Thought: From the Prophet to the Present* (New York: Routledge, 2001), p. 352.

6. Toby E. Huff, *The Rise of Early Modern Science: Islam, China, and the West* (New York: Cambridge University Press, 1993), p. 80.

7. Lawrence Rosen, *The Culture of Islam: Changing Aspects of Contemporary Muslim Life* (Chicago: University of Chicago Press, 2002), chap. 9.

8. John Morris, "Is Creation or Evolution More Empirical?" *Dr. John's Q&A* (April 1995) (among the Institute for Creation Research's monthly publications).

9. Abd al-Jabbar, *Kitab al-Usul al-khamsa*, translated in Richard C. Martin and Mark R. Woodward with Dwi S. Atmaja, *Defenders of Reason in Islam: Mu'tazilism from Medieval School to Modern Symbol* (Oxford, UK: Oneworld, 1997), p. 90.

10. There were other early persecutions and inquisitions, but these were largely directed against "dualists." Bernard Lewis, *Islam in History: Ideas, People, and Events in the Middle East*, 2nd ed. (Chicago: Open Court, 1993), p. 286.

11. Andrew Rippin, *Muslims: Their Religious Beliefs and Practices* (New York: Routledge, 2001), p. 65.

12. Seyyed Hossein Nasr, *Traditional Islam in the Modern World* (London: Kegan Paul International, 1987), p. 102.

13. Remzi Demir, *Osmanlılar'da Bilimsel Düşüncenin Yapısı* (Ankara, Turkey: Epos Yayınları, 2001), pp. 9–10.

14. Lawrence I. Conrad, "The Arab-Islamic Medical Tradition," in *The Western Medical Tradition, 800 BC to AD 1800*, by Conrad et al. (Cambridge: Cambridge University Press, 1995), p. 103.

15. Quoted in Demir, *Osmanlılar'da Bilimsel Düşüncenin Yapısı*, pp. 24–25. "Physics" refers to Aristotelian physics, which does not exactly overlap with physics as a modern science.

16. Richard W. Bulliet, *Islam: The View from the Edge* (New York: Columbia University Press, 1994), chap. 9.

17. Oliver Leaman, *An Introduction to Classical Islamic Philosophy*, 2nd ed. (Cambridge: Cambridge University Press, 2002), p. 160.

18. Howard R. Turner, *Science in Medieval Islam: An Illustrated Introduction* (Austin: University of Texas Press, 1998), pp. 204–205.

19. Recently, the notion of decline, especially uniform decline, has been challenged. See Mohamad Abdalla, "The Fate of Islamic Science between the Eleventh and Sixteenth Centuries: A Critical Study of Scholarship from Ibn Khaldun to the Present" (PhD thesis, Griffith University, Australia, 2003).

20. Rippin, *Muslims*, pp. 120–23.

21. Turner, *Science in Medieval Islam*, pp. 110–11.

22. Ibid., pp. 196–200.

23. Many of them are still available in Islamic bookstores in Istanbul

today, reprinted in the Latin alphabet, and still apparently selling enough to justify their publication.

24. This is not to deny that Islamic technology could be very ingenious; see Ahmed Y. al-Hassan and Donald R. Hill, *Islamic Technology: An Illustrated History* (New York: Cambridge University Press, 1986).

25. Leaman, *An Introduction to Classical Islamic Philosophy*, p. 47.

26. Demir, *Osmanlılar'da Bilimsel Düşüncenin Yapısı*, p. 30.

27. Nasr, *Traditional Islam in the Modern World*, p. 102.

28. See contributions by Azzam Tamimi and S. Parvez Manzoor in *Islam and Secularism in the Middle East*, ed. Azzam Tamimi and John L. Esposito (New York: New York University Press, 2000), pp. 16, 26, 90, 91.

29. Marcia L. Colish, *Medieval Foundations of the Western Intellectual Tradition, 400–1400* (New Haven, CT: Yale University Press, 1997).

30. Huff, *The Rise of Early Modern Science*, pp. 100–102.

31. Ibid., chaps. 4, 5.

32. Demir, *Osmanlılar'da Bilimsel Düşüncenin Yapısı*, pp. 31–32.

33. John C. Greene, *The Death of Adam: Evolution and Its Impact on Western Thought* (Ames: Iowa State University Press, 1959), pp. 8–13.

34. Many Christians think otherwise; for example, Rodney Stark, *The Victory of Reason: How Christianity Led to Freedom, Capitalism, and Western Success* (New York: Random House, 2005) argues that scientific rationalism was a direct outgrowth of rational Christian theology. I am unconvinced.

35. Bernard Lewis, *What Went Wrong? Western Impact and Middle Eastern Response* (New York: Oxford University Press, 2002), p. 7.

36. Muslims were certainly not innocent parties in the bloodletting; the Ottomans committed some amazing atrocities in trying to quell rebellions. In the end, though, they lost. Turks are still remembered with ill feelings for "400 years of occupation" in the Balkans, and I do not think this is all an invented nationalist sentiment.

37. Quoted in Demir, *Osmanlılar'da Bilimsel Düşüncenin Yapısı*, pp. 48–52. Bernard Lewis, *Islam in History*, p. 373, points out that Umar's destruction of the library of Alexandria is a Muslim-invented myth, helping justify the contemporary destruction of heretical Fatimid libraries in Egypt.

38. My modification of a translation on http://www.osmanli700.gen .tr/english/ourselection/select_15.html (accessed December 3, 2006).

39. Lewis, *Islam in History*, chap. 6.

40. Black, *The History of Islamic Political Thought*, p. 268.

41. Abdullah Alperen, *Sosyolojik Açıdan Türkiye'de İslam ve Modernleşme: Çağımız İslam Dünyasında Modernleşme Hareketleri ve Türkiye'deki Etkileri* (Adana, Turkey: Karahan Kitabevi, 2003), pp. 100–54.

42. Javed Majeed, "Nature, Hyperbole and the Colonial State: Some Muslim Appropriations of European Modernity in Late Nineteenth-Century Urdu Literature," in *Islam and Modernity: Muslim Intellectuals Respond*, ed. John Cooper, Ronald Nettler, and Mohamed Mahmoud (London: I. B. Tauris, 2000); Mevlüt Uyanık, *Bilginin İslamileştirilmesi ve Çağdaş İslam Düşüncesi* (Ankara, Turkey: Ankara Okulu Yayınları, 2001), pp. 46–50.

43. Alperen, *Sosyolojik Açıdan Türkiye'de İslam ve Modernleşme*, pp. 18–19.

44. Ibid., pp. 154–92.

45. Quoted in Roxanne L. Euben, *Enemy in the Mirror: Islamic Fundamentalism and the Limits of Modern Rationalism* (Princeton, NJ: Princeton University Press, 1999), p. 106.

46. The "modernist" label is typically used to describe those with *politically* more open attitudes. When it comes to science, political "modernists" and "liberals" often subscribe to the same sort of pseudoscientific approaches as others. For example, Charles Kurzman includes Maurice Bucaille (see chapter 3) as a liberal, in *Liberal Islam: A Sourcebook*, ed. Charles Kurzman (New York: Oxford University Press, 1998), p. 14.

47. Euben, *Enemy in the Mirror*, p. 107.

48. Such a reaction is not special to Islam; it has Russian and Chinese parallels. Ian Buruma and Avishai Margalit, *Occidentalism: The West in the Eyes of Its Enemies* (New York: Penguin Press, 2004), chap. 4.

49. Mehmet Akif Ersoy, quoted in Mehmet S. Aydın, *İslam'ın Evrenselliği* (İstanbul, Turkey: Ufuk Kitapları, 2000), p. 162.

50. Demir, *Osmanlılar'da Bilimsel Düşüncenin Yapısı*, pp. 64–66.

51. Lewis, *What Went Wrong?* pp. 53–54.

52. Innovation remains a problem in Turkish science, and even today, Turkish academics who think the nation should do better often reassert Kemalist arguments from previous generations. For example, see Güneş Kazdağlı, *Atatürk ve Bilim* (Ankara, Turkey: TÜBİTAK Yayınları, 2001), pp. 80–81.

53. David Shankland, *Islam and Society in Turkey* (Huntingdon, UK: Eothen Press, 1999), pp. 76–78.

54. Alperen, *Sosyolojik Açıdan Türkiye'de İslam ve Modernleşme*, pp. 328–52.

55. Nilüfer Göle, *İslam ve Modernlik Üzerine Melez Desenler* (İstanbul, Turkey: Metis Yayınları, 2000).

56. Muhammad Iqbal, "The Principle of Movement in the Structure of Islam," reprinted in Kurzman, *Liberal Islam*.

57. Martin, Woodward, and Atmaja, *Defenders of Reason in Islam*,

points out that fundamentalism existed before modernity, and reacts against rival currents within Islam, particularly the rationalism in Islamic modernism. Euben, *Enemy in the Mirror*, criticizes views that take fundamentalism to be a reaction against modernity, and among other factors, highlights the religious appeal of fundamentalism. Both seem to be necessary corrections, however, as a first approximation, emphasizing the modern and antimodernist reactive characteristics of fundamentalism still seems accurate.

58. Olivier Roy, *The Failure of Political Islam*, trans. Carol Volk (Cambridge, MA: Harvard University Press, 1996), pp. 22–23.

59. Many Islamic countries besides Turkey have had a similar experience. On Egypt, see Raymond William Baker, *Islam without Fear: Egypt and the New Islamists* (Cambridge, MA: Harvard University Press, 2003), pp. 24–28.

60. Thomas W. Simons Jr., *Islam in a Globalizing World* (Stanford, CA: Stanford University Press, 2003), pp. 26–27.

61. The phenomenon is not confined to Turkey. Olivier Roy, *Globalized Islam: The Search for a New Ummah* (New York: Columbia University Press, 2004), pp. 97–98.

62. In many ways, the current state of Islam reminds scholars of the Protestant Reformation: the changing social context of religion, the challenge to traditional religious authorities, the insistence on going back to the sacred sources and reinterpreting them all are very Protestant religious themes. Nevertheless, there are important differences as well, so I will not argue for the analogy.

63. Farid Esack, *The Qur'an: A Short Introduction* (Oxford, UK: Oneworld, 2002), pp. 24–25.

64. Gabriel A. Almond, R. Scott Appleby, and Emmanuel Sivan, *Strong Religion: The Rise of Fundamentalisms Around the World* (Chicago: University of Chicago Press, 2003), p. 124.

65. Euben, *Enemy in the Mirror*, pp. 68–71; Black, *The History of Islamic Political Thought*, pp. 322–23.

66. Roy, *The Failure of Political Islam*; Roy, *Globalized Islam*.

67. Taner Edis, "Democracy vs Secularism in the Muslim World," in *Toward A New Political Humanism*, ed. Barry F. Seidman and Neil J. Murphy (Amherst, NY: Prometheus Books, 2004).

68. Yalçın Akdoğan, *AK Parti ve Muhafazakar Demokrasi* (İstanbul, Turkey: Alfa Yayınları, 2004). For Egyptian parallels, see Baker, *Islam without Fear*.

CHAPTER 3

FINDING SCIENCE
IN THE QURAN

FRAGMENTS OF FAITH

The center of Istanbul, the old city, is always full of tourists. One reason is the natural beauty of a city set on hills overlooking the narrow strait of sea separating Europe from Asia. Another appeal might be Turkish cooking, from hole-in-the-wall establishments claiming to make the perfect meatball to restaurants specializing in dishes originally developed for the Ottoman palace. But for Westerners, a major attraction of the ancient capital must also be the feeling of history, of something exotic yet not entirely incomprehensible.

Indeed, it seems that around every corner in central Istanbul there is an ancient monument or interesting sight, from buildings displaying the architecture of the nineteenth century to crumbling Byzantine walls more than a thousand years old. Tourists flock to the imperial mosques with their high domes and exquisite tilework and walk through the various palaces and museums. They shop in the covered Grand Bazaar, perhaps trying to get the feel of an ancient Oriental bazaar while negotiating a decent price on a carpet. It does not take much imagination to think that a world of turbaned men and veiled women, of slave markets and harems, is not that distant. Europeans once associated the Muslim East with luxury; to relax, a tourist can go to any number of well-appointed Western-style cafés, or perhaps stop at a coffeehouse where young Turkish men and women play backgammon while smoking a narghile.

Istanbul, though, is a city of more than ten million, and the majority live in circumstances far from what appears in the tourist brochures. A more typical Turkish neighborhood coffeehouse is a dingy, smoke-filled area where men—only men, never women—while away their days smoking, playing cards, and sipping strong tea. Many of these men are underemployed or unemployed; if lucky, they might pick up the odd job opportunity that comes by. Most people are either recent immigrants to the big city or their families have been in Istanbul for only a couple of generations. Their neighborhoods are socially similar to villages as well as modern urban areas; often the squatter-villages that make up the vast suburbs of the city consist of immigrants from a single small region in the countryside. Even if they were born and raised in Istanbul, they think of themselves as being from Sivas or Malatya or one of hundreds of dusty Anatolian towns.

The old Ottoman social order is long gone; much of it is as exotic to Turks today as to their Western visitors. A careful observer might notice shadows of the past everywhere, but most Turks are only half-familiar with these cultural reminders, just as they are half-familiar with the United States after a lifetime of watching American television programs dubbed into Turkish. In a city full of crumbling monuments, the population goes about its daily struggles with little sense of history. Some do feel that they have an extensive heritage, that they stand for timeless values that can anchor them in a changing world. But a careful observer might also come to see this as a myth: that in reality almost everything is new, that even nostalgia for Muslim glory is an attempt to press half-understood and never-lived fragments of the past into present service.

Many visitors also expect to see something of Islam in Istanbul—perhaps a strongly held faith with unfamiliar, perhaps even dangerous overtones. Again, they can find much that is different to Western eyes. Turks are certainly among the more religious peoples in the world, though this contrasts more with Western Europe or Japan rather than with the United States or most less-developed countries.[1] An endless series of mosques, mostly shoddy and undistinguished, cover the landscape, recognizable by their prominent minarets. Few are older than a few decades. Most Sunni Turkish homes have a prayer or two in Arabic script framed on their walls, and elderly members of the family make sure to retire to a well-used prayer carpet five times a day. The typically conservative small-business men punctuate their day with the same prescribed prayers, leaving their shops to gather in a nearby mosque. Especially in rural areas and the vast immigrant shantytowns surrounding industrial urban centers, men and women live more or less segregated lives. Restaurants have separate sections not for smokers and nonsmokers but for single men and for "families." Turkey, as with any Muslim land, is unmistakably different, and this becomes most obvious where religion is concerned.

The Grand Bazaar, however, sells plenty of Indian textiles and Central Asian carpets; even in Turkey, labor has become too expensive for certain products. Shopkeepers attend mosque, but the rhythms of bazaar worship are only an echo of two centuries ago. Even when women go about with carefully covered heads, they do not necessarily follow an age-old tradition. It is just as likely that they observe a modern, fundamentalist kind of modesty. Their layers of scarves pulled over long jackets only superficially resemble the dress of nineteenth-century upper-class Ottoman women, and even less the dress of peasants. Nowadays, Islamically correct clothing is big business. At the high end of the market, Islamic dressmakers present their changing fashions to customers at curiously Western-looking fashion shows, including well-covered models on runways. Cultural conservatism invents its traditions as much as drawing on the actual past.

Similarly, the Islam affirmed in some form by almost everyone is not really the old-time religion. It is not even always a contemporary development that remains deeply rooted in the faith of old. Instead, today's Turkish varieties of Islam very often look like patchworks, assembled from fragments of ancient faith and from very modern convictions, put together with little regard for their overall coherence.

After the Turkish Revolution, the stronger, politically ambitious forms of faith went underground or emphasized the quietist strands of Sunni tradition. Rural areas in particular preserved a traditional piety, and the local ulama, though they declined in status and power, retained much of their informal influence. But village life was also eventually disrupted by modernization and by mass migrations to the cities. In any case, the rural ulama were always somewhat distant from the more intellectually sophisticated civilization of urban Islam. Village piety preserved echoes of the medieval intellectual structure behind Muslim belief, but no more. When migration produced a new urban constituency for an assertive religious identity, networks of mutual aid, and ideologies of moral clarity, the fragments of faith preserved by the rural ulama were most available. A new generation of devout thinkers, including political Islamists, would weave these fragments into new ways of being Muslim.

The fragments of faith belonged to the people, not the urban elites who gravitated to military secularism and learned to think in Western political terms. So the modern forms of Islam under construction in Turkey show a strong populist tendency. And this populism can be a common theme within the diversity of Islam. For example, almost no one questions that the Quran is the literal word of God. No doubt this overwhelming consensus is a continuation of historical attitudes in Muslim lands; seeing the Quran as a human document has never been a viable option in Islam. Nevertheless, the Quranic literalism of today has as much to do with modernizing, newly literate populations seeking an anchor for religious authority as with deep-rooted tradition. After all, people expect to find answers to today's questions when they go to the sacred sources— not arcane matters relating to ancient Arabia or medieval scholastic preoccupations. They are less likely to trust established hierarchies, so they seek authority in the divine sources, and they take the sources at face value as much as possible.

Today's Turkish Muslim views on science are strongly influenced by populism and the rural style of piety modified by a newly urbanizing and industrializing population. There is plenty of popular superstition and a tendency to see natural events in terms of divine reward and punishment. For example, after earthquakes in Muslim lands, which result in much more devastation than in technologically advanced countries, some popular preachers will invariably declare that the quake was a divine punishment brought on by the people's sins. Perhaps the people have been too tempted by Western consumer ways, or maybe they allowed too many women to uncover too much of themselves. This embarrasses the educated classes and prompts newspaper editorials denouncing the "ignorant preachers" who confuse Islam with superstition. But the preachers give voice to common public perceptions. In surveys conducted after the 1999 earthquake in Turkey, which killed tens of thousands due to inadequately regulated and incompetent construction in known seismically active areas, three-fourths of respondents identified the source of the quake's devastation as God rather than nature or human faults in construction. They perceived the quake as being a divine warning, punishment, test of faith, or just a result of the fate predetermined by God.[2]

While retaining a prescientific view of nature, most Turks are also aware of modern technologies that affect every aspect of their lives. They have strong supernatural convictions; the secularist vision of a privatized faith that is only a source of personal morality has never caught on. As David Shankland observes, "The original Republican formula, stoic inner belief whilst getting on with one's public duty to serve the nation, thus separating the absoluteness of faith from everyday, practical experience, has turned out to be unacceptable to a large part of a population which has by and large retained its literal faith in divine creation and intervention in all things. Nevertheless, they sense the difficulties raised by technology keenly."[3]

So ideas that promise to resolve such difficulties are especially attractive. There is a tension between the way that modern technological life encourages skepticism about the supernatural and how popular religion demands a clear divine presence in the world. In the orthodox, Sunni tradition, a commonly available solution is to say that scripture itself is a supernatural sign. Historically, Muslim apologists have always presented the Quran as Islam's prime miracle. Some traditions describe spectacular feats such as Muhammad splitting the moon. 54 Al-Qamar 1 has "The end of time has drawn near, and the moon has split"; some hadith describe an occasion where Muhammad split the moon as a demonstration for doubters. This has become one of the favorite miracle stories in Muslim lands.[4] The Quran, however, was supposed to be a much clearer miracle available to everyone. Indeed, the Quran is supposed to be inimitable. In 17 Bani Israil 88, the Quran itself declares so: "Say, 'Even if humans and jinns all gathered together to produce something like this Quran, they could not produce anything like it, even if they helped each other.'"

Urban Sunni movements, then, often sanitize miraculous elements in their beliefs by playing up the supernatural qualities of the sacred sources and becoming stricter in observing the laws and rituals of Sunni Islam. More Sufi-oriented groups embrace the supernatural feats of Sufi masters; some do very well in an urban environment, even among professionals looking for a more New Age style of undemanding, therapeutic religion. Throughout the rapidly changing social landscape of Turkey, however, there is much religious turmoil and experimentation. Intellectuals as well as popular leaders seek new ways to be modern, to fit science with religious convictions.

THE NUR MOVEMENT

A good example of the new approaches to science and modernity that have developed out of Turkish popular Islam is the Nur movement. Based on the teachings of one of the most important twentieth-century religious figures in Turkey, Bediüzzaman Said Nursi, the Nur movement has grown, become very popular and influential in politics as well as culture, and split into many rival groups. Though centered in Turkey and reflecting Turkish religious and social concerns, the way the "Nurcus" have attempted a science-aware form of cultural defense has parallels in the Muslim world as a whole.

The Nurcus have attracted academic attention not just because of their popularity but also because of the distinctly modern flavor of their beliefs and organization. Nurcu and similarly inspired movements have been associated with the increasingly Protestant qualities of Turkish Islam, including an attitude toward work and wealth similar to that of the famous Industrial Revolution–era "Protestant work ethic." Nurcus have thereby contributed to commercial capitalism and economic development in central Anatolia. The economic interests of today's devout middle classes fit together very well with the new political and religious identity constructed by Nurcu-style movements. Indeed, according to sociologist M. Hakan Yavuz, "without a proper understanding of the Nur movement and its societal impact, one cannot grasp the peaceful and gradual mobilisation of an Islamic identity movement in Turkey."[5] The Nurcus have especially acquired a reputation for their positive attitudes toward natural science and technology. Social scientists usually see this positive approach as an important aspect of how the Nur movement proposes to construct a distinctly Islamic form of modernity.

Said Nursi was born in 1877 in one of the rural, eastern provinces of the crumbling Ottoman Empire. He went into religious training and received the traditional madrasa education of the ulama. Even remote regions, however, were not isolated from the troubles of the empire; Nursi soon became aware of the wider crisis facing the Muslim world and the need to face criticisms of Islam. He explored some typically modernist ideas, such as reforming Islamic education in order to revitalize Muslim tradition. Politically, Nursi got into some minor trouble with the Ottoman authorities, gave cautious support to the movement for constitutional monarchy in 1908, and traveled extensively in Muslim lands, all the while trying to materialize his dreams of a reformed madrasa.[6]

Even early on, Nursi affirmed that Western science was useful and could be appropriated for Muslim ends, but he was also disturbed by the impiety that seemed to accompany science. Western thought had considerable influence on the new elites in the Ottoman Empire, and this included critiques of religion. The writings of positivist Auguste Comte, the materialist Ludwig Büchner, and John William Draper, who wrote of the "warfare between science and theology," found a limited but enthusiastic Turkish readership.[7] Since such views were skeptical of Christianity, they could be more acceptable to westernizing intellectuals in Muslim lands—it was easier to move away from religion than to risk coming under the influence of the age-old rival, Christianity. The European Enlightenment promised a universalism based on common human reason, not on faith in any particular revelation. But for devout reforming ulama such as Nursi, such ideas were even more insidious. Nursi decided he had to learn something of modern thought in order to defend Islam.

After the Turkish War of Independence and then the formation of the Republic in the 1920s, however, a "New Said" emerged who departed from the reformist ulama mold typical of many at the end of the Ottoman Empire. Followers present the New Said as a figure similar to al-Ghazali of old: Nursi suffered a personal crisis, withdrew from the world, immersed himself in Sufi contemplation, and ended up deciding that he needed to base his thinking solely on the Quran. He had started out relying on reason and philosophy in order to defend Islam, but this did not satisfy him. Like al-Ghazali, the New Said turned against philosophy without wholly discarding it:

> In his quest for the Sacred in times of turbulence, Nursi remains committed to discovering the best methods of uncovering the secrets of life. He distinguishes between two broad paths of truth: the first is rational and guided solely by reason. The second is mystical and is guided by both reason and heart or intelligence and wisdom. In his words, the 'old Said' used philosophical and rational means to capture the essence of truth; however, this method evaded him and was responsible for much of his emotional anguish and intellectual confusion. It produced a heart that was totally saturated by wounds *(mumakhad bi'l juruh)*. This much-wounded heart sought consolation in the works of the great Muslim saints such as Imam Ghazali, Jalal al-Din Rumi, 'Abd al-Qadir al-Jilani, and Imam Sirhindi.[8]

The antiphilosophical New Said also took a more quietist political stance, though he was profoundly disturbed by the radical secularist turn of the new Republic of Turkey. Nevertheless, he was not completely inactive, and the government worried about his influence. Much of his life continued under surveillance, episodes of internal exile, and the occasional prison sentence, until a conservative government took over after the 1950 elections. In the late 1920s, Nursi began his famous writings answering religious questions and explaining his views of the fundamentals of Islam. These writings, which became known as the *Risale-i Nur* or the *Epistles of Light*, struck a popular nerve. They usually circulated clandestinely, delivered in secrecy by "Nur postmen."

After 1950, Nursi became politically active once again and supported the conservatives in power. The *Epistles of Light* were printed and distributed openly. In 1960 Nursi died, and a few months later a military coup overthrew the conservative government, briefly attempting to restore a revolutionary, secularist direction for Turkey. The military government felt threatened enough by Nursi's influence to destroy his tomb and reinter him in a place that remains unknown.

Nursi's biography is not entirely remarkable; plenty of ulama of his generation responded to the crisis of Islam in similar ways. Many were charismatic enough to have large followings, and many harbored similar ambitions for a revival of an Islam that would be open to technology and economic enterprise while remaining shaped by village piety. But few came close to founding as potent a movement for Islamic renewal—a renewal that, while not disdaining political influence, primarily worked at the level of culture and individual faith. The secret to Nursi's success has to be the *Epistles of Light*. The Nur movement was, first and foremost, a text-based movement. Nurcus organized as study groups reading and discussing the *Epistles*. This textual focus was particularly appealing to devout individuals who were literate and had ambitions to get ahead in a modern world where educational credentials and skills had become important. Moreover, instead of the ancient, excruciatingly dull texts of the sacred sources and scholastic literature, Nurcus could study a new, contemporary text that addressed their concerns and promised to help them interpret the sacred sources for the modern world. Nur study groups did not organize along the traditional model. Knowledge of the important texts—the *Epistles*—did not require madrasa-trained ulama; leadership was open to capable laity.

Though the *Epistles of Light* were always supposed to be intermediate between the sacred sources and Nurcus, they became quasi-scriptures in their own right. Nursi himself encouraged such views: "Nursi had warned that others might not understand what he was writing about because 'I was not writing with my own will and volition, and it seemed inappropriate to arrange or correct what I had written, according to my own thoughts.' He believed that his reflections were inspired by an outside source. He himself reread them in order to gain guidance. He taught his students that the Epistles were their real teacher."[9]

Nurcus certainly treat the *Epistles* as just about divinely inspired, even if they do not state this explicitly. As with many sacred texts or inspirational literature—New Age channelings as well as ancient scriptures—the *Epistles* very often appear opaque, insipid, or even incoherent to outside critics. But to followers, what is incomprehensible becomes a sign of profound depth or divine mystery; what seems empty is only so to those with closed hearts. In any case, the fact that what amounts to a secondary scripture has become so readily accepted in a Muslim environment is testament to the ironclad doctrinal conservatism of Nursi—it is hard to accuse him of challenging orthodoxy.

After Nursi's death, the Nur movement had all it needed to keep going: the *Epistles*. The main focus of the movement was to sustain a loose community of believers and missionary activity based on studying Nur literature. Nurcu leaders, however, soon found that they could also enjoy political influence if they could translate the allegiance of their followers into votes. Over the last few decades, Nurcu groups have continued to be active in conservative politics, often competing against other versions of Islamic revivalism, religious orders, and Islamist mass movements.[10] Their main interest, however, has been to affect modern Turkish culture from below. And in doing so, the Nur movement has developed a signature style of apologetics that often appeals to modern science.

Since Nurcus are so intensely involved with the *Epistles* and Epistle-based secondary literature, much in the Nurcu style can be traced back to Nursi's own positions on science, philosophy, and technology. And Nursi is a perfect example of a religious thinker trying to fuse fragments of medieval faith with superficially understood fragments of modern science.

Nursi conceives of science as a practical enterprise that has to be accommodated within an Islamic theological framework—though he thinks of his views as inspired by the sacred sources rather than being derived from the classical Islamic theology permeating the education of the ulama. And so his early thought about science includes many specifically Muslim theological preoccupations, formulated in ways to defend Islam against nineteenth-century materialism. "Emphasizing the order (*nizam*) of the universe on the one hand, on the other hand they [his "Old Said" works] aim to disprove

in summary fashion evolution, the pre-eternity of matter, the formation of beings from the motion of particles, nature as creative power,
and causality."[11] The New Said is not substantially different. Similarly, when the New Said condemned philosophy—now modern,
especially materialist philosophy, rather than just the Greek rationalism the medieval ulama worried about—he did so because philosophy does not follow divine revelation. Reason, to work properly,
had to be subordinated to revelation.

Nursi also followed tradition in equating knowledge with certainty; he insisted that though the *Epistles* appealed to the heart and to
the intellectual intuition, they also presented certain, verified truths.
As follower Şükran Vahide perceives them, the *Epistle* literature

> deals almost exclusively with the truths of belief and related sub-
> jects. These are proved and demonstrated by means of logic and
> reasoned argument to be rational and necessary. It employs com-
> parison and allegory in a way that makes clear even the most
> obscure questions. A considerable part is based on extensive com-
> parisons between the Qur'an and its wisdom and civilization, and
> Western philosophy and its "results" and Western civilization;
> refuting the latter and its attacks, and demonstrating that it is only
> the Qur'an that can provide humanity's true happiness and
> progress. It also brings together the truths of religion and the
> modern physical sciences insofar as many of these truths are
> demonstrated in the light of science. This point is related to the
> *Risale* when it expounds "the face of the Qur'an that looks to the
> modern age," for inspired by the Qur'an's method of directing
> people to ponder over the divine works manifested in the func-
> tioning of the universe and the manifestations of the divine names
> within it, with the *Risale*, Nursi opened up a new and "direct way
> to reality." At the same time, it answers and refutes materialist phi-
> losophy, disproving in the clearest manner 'nature' and 'causality,'
> the concepts on which it is based.[12]

Though he mostly restated traditional arguments, Nursi did
introduce some new twists on old themes. For example, there is a
large theological literature speculating on the deep meanings of the
traditional Names of God, such as "All Beneficent," "Most Mer-
ciful," "Sovereign," and so forth. Nursi brought renewed emphasis

to the notion that the arts and sciences emanate from the traditional divine Names. The Name "Healer" is linked to medicine, as the Name "All-Wise" has a connection to natural science. The universe is like a book on which God writes his names, his signs; the creation testifies to the attributes of its creator. So a careful, honest inquirer cannot help but be led to faith. Humans are capable of understanding the book of nature: "We are made in such a way that our intellects can apprehend the structures of the universe, and the divine Names that order these structures."[13] Science, the sacred sources, and spiritual intuition all mutually support one another, illuminating each others' truths.

Nursi's writings occasionally make contact with actual science and technology. To bring science into the picture, Nursi took some themes modernist Muslim thinkers had introduced and developed them further by insisting that much in science had been prefigured in the Quran. There is plenty of precedent for this. In the Quran, 16 An-Nahl 89 includes "For We have revealed the Book to you, an explanation of all things, and guidance and mercy, and good news for those who acquiesce"; 6 Al-Anam 38 has "We have not neglected anything in the Book." Muslims have often interpreted these verses to mean that all that was necessary for Muslims was included—at least as broad principles—in the Quran. The ulama certainly believed this was true in a legal context, and when modern science proved so powerful and useful, it was natural to think that science must also be contained in the Quran. As Andrew Rippin points out, "this exegetical approach has an honorable pedigree with classical precedents, for example in al-Mursi (d. 1257) who found astronomy, medicine, weaving, spinning, agriculture, and pearl-diving mentioned in the Qur'an."[14]

So, Nursi looked for modern technology in the Quran. When Moses performs his miracle of striking a rock and bringing forth water, this looks forward to well drilling and irrigation technology. When Solomon flies through the air, this anticipates airplanes. Jesus' healing miracles prefigure modern medicine. Since Nursi did not really know much about basic science, he concentrated on technology. In any case, he was not completely naive about finding modern wonders in the Quran. He argued that the miracles in the Quran were described in obscure terms, to excite the curiosity of

Muslims, to make it clear that wondrous feats were possible so that the believers would get to work to figure out how to realize these feats.[15] In other words, Nursi combined the modernist tendency to naturalize scriptural miracle stories with the more traditional theme of locating all knowledge in the Quran.

After Nursi's death, the Nur movement continued to proclaim the harmony of science and Islam in its publications. In fact, its members put even more emphasis on showing how scientific discoveries were anticipated in the Quran. If a book revealed fourteen centuries ago not only made no scientific mistakes but also contained knowledge not discovered until recently, then it clearly must have a divine author. At the same time, a similar style of science-in-the-Quran apologetics was becoming increasingly popular throughout the Muslim world; the Nur movement joined in with its Nursi-inspired approach. Nurcu-linked publications with titles like *Zafer* (Victory) and *Sızıntı* (Leakage—presumably from the realm of the unseen) serve as popular magazines of science and culture, always including inspirational articles on how science confirms Muslim beliefs and how science can be found in the Quran. The Nur movement and its offshoots such as the branch headed by Fethullah Gülen continue to promise a synthesis of science and Islam,[16] drawing freely on the fringes of science such as parapsychology as well as more traditional science-in-the-Quran apologetics.[17]

Nursi's original approach was more sophisticated than that of the popular Islamic magazines; after all, he guarded against overenthusiastic interpretations by acknowledging that the alleged Quranic references to technology were obscure. Nevertheless, since Nursi had made little reference to actual science, many among his later followers felt a need to develop his thoughts further, to flesh out the connections between Islam and science. So, finding science in the Quran, though not central to the overall structure of Nurcu thought, has become a significant theme in the popular Nur literature. Today, especially with the further development of communication technologies, similar examples are very easy to find throughout the Muslim world. Muslims everywhere repeat similar claims: that the Quran details human embryonic development, that it describes the geology of mountains, reveals brain structure, refers to today's physical cosmology, anticipates modern meteorology, and much more.

SCIENCE IN THE QURAN

Science-in-the-Quran arguments appeal to an audience who respects science and technology and wants to feel more secure about their faith. Science and technology, however, are strongest in the advanced Western world; many Muslims, though they want to use science to affirm their own tradition, also continually look Westward for the best in science. The effect is curious. Naturally, the most commonly available authorities who support finding science in the Quran are people such as Muslim engineering professors. But as usual in science and technology, the best authorities hail from the West. So, Muslims especially value Westerners with technical backgrounds who testify to miraculous knowledge in the Quran.

In fact, some myths about Western scientists being amazed by the Quran have become very well known throughout the Muslim world. According to one of these myths, Jacques Cousteau, the renowned French underwater explorer, discovered the salinity barrier that impedes mixing between the Atlantic Ocean and the Mediterranean Sea. Later, he was awestruck when shown 55 Ar-Rahman 19–20 from the Quran, "having loosed the two bodies of water to meet without overflowing a barrier between them"—clearly this was an accurate description of the very phenomenon he had encountered under the sea. Some versions of the myth go on to claim that Cousteau then converted to Islam.[18] Another famous legend concerns the astronaut Neil Armstrong. When on the moon, the story goes, Armstrong heard some unfamiliar sounds. Later, when visiting Egypt, he discovered that this was the *adhan*, the Muslim call to prayer. He then converted to Islam.

Such myths, though easily dispelled by elementary fact-checking, remain popular. Hundreds of Muslim publications and Web sites continue to proclaim how Cousteau confirmed the miraculous "barrier between the two seas" pronouncement of the Quran. Evidently such stories help bolster the readers' faith or perhaps even appeal to backsliders and prospective converts.

There are, however, some Westerners who have taken up the cause of Quranic miracles, although they are not quite as accomplished as Cousteau or Armstrong. Indeed, the authority perhaps most often cited by Muslims today is Maurice Bucaille, a French medical doctor. In 1976 Bucaille published *La Bible, le Coran et la Science*, a book that compared the Quran favorably to the Bible, asserting that unlike the Christian holy book, the Quran was not vulnerable to modern historical and textual criticism.[19] Bucaille also argued that the Quran's descriptions of nature were far superior, indeed, that the excellent fit between the Quran and today's astronomy, earth science, biology, and medicine was inexplicable if the Muslim holy book was merely a human work from fourteen centuries ago. Bucaille has had a negligible influence outside of Muslim circles, and in the West, his book has mostly been ignored or treated as a mildly interesting example of crank literature. Muslims who were concerned to reconcile science and religion in the manner of the Nur movement in Turkey, however, embraced Bucaille. Bucaille was a latecomer to science-in-the-Quran apologetics, and his general approach was already familiar to Muslims. Still, the fact that Bucaille could be presented as a Western scientist who confirmed the miracle of the Quran meant that his name was soon known throughout the lands of Islam. Indeed, his popularity has led to Bucaille being identified with the search for modern science in the Quran. Muslim critics who prefer a subtler approach complain about "Bucaillism."

Partly due to Bucaille, one of the most common claims of scientific knowledge hidden in the Quran concerns embryology. Some verses scattered throughout the Quran can be interpreted as referring to the divine creation of humans in the womb. 71 Nuh 14 has "who created you in successive forms"; 39 Az-Zumar 6 says, "God creates you inside your mothers, in successive formations, in three darknesses." Bucaille takes such statements to be about "the successive transformations the embryo undergoes."[20] Another Western medical doctor soon joined Bucaille in claiming that the Quran anticipates modern embryology. In 1986 Keith L. Moore published a short paper in the *Journal of the Islamic Medical Association* that confirmed Muslim views about the Quran and embryology. This also became a favorite source for Muslim apologists to cite. Moore elaborated on the same themes as Bucaille, for example, stating that "doctors in the seventh century A.D. likely knew that the human embryo developed in the uterus. It is unlikely that they knew that it developed in stages, even though Aristotle described the stages of development of the chick embryo in the fourth century B.C. The realization that the human embryo develops in stages was not discussed and illustrated until the fifteenth century . . . 'The three veils of darkness' may refer to: (1) the anterior abdominal wall; (2) the uterine wall; and (3) the amniochorionic membrane."[21]

There are numerous other verses in which Moore, Bucaille, and their imitators can find embryology. For example, 23 Al-Muminun 12–14 says, "We created the human being from an extract of earth, then placed it as a drop in a secure repository; then We made the drop a clot, then We made the clot a lump of flesh, then We made the flesh bones, then we clothed the bones with flesh, and then We produced another creature from it. So blessed is God, best of creators." This, apparently, refers to the sperm—or perhaps the zygote—implanted in the uterus, and describes its various stages in uncanny scientific detail until we get a fetus, which might possibly be the "other creature." Moore adds that when 22 Al-Hajj 5 says, "remember that We created you from dust, then from a drop, then from a clot, then from a lump of flesh, formed and unformed," this part of the verse "seems to indicate that the embryo is composed of both differentiated and undifferentiated tissues."[22]

It does not take much medical knowledge to see that Bucaille and Moore's procedure consists of reading modern medical details into some very vague and general statements in the Quran. Moreover, they overlook much more plausible ways of understanding these statements. After all, the scattered verses that refer to the development of humans use this development as one among many examples of God's creative acts. These examples must have been familiar to at least some of those hearing the Quranic message in the first centuries of Islam. So, unsurprisingly, these verses fit ancient medical beliefs better than modern conceptions. As Basim Musallam points out,

> The stages of development which the Qur'an and Hadith established for believers agreed substantially with Galen's scientific account. In *De Semine*, for example, Galen spoke of four periods in the formation of the embryo: (1) as seminal matter; (2) as a bloody form (still without flesh, in which the primitive heart, liver, and brain are ill-defined); (3) the fetus acquires flesh and solidity (the heart, liver, and brain are well-defined, and the limbs begin formation); and finally (4) all the organs attain their full perfec-

tion and the fetus is quickened. There is no doubt that medieval thought appreciated this agreement between the Qur'an and Galen, for Arabic science employed the same Qur'anic terms to describe the Galenic stages: (as in Ibn Sina's account of Galen): *nutfa* for the first, *'alaqa* for the second, "unformed" *mudgha* for the third, and "formed" *mudgha* for the fourth.[23]

Nevertheless, in Muslim popular literature, it is Bucaille's conclusion that has become the established wisdom: "The Qur'anic description of certain stages in the development of the embryo corresponds exactly to what we today know about it, and the Qur'an does not contain a single statement that is open to criticism from modern science."[24]

The search for science in holy writ encompasses much more than embryology. Popular Muslim writers also find much relating to the physical sciences in the Quran. Physics, especially, is the most mature among modern sciences, and physics is known for its ambitious theories about the fundamental nature of the universe. If the creator of all things was dropping hints about science in the divine revelation, surely physics and cosmology should appear alongside minor facts concerning embryos, oceans, or the water cycle.

The Quran does not say much concerning the structure of the universe, but it does draw attention to the marvels of creation as signs of the reality and power of God. In doing so, numerous verses mention the seven layers of heaven or sky. 71 Nuh 15–16 asks, "Haven't you observed how God made the seven heavens in ascending order, and set the moon in their midst as a light, and made the sun a lamp?" 17 Bani Israil 44 says that "the seven heavens and the earth and all beings therein praise God"; 78 An-Naba 12 lists "And We built seven firmaments over you" among the ways God shaped nature; a few others such as 67 Al-Mulk 3, 23 Al-Muminun 17, and 65 Al-Talaq 12 also mention the seven layers of the skies in passing, as something many in the Quran's audience would know as a fact about the universe.

Now, finding anything like seven layers of skies in modern astronomy is a challenge. Bucaille finesses the problem: he interprets the number seven to be no more than a symbolic expression of plurality, so that there are an indefinite number of heavens. He does not say more; when discussing the lowest heaven, for example, he says,

"When however the Qur'an associates material notions intelligible to us, with statements of a purely spiritual nature, their meaning becomes obscure."[25] Others, however, are not satisfied by such excuses. Having set out to find modern science in the Quran, they would much prefer that the seven layers should mean something real.

One such interpreter is Haluk Nurbaki, a Turkish medical doctor who served as a conservative member of parliament in the 1960s and became best known for his vigorous output of writings on Islam, particularly Islam and science. In the early 1980s, he published his most influential book, *Verses from the Holy Quran and Scientific Facts*, which went through many editions and continues in print well after his death in 1997. Nurbaki's book is a classic Bucaillist work, compiling many of the standard science-in-the-Quran arguments current in the Muslim world and adding his own ideas. According to his preface, "after examining all Western publications concerning today's physics and astrophysics" he tries to present "believable scientific facts and the scientific miracles of the Quran" to the reader.[26]

Nurbaki also tackles the matter of the seven heavens, saying that "if you look out toward space from the Earth, or from any planet, seven magnetic spheres surround you." These are

1. The sphere represented by ourselves and the solar system (the first sky).
2. The sphere of space represented by our galaxy (the second sky).
3. The sphere of space represented by our local group of galaxies (the third sky).
4. The central radio magnetic sphere of the universe represented jointly by groups of galaxies (the fourth sky).
5. The cosmic sphere represented by quasars (the fifth sky).
6. The expanding cosmic sphere represented by escaping stars (the sixth sky).
7. The cosmic sphere representing the remaining boundless infinities of the universe (the seventh sky).

Nurbaki continues, claiming that "the Quran does not just mention seven skies and leave it there, but provides it with the most serious physical explanations that fits the astrophysical thought of today."[27]

To a physicist, however, Nurbaki's physical explanations look like a barely intelligible mosaic of misused terminology. Indeed, like Nurbaki, most science-in-the-Quran authors show no evidence of having consulted any actual physicists or other relevant experts.

Any identification of seven skies with information from modern astronomy is arbitrary at best and inevitably incorrect because we find nothing like a layered structure of heavens. But Ptolemaic models of astronomy current until the scientific revolution in Europe described the heavens as consisting of discrete spheres. The total number of spheres varied, including some for the fixed stars or, in Christianized versions, the highest heaven where God and the angels dwelt. The number of *planetary* spheres—Saturn, Jupiter, Mars, the Sun, Venus, Mercury, the Moon—was, however, seven. The Ptolemaic model was one of the crowning glories of Greek astronomy and represented the best cosmology at the time the Quran was put together.

The Greek notion of layered skies influenced Middle Eastern religious thought, including, for example, noncanonical Jewish and Christian literature that narrates the ascent of holy men through various heavens where they meet biblical figures, angels, and so forth. The traditions concerning Muhammad's Night Journey tell a very similar story. But religious texts do not have any single, coherent cosmology. Alongside references to the Ptolemaic layers of sky, the Quran and hadith literature also retain elements of much older Middle Eastern traditions of a flat earth with a heaven above, accessed by gates from "the ends of the Earth," and where the heavens contain windows for snow and rain to fall from storehouses above, and so forth.[28] The earth and the heavens are spread out like a tent: Isaiah 45:12 has God say, "It was I who made the earth and created man upon it; my own hands stretched out the heavens, and I marshaled all their host"; in the Quran, 13 Ar-Rad 3 has "And God it is who spread out the earth, and placed on it mountains and rivers." Religious texts preserve fragments of ancient cosmologies rather than prophesy modern scientific developments.

Still, a determined interpreter cannot fail to find modern physical cosmology in the Quran. 51 Adh-Dhariyat 47, "Even the sky We constructed through agencies while it was We who made the space" is ambiguous and can also be translated "We built the heavens by

Our authority; and We are the Lord of power and expanse." Since this is followed by "and the Earth we cover, spreading it richly" or "We spread the earth a carpet; what comfort we provide,"[29] it seems that this is another picture of God spreading the earth and sky like a tent. In these verses, however, Bucaille, Nurbaki, and others perceive the expansion of the universe, which was only discovered by twentieth-century astronomers.[30]

Then there is 21 Al-Anbiya 30, "Don't the scoffers see that the skies and the earth used to be one solid mass, then We split them, and made all living things from water?" This might seem very much like a version of the very ancient Middle Eastern story of the gods separating the earth from the sky and bringing order from chaos. But for many science-in-the-Quran enthusiasts, this is an expression of the big bang theory of modern cosmology.[31] Nurbaki somehow fails to see this, however, and explains 21:30 in terms of "great magnetic tension in the infinite spheres of the heavens," declaring that this "Quranic physics" solves supposedly inexplicable problems in modern physics concerning gravity, the expansion of the universe, quantum mechanics, and black holes.[32]

The quest for science in the Quran can lead to even stranger results, sometimes ignoring or overturning traditional interpretations of verses and important doctrines just to find some science. For example, Ahmad Mahmud Soliman claims that the Quran's "verses dealing with science need very little explanation. When we read them, they immediately convey their meaning. There is no symbolism or ambiguity."[33] He interprets apocalyptic verses such as 84 Al-Inshiqaq 1, "When the sky bursts open"; 81 At-Takvir 6, "and when the oceans are flooded"; and 75 Al-Qiyamah 9, "and the sun and moon are joined," as descriptions of what will happen in the far future when the sun expires due to the natural course of stellar evolution. He also says that 51 Adh-Dhariyat 49, "And we have made pairs of everything," meaning male and female, applies to positive and negatively charged particles. He ends by discussing 55 Ar-Rahman 19–20, about the two bodies of water that do not mix, except that he says it refers to the Mediterranean Sea and the Red Sea, and signifies the feasibility of building canals that can connect different seas.[34]

THE QUANTUM QURAN

Not all Muslims are impressed with attempts to find scientific miracles in the Quran.[35] After all, *Bucaillism* is a derogatory term used by Muslims who prefer other ways to reconcile Islam with modern science. The search for miracles can badly distort the revealed text, plus, in a curious way, it concedes too much to Western science. Celebrating the Quran because it anticipates science makes science the more secure form of knowledge. Muslims have more traditionally favored putting revelation first.

Another important, though often unsaid, reason to avoid Bucaillism is that it is simply embarrassing. Science-in-the-Quran apologists produce disconnected collections of "facts" to be prophesied by the Quran, including ideas that are speculative or that arise from the fringes of science. The result looks very like medieval bestiaries, with their curious mixtures of natural history, fantastic animals, and religious storytelling. Soliman interprets 17 Bani Israil 85, "They ask you about the spirit. Say, 'The spirit is from the command of my Lord; and you are given but little knowledge,'" to mean that once we have enough knowledge, then we will understand the soul. Fortunately, "This is what recently has taken place. Science now says that the soul, the immortal part of man, is a material being having weight and is nothing less than a body of a different vibration."[36] Presumably he is referring to the efforts of psychical researchers to weigh a departing soul in the early twentieth century—a highly dubious enterprise then, which has no scientific value today. Nurbaki, on his part, encounters some speculations about tachyons (particles that move faster than light, for which no evidence exists) and decides that "this physical approach has a great affinity to the Quranic concept of angels. The invisibility of angels means they have infinite speed."[37] Someone with little knowledge of science might be impressed, but the absurdity of all this is clear otherwise.

Indeed, it is striking how little writers of the science-in-the-Quran genre know about science. They might have mastered some lists of textbook items, and many are accomplished in particular technical specialties such as medicine. But they conceive of science as a set of practical applications and concrete facts to be collected and organized like stamps. This view is not even medieval; medieval science at least enriched its stamp collections with an elaborate God-centered perception of nature. In any case, the science-in-the-Quran genre displays very little awareness of the powerful conceptual schemes that make modern science so compelling to scientists. Getting concepts such as magnetic fields wrong are relatively trivial mistakes, but representing modern sciences such as physics and cosmology as a list of facts indicates a much deeper misconception.

As a rule, efforts to discover Muslim doctrines reflected in modern science rarely engage with the theoretical side of science. A partial exception is the attempt to harness quantum physics for Muslim purposes. This is, perhaps, not too surprising—quantum mechanics is notoriously counterintuitive. It resists any easy visualization and routinely violates commonsense expectations about how physical objects should behave. So quantum physics has, from its inception, attracted mystical speculation and inspired attempts to argue that modern physics describes a fundamentally spiritual universe. Somehow it is easy to confuse conceptual difficulty with mystical obscurity, and even a few physicists who should know better continue to encourage quantum mysticism.[38] Typically, however, religious references to quantum physics appear in the context of the New Age current within Western society, or as a part of arguments for Hindu or Buddhist mystical philosophies. This literature does not suggest any new directions for physics, using physics only as a source of religiously suggestive metaphors. It turns out that there are very similar, quasi-Muslim versions of New Age quantum-abuse, particularly in the Sufi literature appealing to Western spiritual seekers.[39] Such works, however, are of very dubious orthodoxy and have practically no influence within the Muslim world.

A more straightforwardly Muslim appeal to quantum physics comes from authors who defend traditional Muslim doctrines concerning predestination or causality. Some writers declare that quantum physics has overturned the rationalist conception of causality, replacing it with ideas very similar to those in Muslim theology. For example, Murad Hoffmann, a German convert who is a doctor of law, states that "as has been well-known since Werner Heisenberg's discovery of the uncertainty principle in 1925, physics has learned to describe inner-atomic reality not using alternative but *complementary* states (particles versus waves). It was discovered that particle physics can be better grasped using the Islamic theory of pre-destination, that is, its concept of simultaneously determined and undetermined behavior."[40]

Working physicists do not generally refer to medieval Islamic metaphysics as an aid in understanding quantum physics. Still, it is true that modern physics leads us to rethink traditional philosophical concepts of causality, so the temptation to find parallels between quantum mechanics and Muslim occasionalism can be strong. Hoffmann does not develop the connection beyond vague hints. Some Nurcus in Turkey, however, take up the cause, inspired by Said Nursi's attacks on causality.

For example, Muhammed Bozdağ, a political scientist, notes that the quantum vacuum is not a bare emptiness—which is true as far as it goes—but also attaches some obscure metaphysical properties to the quantum vacuum, perhaps because he takes the "Indian physicist Maharishi Mahesh Yogi" as an important authority on quantum physics.[41] The Maharishi, the spiritual leader of the Transcendental Meditation movement, is notorious for promoting dubious interpretations of quantum field theories and disreputable claims that modern particle physics describes a unified field of consciousness that underlies Hindu metaphysics and various paranormal phenomena. Bozdağ then says that causality has collapsed and that everything in modern physics makes sense in the light of the notion of *tawhid* (divine unity) revealed fourteen centuries ago. Bozdağ declares that the quantum vacuum is nothing but the *"melekut alemi"* in Neoplatonism-inspired medieval Muslim philosophy: a higher, invisible sphere of reality containing spiritual beings responsible for the movement of the planets. He says that passages in Said Nursi's *Epistles of Light* where Nursi refers to the realm of the *melekut* as the hidden spiritual cause of visible phenomena are an illustration of how quantum physics overlaps with Nursi's framework of Quranic interpretation.

According to Bozdağ, though modern physics confirms Nurcu readings of the Quran, it also suffers from some blind spots. To become more complete, science needs to accept Nursi's ideas about causality and acknowledge that even in the absence of superficial material causes, more profound spiritual causes can operate to produce miraculous events. Supposedly documented examples include "the ability of some Yogis to fly even in the absence of the superficial causes demanded by natural law, how some are able to dance on burning fires without any material protection, the followers of some Sufi orders being able to insert sharp objects into their bodies without natural consequences such as pain or bleeding, the bilocation of saints, the Holy Prophet splitting the moon in two by pointing his finger, waters sufficient to an army flowing from the ten fingers of the beloved Messenger, some people being able to move objects at a distance through psychokinesis or read with their fingers or smell through their heels."[42] In other words, some writers within the Nur movement draw freely on New Age quantum abuse and parapsychology alike and present it all as science validating Islam. What physicists see as the uncaused, random events of quantum mechanics become choices of the free divine will. What scientists reject as magical thinking become documented paranormal realities revealing that the personal intent of an infinite spiritual being underlies the universe.

Writings such as Bozdağ's can be hard to take seriously, but the impulse behind them is not so easy to dismiss. After all, some respectable theologians and scholars of religion in the West also believe that parapsychology promises to overturn materialism and restore a notion of irreducible "agent causation" to modern science.[43] Many Christian thinkers express ideas similar to Bozdağ and Hoffmann when trying to reconcile the fundamental randomness in physics, and the important role chance plays in theories such as Darwinian evolution, with a theistic view of nature.[44] Most Abrahamic monotheists think that in the end, nothing is really random in nature. All is ultimately caused by the divine will, however inscrutable.

Equating randomness with divine choice is not, however, just a metaphysical gloss on modern science—it is a serious misreading of the physics. True randomness corresponds to a complete lack of pattern. In quantum mechanics, individual events such as radioactive decays are completely unpredictable; we can only calculate probabilities for them. But precisely because of this individual unpredictability, we can make reliable statistical predictions for large numbers of events. The randomness in fundamental physics does not signify mere ignorance. Neither does it stand in for causes set in motion by inscrutable personal agents—quantum mechanics presents nothing like the sort of patterns in data that would allow us to infer any intent or purpose behind apparently random events. Quantum mechanics, as far as we understand it, appears to describe a world that is genuinely random in its most fundamental physical operations. Moreover, everyday cause and effect are not basic features of the world; they are built on a substrate of uncaused events and large-scale statistical regularities.[45]

So it is true that the commonsense and traditional philosophical notions of causality are inadequate, and that medieval philosophical rationalists criticizing orthodox Muslim views were not entirely correct about causality. This does not mean, however, that medieval Muslim occasionalism was on the right track. Muslims have traditionally placed more emphasis on God's total sovereignty than have Western Christians. They have demanded less of a reason behind divine acts beyond a vague sense of a moral providence governing the world. So, in Islamic conceptions, God might be easier to imagine as a power pulling the strings behind the random-appearing events of the material realm. Nevertheless, the centrality of legal considerations in the Muslim religious consciousness means that God's decisions, though always beyond full comprehension, are never entirely random. Although the divine will cannot be constrained by human reason, it is not completely arbitrary—it is purposeful. Muslims can extrapolate from one legal situation to another, similar situation. Indeed, the traditional Islamic discomfort with concepts of natural causation has less to do with philosophical worries or any appreciation of randomness than the intensely personalistic way Muslims have perceived the world. As described by Lawrence Rosen, "The world is thus seen as quintessentially relational, as being described by the ties among sentient beings that bring still further relationships into existence. Causality is largely a matter of agency, of the actions of reasoning beings, and thus a proper explanation of what happened is incomplete without considering who was involved in its occurrence—both in initiating the event and in experiencing its consequences. What is downplayed is the sense that events cause other events."[46]

As far as the physical world is concerned, Muslim thinking about causality may drift toward occasionalism, but this sense of personal agency and purpose remains. And divine purpose is more fundamental to Muslim thought than metaphysical doctrines about causality. Theologian Mehmet Aydın, for example, argues that Muslim thinkers including al-Ghazali have always accepted causality, since they never went so far as to deny the divine order or nizam evident in the world. He also says that the idea of order comes to mind together with the idea of creation, and that order implies purpose.[47] Moreover, this divine purpose has a deeply moral quality. The nizam of the world is supposed to be a personal and moral order.

In other words, Muslims are typically committed to a view where the universe is morally ordered and where the revealed text confirms this moral order in creation. All this is very different than the picture of the world developed by modern science, in which everything is built up from impersonal physical processes. Our modern understanding departs from strict mechanistic causality by emphasizing the fundamental role of chance in physics. Muslims reflecting on quantum mechanics, in contrast, want to replace mechanistic causality with a more personalistic view, where everything is ultimately explained by divine intentions.

Muslim theology has the resources to construct more sophisticated views of physics than the efforts of Nurcu apologists. Still, even when much better grounded in Muslim traditions, attempts to harness modern physics to serve Islam are inevitably similar to science-in-the-Quran claims. The world of quantum mechanics is too different from anything imagined in ancient religious texts or medieval theologies. Bringing them together always starts with hunting for superficial parallels, and ends up bending both sacred texts and modern science beyond recognition.

FRAGMENTS OF SCIENCE

Claims that scripture anticipates science or that modern science can be interpreted to support medieval theology are not unique to Islam. Conservative religious believers from many traditions try to combine fragments of faith with fragments of science—the motley collection of "scientific facts" dug up from their sacred texts. The modern world presents similar challenges to religious communities, and these communities often respond in similar ways. So Hindus, for example, or orthodox Jews can be just as eager to proclaim that science supports their revelation. Many Buddhists, no less than Nurcu Muslims, like to say that paranormal phenomena are real and validate their doctrines. American Christians, living in one of the most technologically advanced societies in the world, produce some apologetics very similar to popular Muslim literature. One Baptist text says that Job 38:35, "Can you dispatch the lightning on a mission and have it answer you, 'I am ready'?" is an "anticipation of radio."[48] Henry M. Morris, the leading figure in Protestant creationism, regularly writes about matters such as how the Christian Trinity is reflected in the three dimensions of space or how the universe supposedly is a "Space-Matter-Time continuum," so that "there is a remarkable tri-unity pervading the physical universe, and also one throughout the biological creation."[49] Indeed, Morris says the Bible mentions everything from the conservation laws of physics to dinosaurs—the "behemoth" appearing in Job 40:15–24.[50]

The Internet is an especially good source for such claims, as it is the more technologically aware segments of a population that have the greater motivation to combine ancient religion and modern technology. Clearly, the notion that science confirms deeply held spiritual beliefs is attractive to many different religious communities. Is there, then, anything distinct about Muslim efforts to find science in the Quran? Why should Muslim distortions of science be especially worthy of attention?

One reason is that, especially when compared with Christian parallels, the Muslim world supports more prominent examples of science-in-scripture apologetics. They are very popular and have a significant influence on the Muslim public perception of science. While Christian efforts to discover science anticipated in the Bible exist, they are less known even within the conservative Christian subculture. Christians defending the divine nature of the Bible regularly misrepresent historical and archaeological knowledge to claim that the Bible is without error or that biblical prophecies have been fulfilled. Nevertheless, the notion that natural science appears in the Bible has never become as popular. More important, the influence of science-in-scripture apologetics like that of Henry M. Morris is confined to a fundamentalist subculture. Morris is popular among conservative Protestants only; his work does not get any respect outside this large but limited constituency. In the Muslim world, thinkers such as Morris are more common, and their influence is more penetrating.

Popular Muslim literature about science starts with science-in-the-Quran writings, and these blend into a heady mix of Islamic reflections including Nurcu-style themes and strange relics of medieval Sufi numerology.[51] This is an extensive literature available everywhere; it is not confined to any sect, movement, or nation. More sophisticated religious thinkers naturally downplay such ideas. But even then, it is not too surprising to find crude science-in-the-Quran apologetics in works by academics and scientists. For example, Turkish sociologist Adil Şahin tries to provide a sociological perspective on science and religion, but in the middle of his book he says,

> The value attributed to science is due its enabling of technological progress. As these changes take place in full view of humanity, they cast a spell on people, distancing them from immortal and eternal truths. In this context, science is thought to have a more important status than religion. However, science still needs to go a long way to achieve the technological goals anticipated by religion. Humanity has been able to transmit sound with the telephone and images with the television, but has not yet been able to do matter transmission. The Quran lets us know that this also is possible, that this too has a science that makes it possible, and that someone who possessed this knowledge (an angel or the vizier of the Prophet Solomon) instantly transported the throne of the Queen of Sheba from the land of Yemen to the presence of the Prophet Solomon.[52]

The Pakistani physicist Pervez Hoodbhoy gives many examples of Muslim natural scientists and engineers engaging in the same sort of popular apologetics, claiming all sorts of miraculous knowledge in the Quran.[53]

Intellectual life in Muslim countries is more open to populist religious influences. The technologically advanced West might have a different problem, where knowledge is divided up into domains of specialized, autonomous expertise, and it can be difficult to achieve a more integrated perspective. Especially in the United States, the serious divide between the academic world and the devout population can have unfortunate consequences, as the unending controversy over evolution in public science education illustrates. Still, in the West, conflicts between academic science and religious populism usually have been easier to contain. In the Muslim world, the price of harmony is often a larger influence for religion.

Another difference in the Muslim case is that most modern forms of Islam are very *text*-centered. It is often said that for devout Muslims, the Quran occupies a similar religious position that Jesus does in most versions of Christianity. The Quran is the central sacred object; its divine nature and freedom from error are not negotiable. In fact, textual fundamentalism is very attractive in an environment where more believers than ever are literate and unsatisfied with traditional structures of religious authority. Popular Islamic movements promise the faithful access to the sacred texts—the Quran, hadith, and perhaps secondary texts like the *Epistles of Light*—and the guidance to be derived from the texts. This promise is enormously successful in winning over the faithful.

So even though science-in-the-Quran arguments largely featured in the popular literature have an air of disreputability about them, they highlight a difficulty that modernizing Muslims feel keenly. The Quran is *the* sacred text, and even if it may become more open to different readings, this cannot go so far as to make its meanings too obviously a product of human interpretation. And at face value, many of the Quran's fact claims cannot be reconciled with modern knowledge. If modern science has a good handle on the universe, then the Quran is just mistaken about the seven layers of skies or the nature of mountains. It could hardly have been otherwise, since the Quran presents a mishmash of ancient Middle Eastern and Hellenistic notions about the natural world.

Modern secular thinkers resolve such problems by accepting that holy writings are human creations, valuing them for the meaning and inspiration they can provide even if they are wrong about many matters of fact. Western intellectuals, including liberal Christians, often naively ask Muslim thinkers to accept that the Quran is a human literary creation, while still taking it as the primary religious text.[54] Someday this may happen, but for now, such a secularized interpretation of the sacred sources is, far from being obvious, not even an option for all but a very small minority of Muslims. Some devout Muslims interpret statements about the seven skies as vague metaphors, conceding that such statements give no useful scientific information without admitting any mistake. It would be hard to find many who are willing to go further.

For many Muslims, even such metaphorical reinterpretations come uncomfortably close to introducing a nondivine element into the text. Some prefer to respond by denying that modern science should be allowed to dictate how the universe works. If there is any apparent conflict, the divine word is by far the more trustworthy source. So a popular Muslim Web site tells a reader puzzled about some traditions that "the believer's responsibility with regard to reports of the unseen is to accept and submit to them, and not to ask how or why. This is the foundation on which our 'aqeedah [faith] must be built, because this is a matter that is beyond your comprehension. So you have to accept it and submit and say, 'We believe. We believe that the sun will be brought close to mankind on the Day of Resurrection until it is one mile away from them.' Asking any further questions about that is a kind of innovation (bid'ah)."[55]

Even in the here and now, the Quran comes first. So, in 1966, Sheikh Abdulaziz bin Baz, the respected mufti of Saudi Arabia, announced that according to the Quran and the traditions, the sun revolves around the earth.[56] This may seem absurd to anyone with a modern education, but for a traditional scholar who refuses to let modern ideas influence how the sacred sources are read, this is a perfectly legitimate conclusion. Bin Baz's approach is, in fact, curiously compelling in its rigor and consistency. Nevertheless, it is not sustainable today. It might work for groups willing to withdraw from the modern world in order to live their faith as purely as possible. Some Muslim religious orders try this, in isolated, tight-knit sects similar to ultraorthodox Jewish communities. Few can live this way, and even those who do depend on the existence of a wider, less rigorous community of coreligionists.

For most modern-day Muslims, the best option is to seek a kind of compromise. They accept technology without reservation and acknowledge modern knowledge in the form of usable fragments of science, joining these with the fragments of faith that survive the ruin of Islam's encounter with the West. They try to achieve a kind of harmony, regardless of any intellectual difficulties either scientists or traditional ulama might perceive. For as is clear in the success of the Nur movement and similar religious currents in the Muslim world, strategies such as science-in-the-Quran apologetics *work*. They allow devout people not far removed from traditional social backgrounds to join the modern world.

Still, to secularists who worry about science in the lands of Islam, the superficially science-positive attitude of Nurcus and similar movements is not much comfort. The problem Muslims face is not just assimilating current technology but sustaining a local scientific community that can generate new knowledge. And it is unclear whether in the long run movements such as the Nurcus will help or hinder in this regard.

NOTES

1. Pippa Norris and Ronald Inglehart, *Sacred and Secular: Religion and Politics Worldwide* (New York: Cambridge University Press, 2004).

2. Talip Küçükcan and Ali Köse, *Doğal Afetler ve Din: Marmara Depremi Üzerine Psiko-Sosyolojik Bir İnceleme* (İstanbul, Turkey: Türkiye Diyanet Vakfı, 2000), pp. 91–105. Such reactions are not a Turkish idiosyncrasy. As I write this after the 2005 earthquake affecting Pakistan and India, I can easily find newspaper reports of similar reactions and of Muslim preachers attributing the quake to divine punishment.

3. David Shankland, *Islam and Society in Turkey* (Huntingdon, UK: Eothen Press, 1999), p. 80.

4. Annemarie Schimmel, *And Muhammad Is His Messenger: The Veneration of the Prophet in Islamic Piety* (Chapel Hill: University of North Carolina Press, 1985), pp. 69–71.

5. M. Hakan Yavuz, *Islamic Political Identity in Turkey* (Oxford: Oxford University Press, 2003), p. 11.

6. I take many of the details of Nursi's life in this section from Şükran Vahide, "A Chronology of Said Nursi's Life" and "Toward an Intellectual Biography of Said Nursi," in *Islam at the Crossroads: On the Life and Thought of Bediuzzaman Said Nursi*, ed. Ibrahim M. Abu-Rabi' (Albany: State University of New York Press, 2003).

7. Bernard Lewis, *What Went Wrong: Western Impact and Middle Eastern Response* (New York: Oxford University Press, 2002), p. 78.

8. Ibrahim M. Abu-Rabi', "How to Read Said Nursi's *Risale-i Nur*," in Abu-Rabi', *Islam at the Crossroads*, p. 66.

9. Yvonne Yazbeck Haddad, "*Ghurbah* as Paradigm for Muslim Life: A *Risale-i Nur* Worldview," in Abu-Rabi', *Islam at the Crossroads*, p. 245.

10. Oral Çalışlar and Tolga Çelik, *Erbakan-Fethullah Gülen Kavgası: Cemaat ve Tarikatların Siyasetteki 40 Yılı* (İstanbul, Turkey: Sıfır Noktası Yayınları, 2000).

11. Vahide, "Toward an Intellectual Biography of Said Nursi," p. 14.

12. Şükran Vahide, "Said Nursi's Interpretation of *Jihad*," in Abu-Rabi', *Islam at the Crossroads*, pp. 101–102.

13. Kelton Cobb, "Revelation, the Disciplines of Reason, and Truth," in Abu-Rabi', *Islam at the Crossroads*, p. 137.

14. Andrew Rippin, *Muslims: Their Religious Beliefs and Practices* (New York: Routledge, 2001), p. 238.

15. Cobb, "Revelation, the Disciplines of Reason, and Truth," p. 135. M. Sait Özervarlı, "Revitalizing Contemporary Islamic Thought," in Abu-Rabi', *Islam at the Crossroads*, p. 327.

16. Ali Bayramoğlu, *Türkiye'de İslami Hareket: Sosyolojik Bir Bakış (1994–2000)* (İstanbul, Turkey: Patika Yayıncılık, 2001), pp. 247–57.

17. M. Fethullah Gülen, *Essentials of the Islamic Faith* (Fairfax, VA: Fountain, 2000).

18. For example, Haluk Nurbaki, *Kur'an-ı Kerim'den Ayetler ve İlmi Gerçekler*, 7th ed. (Ankara, Turkey: Türkiye Diyanet Vakfı, 1998), p. 64.

19. Maurice Bucaille, *The Bible, The Qur'an and Science*, trans. Alastair D. Pannell and Maurice Bucaille (Indianapolis, IN: American Trust Publications, 1979).

20. Ibid., p. 200.

21. Keith L. Moore, "A Scientist's Interpretation of References to Embryology in the Qur'an," *Journal of the Islamic Medical Association* 18 (1986): 15. This has also found its way into Saudi medical texts; for example, Keith L. Moore et al., *Human Development as Described in the Quran and Sunnah* (Makkah, Saudi Arabia: Commission on Scientific Signs of the Quran and Sunnah, 1992).

22. Ibid.

23. Basim Musallam, "The Human Embryo in Arabic Scientific and Religious Thought," in *The Human Embryo: Aristotle and the Arabic and European Traditions*, ed. G. R. Dunstan (Exeter, UK: University of Exeter Press, 1990), pp. 39–40.

24. Bucaille, *The Bible, The Qur'an and Science*, p. 205.

25. Ibid., p. 158.

26. Nurbaki, *Kur'an-ı Kerim'den Ayetler ve İlmi Gerçekler*, p. 9.

27. Ibid., pp. 146–47.

28. J. Edward Wright, *The Early History of Heaven* (New York: Oxford University Press, 2000).

29. Alternate translations from Ahmed Ali's version, 1984.

30. Bucaille, *The Bible, The Qur'an and Science*, pp. 166–67. Nurbaki, *Kur'an-ı Kerim'den Ayetler ve İlmi Gerçekler*, pp. 197–200. Ahmad Mahmud Soliman, *Scientific Trends in the Qur'an*, rev. ed. (London: Ta-Ha Publishers, 1995), p. 25.

31. Footnote to Ahmed Ali's translation of *The Qur'an* (New York: Quality Paperback Book Club, 1992), p. 282.

32. Nurbaki, *Kur'an-ı Kerim'den Ayetler ve İlmi Gerçekler*, pp. 137–42.

33. Soliman, *Scientific Trends in the Qur'an*, p. 14.

34. Ibid., pp. 27, 95, 107–108.

35. Mevlüt Uyanık, *Bilginin İslamileştirilmesi ve Çağdaş İslam Düşüncesi* (Ankara: Ankara Okulu Yayınları, 2001), p. 88. Shabbir Akhtar, *A Faith for All Seasons: Islam and the Challenge of the Modern World* (Chicago: Ivan R. Dee, 1991), pp. 53–55.

36. Soliman, *Scientific Trends in the Qur'an*, p. 101.

37. Nurbaki, *Kur'an-ı Kerim'den Ayetler ve İlmi Gerçekler*, p. 134.

38. For critiques, see Victor J. Stenger, *The Unconscious Quantum: Metaphysics in Modern Physics and Cosmology* (Amherst, NY: Prometheus Books, 1995); Taner Edis, *The Ghost in the Universe: God in Light of Modern Science* (Amherst, NY: Prometheus Books, 2002), chap. 3.

39. For example, Pir Vilayat Inayat Khan, *Thinking Like the Universe: The Sufi Path of Awakening* (New York: Jeremy P. Tarcher/Putnam, 1999).

40. Murad Hoffmann, *Islam: The Alternative*, 2nd ed. (Beltsville, MD: Amana, 1999), pp. 53–54.

41. Muhammed Bozdağ, "Mutlak Gerçeklik Arayışında Bilim ve Din," *Köprü* 53 (1996), available at http://www.koprudergisi.com (accessed December 3, 2006).

42. Ibid.

43. Michael Stoeber and Hugo Meynell, eds., *Critical Reflections on the Paranormal* (Albany: State University of New York Press, 1996). David Ray Griffin, *Parapsychology, Philosophy, and Spirituality: A Postmodern Exploration* (Albany: State University of New York Press, 1997).

44. John Polkinghorne, *Belief in God in an Age of Science* (New Haven, CT: Yale University Press, 1998).

45. Edis, *The Ghost in the Universe*, chap. 3; Taner Edis, *Science and Nonbelief* (Westport, CT: Greenwood Press, 2006), chap. 2.

46. Lawrence Rosen, *The Culture of Islam: Changing Aspects of Contemporary Muslim Life* (Chicago: University of Chicago Press, 2002), p. 115.

47. Mehmet S. Aydın, *İslam'ın Evrenselliği* (İstanbul, Turkey: Ufuk Kitapları, 2000), p. 81.

48. Harold L. Fickett Jr., *A Layman's Guide to Baptist Beliefs* (Grand Rapids, MI: Zondervan, 1965), p. 16.

49. Henry M. Morris, "The Tri-Universe," *Back to Genesis* 204 (2005).

50. Ibid.; Henry M. Morris, "Dragons in Paradise," *Impact* 241 (1993).

51. For example, Bahaeddin Sağlam, *Yaratıcı Evrim ve Adem Meselesi* (İstanbul, Turkey: İnsan Yayınları, 2001).

52. Adil Şahin, *İslam ve Sosyoloji Açısından İlim ve Din Bütünlüğü* (İstanbul, Turkey: Bilge Yayınları, 2001), p. 81.

53. Pervez Hoodbhoy, *Islam and Science: Religious Orthodoxy and the Battle for Rationality* (London: Zed Books, 1991).

54. Akbar S. Ahmed, *Postmodernism and Islam: Predicament and Promise* (London and New York: Routledge, 1992), p. 42.

55. Shaykh Muhammad ibn 'Uthaymeen, question 43314 on http://www.islam-qa.com/ (accessed December 3, 2006).

56. Milton Viorst, *In the Shadow of the Prophet: The Struggle for the Soul of Islam* (Boulder, CO: Westview, 2001), p. 207.

CHAPTER 4

CREATED NATURE

THE TROUBLE WITH EVOLUTION

Modern science and conservative monotheistic religions most often clash over evolution. This is certainly true for those Muslims who seek traces of science and technology in the sacred sources. Publications associated with the Nur movement will print interpretations of black holes in terms of Muslim views about the end of the universe and insist that the Quran contains hints about the structure of the atom. They project a sense of harmony between science and Islam. But they also give voice to conflicts, most frequently through articles denouncing Darwin and evolution.

The trouble with evolution goes deeper than Muslim concerns that every word in the Quran must be true. After all, though the Quran describes God as the one who created the heavens and the earth in six days—in 7 Al-Araf 54, 10 Yunus 3, 11 Hud 7, and 25 Al-Furqan 59—it does not provide any detailed creation story like those in the book of Genesis. Biblical literalists have to worry about the age of the earth and the sequence of events in the days of creation, and many of them conclude that the earth and the universe must have been created in six literal days just a few thousand years ago. Muslims, in contrast, are less interested in the age of the earth. Maurice Bucaille says that since the Quran is vague about the matter, it is easy to interpret the "six days" as six very long periods.[1] Biological evolution is harder to fit into the Quranic picture, but many Muslims agree that some forms of life could very well be related to one another, as long as humans are acknowledged to be specially created as described in the Quran: made out of clay, and descended from Adam and Eve.

In fact, devout Muslims hold a wide variety of positions concerning common descent—evolution in the sense that a sparrow and a butterfly have a common ancestor. Though many are suspicious of common descent, Muslims who think evolution can be accommodated are not rare. Muslims are more united in resisting *Darwinian* evolution—the prevailing view in modern biology that natural mechanisms alone suffice to explain the history of life. As prominent Turkish creationist Adem Tatlı explains, "In the end, the theory of evolution states that all creatures come about through accidents without a prior plan or guidance, or that they originate by chance. Creationists state that everything from atoms to galaxies was created in a conscious, planned, wise, and purposeful fashion. This is the point where the theory of evolution conflicts with religions."[2] So evolution is a flash point, not because of individual verses from the Quran or any handful of scientific fact claims, but because the modern theory of evolution is embedded in a thoroughly naturalistic picture of the world. The world, naturalists claim, is best explained without supernatural realities. Muslims oppose this naturalism, presenting an alternative picture where divine harmony and moral significance are visible in the very fabric of nature.

Indeed, for Muslims who want to slay the dragon of modern naturalism, evolution is a most appropriate target. Naturalism is inspired by physics as well as biology: it builds on the success of modern physics, expecting that the universe is describable in terms of combinations of physical laws and random events. As biologist Jacques Monod put it, modern science has tended to reduce everything to "chance and necessity."[3] Instead of referring to the purposes and actions of supernatural agents, physicists expect that nature is best explained in fundamentally impersonal, mathematical terms. And so, the most ambitious forms of naturalism today claim that every process in existence, including life and mental activity, is physically realized.[4] A naturalistic account of evolution is central to such ambitions because it explains functional complexity in strictly physical terms. Intuitively, for most people, the intricate interlocking complexity of life is a clear sign that a supernatural intelligence has designed nature. But the Darwinian mechanism relies on accidents to generate novelty, and on natural selection to pick out the novelties that produce a reproductive advantage. Darwinian evolution is not just a theory explaining evidence such as the fossil record but a theory that locates *creativity* in the physical world. After Darwin, naturalistic scientists and philosophers had a good idea how the complexities of life and mind bubbled up from the lifeless, mindless processes described by physicists. Today, Darwinian variation and selection is central to biology, helping explain development and somatic adaptability as well as evolution on the grand scale.[5] And Darwinian thinking is no longer just the province of biologists. Anywhere scientists try to understand functional complexity, whether it is in cosmology, artificial intelligence research, or cognitive neuroscience, Darwinian ideas regularly come into play. When scientists explain moral perceptions and behavior, and even when they investigate the almost universal human belief in supernatural agents, evolution is a central element of the best theories. As a result, Daniel C. Dennett likens Darwinian evolution to a "universal acid" eating away at all supernatural ideas.[6]

While physics provides the framework for modern naturalism, the specifically physical arguments relevant to naturalism are invariably complex and technical. Discussions about the origin of the universe, for example, involve some very counterintuitive ideas in physical cosmology that make the traditional philosophical disputes over the eternity or finiteness of the universe irrelevant—modern physics forces us to rethink our basic concepts of time and causality.[7] None of this directly touches on everyday human concerns; physical cosmology has little relevance for existential questions or moral worries. Evolution, however, is different. Although modern evolutionary theory is also very technical and hard to grasp intuitively, its conflicts with common supernatural beliefs are much more obvious. By casting doubt on scriptural notions of special creation, evolution directly challenges orthodox doctrines. And there is a deeper problem as well. Evolution goes against traditional views of cosmic history and the place of humans in nature. Instead of a special divine creation midway between the angels and the beasts, we become a very intelligent species of animal.

Muslim intellectuals are well aware of such troublesome aspects of evolution. Moreover, much Muslim thinking about science, whether it addresses the general public or a more intellectual community, is driven by concerns to assimilate technical knowledge while guarding against secular, naturalistic influences. Such concerns contribute to the Muslim suspicion of evolution. After all, from its very inception, Darwinian theory has provided scientific support for the ongoing secularization of Western intellectual culture. Western science appears to Muslims with enticing benefits, such as improved medical technology, but these benefits come wrapped in theories that suggest humans are just part of an impersonal natural order. So the theory of evolution becomes a symbol of the godless, dangerous path taken by secular Western science. It inspires resistance.

Many conservative Christians and Jews also resist evolution, for very similar reasons. In the United States, a politically powerful religious conservatism continually attacks evolution as part of its culture wars. Many Americans share a populist distrust of evolution and the scientific and educational elites who favor evolution. At this grassroots level, a literally read Bible confronts evolution, caricaturized as the notion that complex objects can be assembled by pure chance. Young-earth creationists insist that science, when done properly without a prior commitment to a materialistic philosophy, affirms that the world was created in six days just thousands of years ago, and that "molecules to man macroevolution" is a gross scientific impossibility. Conservative Protestants in the United States generate an extensive pseudoscientific literature and support organizations such as the Institute for Creation Research. And compared to the rest of the technologically advanced Western world, this kind of creationism looks very much like a sectarian preoccupation of a powerful but narrow segment of American Protestantism.

Even in the United States, however, religious ambivalence about evolution is not confined to the crude religious populism of the young-earth creationists. Recently, opposition to evolution has been coalescing around the intelligent design (ID) movement, which attempts to present a more intellectually respectable rejection of Darwinian evolution. ID proponents include a number of philosophers and a handful of scientists; they argue that Darwinian variation and selection cannot account for the creation of new information. Though ID looks like a complete failure as a scientific claim,[8] it has become politically influential in the United States, continually trying to make inroads into science education. Significantly, ID proponents attack Darwinian evolution not just because they mistakenly consider it a biological failure but because they correctly perceive that Darwinian thinking is a centerpiece of modern naturalism. They claim that chance and necessity are not sufficient to explain our world, that intelligence and the products of intelligent design cannot be captured by physical explanations. They are wrong—there are very good reasons to think that no ID-like argument can succeed, indeed, that human intelligence itself is enabled by broadly Darwinian processes in human brains.[9] Nevertheless, the ID movement enjoys some success because it is based on broad intellectual themes and intuitions concerning divine design shared by most theistic religious traditions.[10]

Muslim critics of evolution have similar motivations and rely on the same kind of arguments as their Christian and Jewish counterparts. In the Islamic case as well, the grassroots constituency for creationism favors crude scripture-based arguments: creationism starts at the same level as science-in-the-Quran apologetics. After all, attempts to present modern science as rediscovering Quranic wisdom can only go so far; modern audiences eventually become aware of scientific ideas, like evolution, that challenge traditional Islamic views. So even popular apologists must confront modern science as well as try to enlist science in the service of faith. Islamic creationism serves this purpose.

Moreover, in the Muslim world no less than in Christian lands, conservative populism alone can enjoy only a limited success. Since naturalistic ideas have a significant influence in intellectual circles and in the educational establishment, more sophisticated forms of resistance also have a role to play. Muslim intellectuals need to present an alternative to the naturalism drifting in from the West and maybe even point the way for scientific institutions to restore God to the center of their conception of nature. So Muslims also have their equivalents of ID proponents sporting PhD degrees.

There is, however, also an important difference between Christian and Muslim creationism. In Western Europe, creationism is negligible except in fundamentalist enclaves. Very often, immigrant Muslim communities generate the loudest objections to evolution in public education.[11] In the United States, even though Christian conservatism is very strong, creationists remain intellectual outsiders. They enjoy considerable popular support; polls regularly indicate that roughly half of Americans agree with outright creationist views, with most of the rest accepting a non-Darwinian, divinely guided version of evolution. In intellectual life, however, Christian doubters of evolution continually struggle to recover an all-but-defeated tradition. Muslim creationists, in contrast, can count on more than popular religious sympathy. They certainly have popular support: the Muslim world is perhaps the part of the world in which evolution has penetrated the least and where the strongest forms of creationist pseudoscience can be found. In a 2005 survey measuring the proportion of adults who accept evolution in thirty-one European countries plus Japan, the United States, and Turkey, the United States ranked thirty-third, while Turkey came in last. In most European countries, over 60 percent of those surveyed accepted evolution, while around 25 percent were sure evolution was false. In Turkey, about 25 percent favored evolution while just over 50 percent opposed evolution.[12] But there is a more important factor than popular opposition to evolution. Muslim creationists do not oppose the consensus of their own intellectual high culture—naturalism has penetrated very little into their culture and an ID-like view remains the common intellectual background. Darwinian evolution comes as an import from the West, defended by westernizing elements. And so Muslim antievolutionary thought does not aim to reverse a defeat but to reassert the authentic local tradition. Muslim creationists are insiders.

MUSLIMS RESPOND TO DARWIN

Soon after *The Origin of Species* was published, Darwin also came to the attention of intellectuals in the Ottoman Empire. A small but influential westernized, Western-educated elite had already been fascinated by scientific developments in Europe; they were especially interested in cases where it seemed that science exposed the errors of religious obscurantism. In Europe, evolution had become a much-discussed topic—even more for its cultural and philosophical implications than for its insights into biology. Westernized Ottoman Turks and Arabs reacted the same way. Some enthusiastically embraced evolution, taking it as a particularly striking component of nineteenth-century philosophical materialism. They cared about the prospect of progress and enlightenment and about confirming that the ulama were mired in archaic superstition, not about fossils or biogeography.

More devout Muslim thinkers, however, were not prepared to respond positively to the implicit materialism of theories such as Darwinian evolution. Most were suspicious, especially since Darwinian ideas were introduced and defended by radical westernizers who included people who flirted with a more explicit materialism. Since evolution was a product of science, and since most intellectuals advocated some measure of reform and wanted to import much of Western knowledge, evolution inevitably became a minor topic of public discussion. Among Arab intellectuals as well as Turks in the center of the Ottoman Empire, the new ideas about evolution filtering in from Europe aroused interest.[13] Still, the more moderate westernizers, who hoped to borrow Western science but purify it of materialist elements, acted with ambivalence. Prominent early Islamic modernists, in fact, rejected evolution outright. Jamal al-Din al-Afghani denounced the theory, finding it absurd and unacceptable.[14] The political climate within the 1870s Ottoman Empire also did not favor open discussion of Darwinian ideas. Religious scholars issued rulings saying that those who discussed the Darwinian hypothesis might be considered apostates, a condition that invited dire punishments. The Ottoman state appears to have found it most expedient to cool down the situation by tightening censorship.[15]

So Darwinian ideas remained confined to a small section of a westernized elite. Outside this group, evolution was either unknown or considered to be impious and incompatible with Islam. This early reaction against Darwin limited the penetration of evolutionary ideas. And with little public knowledge or discussion of evolution, no active opposition to Darwinian evolution developed beyond the occasional superficial rejection. The vast majority of the Muslim population, including most devout Muslim intellectuals, knew little about Darwinian evolution and held a naively creationist view of life.

Secularists continued to admire Darwin. For example, Mustafa Kemal Atatürk, principal founder and leader of the Turkish Republic, was known to have been very interested in the Darwinian theory as a student in the Ottoman War Academy.[16] The radical westernizers who took power in Turkey in the 1920s made sure that the modern education system that they implemented included plenty of instruction in natural science, including topics such as Darwinian evolution. Again, however, this did not inspire much active creationism. As far as religious conservatives were concerned, the new secular education system included more serious insults to traditional religion than a few paragraphs in biology textbooks. So, curiously, the secularist embrace of Darwin did not lead to much explicit opposition to evolution since evolution remained only a minor point of friction among much more important challenges to traditional beliefs. The Nur movement and similar religious currents always rejected Darwinian thinking, and the occasional antievolutionary statement appeared in religious publications. But few outside of modernized elites wholeheartedly agreed with evolution, and people passively resisting official secularism extended their distrust to evolution without singling out Darwin for special criticism.

In 1970s Turkey, evolution started to generate more controversy. The creationist literature of this decade was no different than before: largely Nurcu-linked publications denouncing evolution as going against religion and true science alike. They included some typical creationist claims, such as the notion that the extreme improbability of protein formation by pure chance demonstrated that evolution was impossible.[17] These arguments appear to have been constructed independently of Western creationist movements. After all, there are a limited number of ostensibly scientific creationist arguments possible. The more notable development came when some governments in the 1970s included an Islamist party as a junior coalition partner.

Some members of parliament from this party objected to the presence of evolution in textbooks.[18] Nothing much came of their complaints, but the ensuing debate showed that religious conservatives were becoming more vocal about their discomfort with evolution— or that they began to see ideas such as evolution as targets in a culture war, as a way of indirectly opposing official secularism.

The big opening for Turkish creationists came in the mid-1980s, in the aftermath of the military dictatorship of 1980–1983.[19] The civil strife and continuing failures of the political process in the late 1970s led to a military takeover, and even though the generals cited Islamist extremism among the reasons that led to their coup, they considered the political left to be a more serious threat. So they decided to put more emphasis on Islam as a force for national unity. For example, they imposed a new constitution that reaffirmed secular government but also included features such as mandatory religious instruction in schools. A few high schools in liberal urban areas treated this as a "world religions" course, but in practice, the constitutional requirement almost always meant a class in Sunni Islam.

The educational and cultural policies of the dictatorship period showed a strong cultural conservatism. A 1983 report of the State Planning Organization, on the subject of a national cultural policy, endorsed the idea of a "Turkish-Islamic Synthesis," which appeared to be on its way to becoming a quasi-official ideology.[20] The report is especially curious when it comments on history and science. Along with pseudohistory about the pre-Islamic culture of Central Asian Turkic peoples, the report includes attacks against Darwin as an apostle of materialism: "Prominent among naturalist views that reduce humans to nature, count them as part of it, and deny human spiritual superiorities that do not exist in nature and cannot be derived from nature, is Darwin [sic]. This biological hypothesis has declared humans to be of monkey origin, and asserted that the mechanistic workings of nature are completed with the last stage of evolution progressing from monkey to human."[21]

The generals soon handed power over to a civilian government in a restricted election. A conservative party emerged as the winner and continued similar cultural and educational policies. One of the main factions of this party were religious conservatives; they took over the Ministry of Education. As a result, Turkey took an official turn toward creationism. And in bringing about this change, Muslim conservatives sought inspiration from an unusual source: "scientific creationists" among American Protestants. A publication of the Institute for Creation Research (ICR) describes the events as: "Sometime in the mid 1980s, the Turkish Minister of Education, Mr. Vehbi Dinçerler . . . placed a call to ICR. . . . [H]e wanted to eliminate the secular-based, evolution-only teaching dominant in their schools and replace it with a curriculum teaching the two models[.] As a result, several ICR books which dealt with the *scientific* (not Biblical) evidence for creation were translated into Turkish and distributed to all Turkey's public school teachers."[22]

The American creationists had long had contacts in Turkey due to their ever-fruitless but always hopeful expeditions hunting for the remains of Noah's Ark in the mountains of eastern Turkey. Suddenly they found themselves in the position of Western experts consulted by the Turkish government. Just as secularists looked toward the West for scientific knowledge, the religious conservatives would do the same—even if the authorities they sought out were not at all taken seriously in Western scientific circles.

Minister Dinçerler also enlisted local talent, such as Adem Tatlı, a university professor and creationist connected to the Nur movement. In 1985 Dinçerler asked Tatlı to prepare an extensive report on the theory of evolution. Tatlı recalls commenting, "Darwinism, along with Marxism and Freudism, constitutes the basis of materialist philosophy. Your opposition to evolution theory may, I fear, lose you your position." The minister replied: "I feel the spiritual responsibility of 15 million children of the nation on my shoulders. The faith of our youth is shaken by the one-sided presentation of such a theory. For the truth of this matter to be understood and be set in its proper course, let not only one, but a thousand Vehbi positions be sacrificed." Tatlı's report describes evolution as "a theory that has not been able to become a law for 120 years," and recommends "inclusion in the curriculum of the shortcomings of this theory and opposing opinions."[23] Tatlı takes most of his arguments directly from the American creationist literature; he often cites leading figures of ICR such as Henry Morris and Duane Gish, presenting them as Western scientists who have come to see the flaws in evolutionary theory.

Intellectually dubious, ideological government reports are not a rarity. Starting in the 1980s, however, Tatlı's report reflected and inspired official policy. The Ministry of Education translated books by leaders of the ICR and distributed them to teachers free of charge. Creationism appeared in high school biology textbooks, some of which presented evolution as a failed and implausible theory, leading up to the conclusion that the universe and all within were specially created by God.[24] Religious conservatives have been in and out of power since, and how evolution appears in Turkish textbooks depends largely on who controls the Ministry of Education at any moment. At present, with moderate Islamists in power, biology textbooks tend to give creationism equal standing with evolution. Moreover, many high school biology teachers teach creationism. Those who teach evolution can face enormous social pressure; some have even been suspended by hostile administrators.[25]

Turkey is perhaps the Muslim country in which Darwinian ideas penetrated the most, accompanying the radical secularism of the early Turkish Republic. In Turkey, there was at least enough evolution to bother religious conservatives. In the 1980s, a creationist pseudoscience began in Turkey that went beyond simple religiously based rejection of evolution. The Nur movement was instrumental in this transformation, connecting antievolutionary views with the same habits of thought that found science all over the Quran. In the 1990s, Turkey would take the next step, becoming the center for an aggressive Islamic creationism that enjoyed influence throughout the Muslim world.

HARUN YAHYA

After achieving sporadic official endorsement, Turkish creationism continued to flourish. Islamist intellectuals paid more attention to evolution, typically treating it as a materialist myth with insidious effects on morals and religion. In Turkish academic circles, a few scientists with backgrounds in Nurcu and similar religious movements felt encouraged to proclaim an "alternative biology" that replaced Darwinian evolution with a view that emphasized traditional Islamic perceptions of divine design in nature.[26] But the most important development came toward the end of the 1990s, when Turkish creationism became a modern, media-driven, popular pseudoscience.

The work of "Harun Yahya," said to be a pseudonym for Adnan Oktar, was central to the newest wave of creationism. Oktar was already known as a charismatic and controversial leader of a small Muslim sect notorious for attracting the children of social elites. Surprisingly, around 1997, he reappeared as the leading figure of Turkish creationism. A number of books under the name of Harun Yahya hit the shelves, promoting creationism alongside some other preoccupations of Islamic conservatives in Turkey. An organization called the Science Research Foundation promoted the Yahya books and made creationism a centerpiece of its views on science and culture. These efforts tied in with a series of "international conferences" promoting creationism, in which Turkish creationist academics shared the stage with American creationists from ICR and similar organizations.[27]

From the beginning, the distinguishing feature of Harun Yahya's creationism was its very modern, media-savvy nature. Previously, Turkish creationism was a low-budget operation, even when it found official endorsement. Devout Muslim intellectuals wrote articles and books railing against Darwin and lobbied for state cultural and educational policy to reflect their views. They wrote for the already committed conservative Muslim public, making little effort to appeal to a wider readership. Yahya's operation changed all this. The books that appear under Harun Yahya's name are attractive, well produced, lavishly illustrated, on good quality paper. In a poor country such as Turkey, this means that creationist literature looks better packaged than books popularizing mainstream science. Moreover, Yahya did not stop at books, or even at advertising creationism through "conferences," op-eds, and media events. Soon well-made videos and slick monthly magazines promoting Yahya's creationism appeared on the market. Indeed, there must have been few forms of media that escaped Harun Yahya's attention. For the many Turks who cannot afford DVDs, there are creationist videos in the cheaper and quite popular VCD (Video CD-ROM) format. For those put off by the price tag on slick books—though their prices are artificially low—there are cheap booklets on low-quality paper, giving abridged versions of Yahya's prodigious output. These have occasionally been distributed free of charge. Those online can visit one of the many Web sites devoted to Harun Yahya and creationism, from those that claim to expose the many lies of Darwinist media to the main site that makes practically everything written under the Yahya name available at no cost.[28]

Yahya's creationism appeals beyond the core audience of conservative religious believers. There are many pious but also modernized people, many who work in a high-tech world but seek to anchor themselves in tradition and spirituality. So the Harun Yahya material is distributed in secular book and media outlets, not just in religious bookstores or stalls adjoining mosques. They are available in some supermarket chains, just like Christian inspirational books are found in Wal-Marts across the United States. Even the way the Yahya material uses the Turkish language indicates a desire to reach a broader audience. Conservative Muslim intellectuals in Turkey typically use an older version of Turkish that hearkens back to Ottoman times, especially in its heavy use of Arabic and Persian loan words. After the Turkish revolution, secular nationalists pushed for a more purely Turkish language, which was supposed to bring official and intellectual language more in line with everyday speech. The language in the media, literature, and daily use diverged from the more archaic imperial Ottoman form that conservative Muslims tended to favor. The Yahya material uses a simpler, less Arabized everyday Turkish—the books and videos are not marked out as belonging to the orthodox, conservative subculture that is not always attractive to every Turk.

The way Adnan Oktar and others associated with the Yahya material present themselves also reinforces the modern image of the new creationism. Yahya and the Science Research Foundation literature support modern Turkish nationalism; far from indulging in the conservative religious hostility toward Atatürk, founder of the secular Republic of Turkey, they miss no opportunity to proclaim their admiration of the great man. They do not insist on traditional cultural symbols such as Islamic dress; in fact, they conspicuously endorse modern clothing and modern lifestyles. Their image is that of modern, technologically sophisticated people who enjoy success in a global capitalist economy. They are not reactionaries but leaders who have a key to reconciling science and religion, a way of affirming tradition and spirituality while enjoying the benefits of modern life.

The impressive scope of Yahya's media operation raises questions about its financial resources. Sales alone cannot suffice, especially since Yahya material is often given away free and is available through numerous Web sites. Advertising is also negligible on creationist media. For example, the August 2002 issue of *Mercek*, a Yahya-linked "monthly scientific and cultural magazine" sold for about $1.80. A well-produced, full-color magazine printed on glossy paper, it also included two VCDs. The only ad for non-Yahya merchandise it contained was for a series of materials to learn English, an important skill for the upwardly mobile. In 2005 the price had gone up to about $3.20, but *Mercek* continued to include bonus merchandise, for example, full-color, full-length books that would normally be valued at over $15. Yahya's backers must be pouring a lot of money into all these efforts. Yet the details of the organization behind Yahya, and the sources of its finances, are virtually unknown. The Turkish state, notoriously unable to bring the underground economy under control, or even collect taxes from many businesses, cannot reliably enforce regulations on religious foundations who enjoy political protection. The Science Research Foundation claims to be supported by donations. Adnan Oktar's affairs are just as murky. He has often had to defend himself in court, but in Turkey, it is easy to suspect political machinations behind his prosecutions as well as the protection he enjoys.[29] In any case, the resources and clout of Turkish creationists are the envy of American Protestant creationists. As John Morris, president of the ICR, observes, "they have access to more than adequate financial resources, as well as to the media, and are able to blanket the country with creation information."[30]

There is much less novelty in the content of Harun Yahya's creationism. His views, elaborated and repeated in his endless stream of publications, are a grab bag of classic Islamic objections to evolution, arguments copied directly from Christian young-earth creationists and intelligent design proponents, and other snippets from Western writers who claim to find signs of God in some area or other of modern science. Yahya touches on just about all the typical creationist themes, alleging that transitional fossils do not exist, that functioning intermediate forms are impossible anyway, that the evidence for human evolution is fraudulent, that radiometric dating methods are unreliable, that physical cosmology produces clear signs that the universe is a divine design, and that evolution at the molecular level is statistically impossible. Yahya also explains why Western scientists and Turkish fellow-travelers are so enamored of evolution if it is so clearly false. Like Christian creationists, Yahya thinks that beguiled by the secular philosophies of the European Enlightenment, scientists got caught up in a long war against God.[31]

Turkish creationists do not borrow indiscriminately from Christians. For example, they omit ICR's signature doctrine of flood geology, since geological time scales are a lesser problem for Muslim conceptions of history. Although ICR rejects all of modern physical cosmology, Harun Yahya favorably cites old-earth creationists who proclaim that the big bang proves the existence of God, and enthusiastically adopts the intelligent design view that physical constants are fine-tuned to produce intelligent life and that this fine-tuning cannot have any naturalistic explanation. Yahya is an opportunist: he uses any suggestion that Darwin was wrong or that the universe is a divine design, weaving it all together with little regard for the overall coherence of his claims. In all this, Yahya is a very traditional Muslim creationist. Like those who seek science in the Quran, he goes in search of isolated arguments or claims that he can use to support his views. Science, as usual, ends up as a stamp-collecting activity, supplying the "facts" that confirm religious beliefs.

Another interesting difference emerges when Yahya explains how a godless conspiracy established evolution: apparently, the main forces behind the promotion of evolution are Masons and Jews. Anti-Semitism is common among Muslim apologists; indeed, when Harun Yahya first appeared on the scene, he was also listed as the author of a book titled *The Holocaust Hoax*, which borrowed much from well-known American holocaust deniers. The perfidy of Masons is also a common motif in popular Islamic literature, where Freemasonry, as for many Christian conspiratologists in the past, serves as a symbol personifying the Enlightenment culture that helped to erode traditional religiosity.

Adnan Oktar almost certainly does not write more than a fraction of the material appearing under the Harun Yahya name. The intellectual prowess of leaders of religious orders are commonly exaggerated—tales of incredible intellectual productivity function like miracle stories, magnifying the stature of a charismatic teacher.

And attributing writings to a teacher is not out of place in the traditions of Islamic religious orders. In any case, Oktar has no background in science, not even enough for an organized distortion of science. And the sheer volume put out in his name is daunting—not only tracts about creationism and how science proves the existence of God, but also pleas for religions to unite against the Darwinian materialists, writings on devotional and moral themes, praises of Said Nursi and expositions of Nurcu beliefs, and more. As might be expected, consistency is not the hallmark of such a collection. For example, more recent writings under the Harun Yahya name no longer flirt with Holocaust denial, but blame Darwinian thinking for Nazism and the Nazi crimes against the Jews. Still, Yahya always manages to return to his main theme. One book accusing Darwinism of leading to Nazism begins with a "To The Reader" section, where Yahya explains that evolution is at the root of evil today:

> The reason why a special chapter is assigned to the collapse of the theory of evolution is that this theory constitutes the basis of all anti-spiritual philosophies. Since Darwinism rejects the fact of creation, and therefore the existence of God, during the last 140 years it has caused many people to abandon their faith or fall into doubt. Therefore, showing that this theory is a deception is a very important duty, which is strongly related to the religion. It is imperative that this important service be rendered to everyone. Some of our readers may find the chance to read only one of our books. Therefore, we think it appropriate to spare a chapter for a summary of this subject.[32]

The same antievolutionary chapter also appears in *Islam Denounces Terrorism*, a book in which Yahya argues that the true responsibility behind events like the September 11, 2001, terror attacks on the United States lies in Darwinian theories. Apparently, "the way to stop acts of terrorism is to put an end to Darwinist-materialist education, to educate young people in accord with a curricula [*sic*] based on true scientific findings and to instil in them the fear of God and the desire to act wisely and scrupulously."[33]

As a growing media operation, the natural next step for Harun Yahya was to go global. Harun Yahya books, articles, videos, and Web materials were made available first in English, French, German,

Malay, Russian, Italian, Spanish, Serbo-Croat (Bosniak), Polish, and Albanian. Interestingly, Western languages and languages used in the periphery of the Islamic world preceded languages of the Islamic heartland. This is not a great surprise—creationism finds its largest market in partially westernized countries like Turkey and in the Muslim immigrant communities in the West. Evolutionary ideas first have to be widely available before they lead to widespread religious worries. Still, translations into Urdu and Arabic soon followed, as did Indonesian, Estonian, Hausa, Bulgarian, Uighur, Kiswahili, Bengali, and more. Harun Yahya books are now available in many Islamic bookstores around the world, especially as English translations have been printed in London, the global center of Islamic publishing.

This global venture appears to be another success. Harun Yahya has become popular throughout the Muslim world; he is no longer just a Turkish phenomenon. Articles under Yahya's name regularly appear in Islamic publications all over the world. Even in the United States, mass-market introductory books such as *The Complete Idiot's Guide to Understanding Islam* present Yahya as a "top" Muslim scientist with a worthwhile critique of evolution.[34] From small meetings in San Francisco to a series of public presentations in Indonesia, from books to videos to the small Creation Museums that opened in Istanbul in 2006, the gospel of Yahya's Islamic creationism continues to spread. The popularity of creationism might be a sign of modernization in the Islamic world—evidence that Darwinian ideas have finally penetrated enough to inspire a response beyond just reiterating that orthodox doctrines do not allow evolution. Still, the scale and success of enterprises such as that of Harun Yahya do not inspire confidence for the future of science in Islamic lands.

HIGHER LEVELS OF CREATIONISM

Yahya represents a hard-core creationism completely at odds with how modern science pictures the world. Moreover, Yahya stands for a crude, popular point of view. His work does not engage in serious intellectual debate; it is hard to conceive of more sophisticated and scholarly Muslim thinkers joining the Yahya effort.

Still, Turkish creationists seem to have little difficulty finding academic voices to lend them legitimacy in public presentations they call "conferences." Though Oktar has been embroiled in controversy, Harun Yahya has still managed to attract endorsements and encouraging messages, including some from Turkish academic theologians. These messages do not support or elaborate on any specific claim in the Yahya corpus. Instead, they express appreciation for Yahya's overall project. Muslim intellectuals need not be entirely happy about the style or particular substance of Yahya's creationism. There appears, however, to be considerable sympathy for the notion of combating materialism in the form of evolution—prominent Turkish theologians regularly express skepticism about Darwinian evolution, quite independently of the Harun Yahya phenomenon.[35] In however unscholarly a manner, Yahya popularizes a top-down, purposeful view of nature. For Muslim thinkers who want both to claim the power of modern science and to reaffirm the traditional God-centered view of reality, Yahya's overall vision is more important than the details of his arguments.

In fact, many respected academic thinkers among Muslims adopt a less crude and more traditional creationism. For example, philosopher of science Osman Bakar, who was vice-chancellor of the University of Malaya before moving to Georgetown University in 2000, considers evolutionary theory to be a materialist philosophy that attempts to deny nature's manifest dependence on God, its creator.[36] Seyyed Hossein Nasr, a well-known scholar of Islam who has long been based in American universities, argues that Darwinian evolution is a logically absurd idea that is incompatible with the hierarchical view of reality demanded by all genuine religious traditions.

Both Bakar and Nasr rely on classic creationist arguments that would not be out of place in Yahya's writings. Nasr starts by arguing that mathematics and information theory preclude evolution: "One cannot study the cell as it is done today, accept information theory and at the same time accept the current interpretations of the theory of evolution according to which, through temporal processes and without an external cause, which itself must be of a higher order in the sense of being able to increase the information contained within a gene, the amount of information contained within the genes does increase and they 'evolve' into higher forms." Nasr goes on to endorse some very typical creationist claims. He says, for example, that life opposes the second law of thermodynamics, which means that "inert matter evolving into life forms" is impossible. He believes that "the paleontological record hardly supports the evolutionary hypothesis no matter how far it is stretched and how far-fetched is its interpretation," that the Cambrian explosion is inexplicable by evolution, that mutations can only lead to very limited change, and so on.[37] The "scientific" sources Nasr cites include works by Christian creationists associated with the Institute for Creation Research. This ill-informed denunciation of evolution does not appear in a popular text intended for a conservative Muslim market but in an academic book in religious studies put out by an American university press.

Thinkers such as Bakar and Nasr, however, are not primarily concerned with enumerating supposed scientific flaws in evolution. They take the failure of evolution for granted; they are more interested in constructing an alternative view of nature, indeed of science itself—a view that is grounded in classical Muslim conceptions of reality. Bakar supports efforts to develop an alternative "Islamic science" that would incorporate a traditional Muslim perspective into its basic assumptions directing how nature should be studied.[38] Nasr calls for a revival of the traditional Muslim religious sciences, including the more occult and metaphysical sciences, to redirect and sacralize Western science. In his conception, lower levels of reality depend on higher, more spiritual levels, which leads to a satisfactory alternative to evolution:

> Even today, certain scientists who realize the logical and even biological absurdity of the theory of evolution and some of its implications and presuppositions believe that the only other alternative is the *ex nihilo* doctrine, unaware that the traditional metaphysical doctrine interprets the *ex nihilo* statement as implying an elaboration of man's being *in divinis* and through stages of being preceding his appearance on earth. This doctrine of man, based on his descent through various levels of existence above the corporeal, in fact presents a view of the appearance of man which is neither illogical nor at all in disagreement with any scientific facts—and of course not necessarily hypotheses and extrapolations—provided one accepts the hierarchy of existence, or the multiple levels of reality which surround the corporeal state. . . . [T]he whole

> modern evolutionary theory is a desperate attempt to substitute a
> set of horizontal, material causes in a unidimensional world to
> explain effects whose causes belong to other levels of reality, to the
> vertical dimensions of existence.[39]

Again, though such ideas find no support from today's science, they differ from the popular pseudoscience of Harun Yahya. These are ideas that receive serious attention in the highest levels of Muslim intellectual culture. Western scientists are used to working in an environment where the kind of metaphysical and theological doctrines expressed by Nasr or Bakar no longer affect either the practice of science or the way most modern intellectuals perceive the world. In the Muslim world, it is not as easy to ignore theology. Nasr's ideas resonate; his work is well known among Turkish thinkers. Indeed, many others toy with similar notions of reviving and modernizing medieval Muslim views of knowledge, and Nasr's Ismaili Shii background is usually a more weighty reason for controversy than any of the scientific deficiencies of his views.

Still, many Muslims also perceive that an intellectually higher-level creationism is not enough. The notion of rebuilding science with Muslim foundations is very attractive, but since Nasr-style ideas do not make much contact with science—actual, productive science—they are not entirely convincing as a framework for claiming science for Muslim ends. Here, Muslims again have to look toward the West. The intelligent design movement that has been gathering steam in the United States defends many intuitions about design and creation common to a wide variety of religions. When Nasr speaks of the impossibility of creating information within nature, and when he suggests that information and creativity are injected into the material world from above, from higher levels of reality that are not reducible to material causes, he expresses the main themes of intelligent design.

Since the ID movement only crystallized in the 1990s, and its challenge to evolution has only very recently attained a high public profile in the United States, ID has not had time to deeply influence Muslim thinking. Parallels to ID are easy to find in Muslim antievolutionary literature, but these arise from common religious themes rather than direct influence. Nevertheless, ID has begun to penetrate.

First of all, ID attracts attention just because it opposes evolution. Harun Yahya's recent writings include quotations from and citations of major ID proponents. The Islamic press in Turkey has drawn attention to ID in the United States; books by major ID figures have quickly been translated into Turkish and are available in secular bookstores alongside mainstream popularizations of science. There are also a few minor institutional links between Muslim opponents of Darwinian evolution and American ID proponents. For example, Muzaffar Iqbal is listed as a fellow of the International Society for Complexity, Information and Design, a loose organization of philosophers and scientists who support ID and similar ideas. Iqbal is also part of the Center for Islam and Science, a group of Muslim intellectuals promoting "Islamic science." Their journal occasionally publishes papers incorporating ID into proposals for an Islamic view of nature.[40] These linkages, however, seem minimal.

In Turkey, a leading figure promoting ID is Mustafa Akyol, a journalist and up-and-coming modernist Muslim intellectual. Akyol takes care to steer clear of the antagonism toward the West that characterizes some political Islamists; indeed, he sees ID as a means of rapprochement between Islam and a revitalized Christianity. In an article for an American readership, he writes that Muslims often distrust the West because of the materialism within Western intellectual currents, as manifested in theories such as Darwinian evolution. ID, however, presents a more acceptable side of Western civilization:

> By its bold challenge to Darwinian evolution—a concept that claims it is possible to be an "intellectually fulfilled atheist"—ID is indeed a wedge that can split the foundations of scientific materialism. ID presents a new perspective on science, one that is based solely on scientific evidence yet is fully compatible with faith in God. That's why William Dembski, one of its leading theorists, defines ID as a bridge between science and theology.
>
> As the history of the cultural conflict between the modern West and Islam shows, ID can also be a bridge between these two civilizations. The first bricks of that bridge are now being laid in the Islamic world. In Turkey, the current debate over ID has attracted much attention in the Islamic media. Islamic newspapers are publishing translations of pieces by the leading figures of the ID movement, such as Michael J. Behe and Phillip E. Johnson. The

Discovery Institute is praised in their news stories and depicted as the vanguard in the case for God, and President Bush's support for ID is gaining sympathy. For many decades the cultural debate in Turkey has been between secularists who quote modern Western sources and Muslims who quote traditional Islamic sources. Now, for the first time, Muslims are discovering that they share a common cause with the believers in the West. For the first time, the West appears to be the antidote to, not the source of, the materialist plague.[41]

The ID movement is in turn happy to enjoy Muslim support. Since ID commonly faces the accusation that it is merely a clever repackaging of conservative Christian creationism, ID proponents take pains to highlight how people from diverse religious backgrounds support ID. In 2005 Akyol testified in support of ID in hearings held by the Kansas State Board of Education and appeared in American media as a Muslim voice for ID.

So it is easy to expect increasing ID influence on more sophisticated Muslim thinking about evolution, even though ID is almost universally rejected by the Western scientific community. There is much common ground, even in ambitions to reconstruct science to restore God to the way we understand nature. Some Christian philosophers sympathetic to ID dream of a "theistic science" that counters the way mainstream science has veered toward naturalism with a built-in perspective that recognizes divine design.[42] Muslim hopes to Islamize science may yet develop in a more ecumenical direction.

At the very least, ID will help harden Muslim resistance to evolution in intellectual as well as popular religious circles. Yet the way ID can supply the illusion of scientific substance to Muslim as well as Christian creationism should not obscure the deeper resonance ID has with common Muslim ways of thinking. Muslim high culture—the culture of devout scholars and public intellectuals—was already steeped in ID-like convictions long before American ID proponents appeared on the scene. Most devout Muslim thinkers take it to be self-evident that life-forms and nature as a whole are intelligently designed, that the cosmos is a divinely guided, harmonious place where Muslim metaphysics and morality is seamlessly joined with the orbits of the planets and the songs of the birds.

GUIDED EVOLUTION

Many Muslims seek to reconcile Islam and evolution. Some theologians find inspiration in Quranic verses such as 24 An-Nur 45, "And God created all animals from water: some of them travel on their bellies, some travel on two legs, some travel on four. God creates what God will; God is capable of all things." In the tradition of finding science in the Quran, they declare that this verse sounds very much like the modern scientific scenario in which life on Earth originated in the oceans. It could even be compatible with life-forms gradually evolving. Strict creationists, naturally, are not happy with such interpretations. Just like those Christian creationists who object to their compromising brethren, Harun Yahya insists that evolution is incompatible with Islam and criticizes those who seek a middle road.[43] Seyyed Hossein Nasr also sounds a warning: "The evolutionary thesis has also penetrated into the Islamic world through the writings of many of the modernists who picked up the idea either in its scientific or philosophical sense. They then tried to extend the meaning of certain verses of the Quran to include the idea of evolution, although the Quran, like other sacred scriptures, states clearly that the world and all creatures were created by Allah and that the origin of man is not some prehistoric animal but the divinely created primordial man who in the Islamic tradition is called Adam."[44]

The distinction between Nasr's position and that of those who accept some evolution is, however, murky. Muslims who seek a middle path typically only allow evolution in a limited sense and are especially cautious about human origins.

More liberal-minded Muslims certainly have the option of interpreting evolution as a divine means of creation. They can accept biological evolution in the minimal sense, that living things have a common ancestor. This still leaves the question of exactly how life developed and diversified, and it is tempting to say that evolution was a divinely guided unfolding of life, progressing toward greater complexity and spiritual potential. The Adam story might metaphorically describe what happened after human souls were created and joined to material bodies. Indeed, similar reinterpretations are commonly used by Christians who accept that there is considerable truth in the theory of evolution.

Unfortunately, such a non-Darwinian conception of evolution, though conciliatory, has also become intellectually irrelevant to science. Harun Yahya and other creationists correctly point out that it is far from the view current in natural science today. After the mid-twentieth century, no purposive or intrinsically progressive forces survived in biological theories. Scientists understand the history of life and complexity in terms of physical mechanisms combining chance and necessity. Even the notion of developmental constraints, which to a small minority had held out some hope for a built-in direction for evolution, has been subsumed within a Darwinian framework with advances in developmental and molecular biology.[45] So, from the perspective of today's science, if guided evolution means any sort of detectable purposive intervention in evolution, it is very likely false. And if guided evolution stands for a divine power directing evolution from behind the scenes, but in such a way as to make the process indistinguishable from the mindless working out of physical events, it just becomes a questionable metaphysical gloss on evolution. In either case, the notion of divine purpose becomes useless for understanding nature.[46]

Still, the idea of guided evolution has a great virtue: it helps dampen cultural and institutional conflicts between science and religion. Especially in the form of a metaphysical gloss, it allows biologists to remain religious while preventing any overt supernatural influence on the objects of their research. And liberal religious thinkers can, in turn, declare that the fact that life-forms developed over time does not conflict with their faith. So guided evolution is an attractive option for more liberal Muslims, even though, as Nasr points out, mismatches with traditional interpretations of the Quran remain a real concern. But then, this merely means that Muslims have to catch up to the Christians in the art of reinterpreting scripture to make it conform to modern knowledge.

So, unsurprisingly, many modernist Muslim thinkers try to incorporate some evolution into their reformed visions of Islamic metaphysics. For example, the Sudanese liberal Mahmud Muhammad Taha incorporates influences from Marxism, evolution, and psychoanalysis, along with more traditional sources of inspiration such as Sufi mysticism.

[Taha] does not see evolution in linear, but rather cyclical and spiral terms—while he insists on the ultimate unity of all phenomena which in the end are destined to dissolve in God. Hence his constant reminder that differences between things are intrinsically of degree and not of kind. With this evolutionism goes a commitment to the idea of progress and a pronounced meliorism. Taha sees human history in Hegelian, progressive, optimistic terms. The Hegelian Idea is replaced by a Sufi concept of God as an active agent of change on one hand, and as the ultimate end of history on the other hand. Man's history is described in terms of perpetual ascent from lowlier to higher states in an infinite process of self-realization.[47]

Taha's "evolution" has more in common with the mysticism of Pierre Teilhard de Chardin or current New Age and metaphysical conceptions of cosmic evolution than any theory used by biologists. Indeed, from a strictly scientific point of view, such ideas seem nearly as mistaken as Harun Yahya's views—except that they do not challenge modern science as directly.

Most Muslims are less enthusiastic about Taha-style metaphysical excursions, especially if they happen to be wary of Sufism. Indeed, Taha was executed for heresy in 1985, mainly for political reasons. Still, many cautiously accept evolution in a minimal sense. The Turkish theologian Muhammet Altaytaş, for example, has a typical view. He insists that evolution does not conflict with Islam, "provided that this theory stays within scientific boundaries and is not confused with metaphysics and does not present certain hypotheses as 'scientific facts'"—for example, the claim that "everything exists through chance and without purpose."[48] This sounds reasonable enough, but since the central achievement of Darwinian evolution is to explain life and complexity without invoking any external purpose, it is hard to see more than a lukewarm acceptance of the possibility of common descent in such pronouncements.

More interestingly, Altaytaş and some other Turkish thinkers add another reason that evolution in the minimal sense might be acceptable: long before Darwin, Muslim philosophers had come up with the idea of evolution anyway. This claim is based largely on the work of Mehmet Bayrakdar, who examines some writings on nature by Muslim philosophers of the ninth to eleventh centuries and calls for a revival of the "evolutionary creation theory" in Islam.[49] In fact, some Muslim philosophers did elaborate on the idea of the Great Chain of Being that they inherited from Greek philosophy. Accepting that all things were related, occupying various levels on a chain stretching from rocks to metals to plants to animals to humans to angelic beings to God, some even speculated about local adaptations and the relations between species. While interesting, none of this anticipates Darwinian evolution. The handful of medieval Muslim philosophers who showed a passing interest in the subject never broke free of conceiving of species as defined by Platonic essences and did not propose any entirely nonteleological mechanism for biological change. Still, Bayrakdar's work highlights the fact that rigid special creation is not the only option with roots in Muslim tradition.

Muslim writers who support evolution, then, typically have a very non-Darwinian concept of evolution. They accept common descent but maintain an explicit divine design in creation. In many ways, this is an ID-lite approach. After all, many Christian intelligent design proponents agree with evolution in the sense of common descent; they just do not think that Darwinian and other unguided mechanisms can create new information. And ID is just one minority option for theologians and religious-minded scientists to try to impose divine guidance on evolution. ID themes such as information being injected into the evolutionary process from outside nature are not exclusive to the movement calling for ID in public education.[50] ID-lite ideas are common among Christians who accept evolution; it is no great surprise that the same should be true for liberal Muslims.

The strongest support for Darwinian evolution comes from academic biologists and from secularists—heavily Western-influenced minorities. In Turkey, they have only weakly responded to creationism. Some secular scientists and intellectuals comment on the recent waves of creationism and on writers such as Harun Yahya. They do little but deplore the situation and describe creationism as yet another antimodern, threatening aspect of conservative Islamic culture and Islamist politics.[51] While secularists usually reassure their readers that there is no conflict between a properly understood Islam and evolution, they appeal to a privatized concept of faith that few

Muslims share. Strict secularists propose to remove religious faith from the public realm, including the scientific investigation of nature. This achieves compatibility between science and religion, but at a heavy cost. And in practice, while secularists defend Darwin as an icon in their culture war with conservative Islamic movements, other, more immediate political concerns come to the fore when mobilizing secular constituencies. In any case, strict secularism is not greatly popular, and so associating Darwinian theory with secularism is not necessarily the best way to increase support for evolution.

Scientists themselves, then, might be the best people to defend evolution, or at least to take the debate out of the political realm. Soon after Harun Yahya's creationism appeared, some Turkish academics reacted. The Turkish Academy of Sciences (TÜBA) condemned creationist efforts in a press statement, emphasizing that evolution is a well-confirmed part of modern science. The academy pointed out that creationism was spread by Christian groups but had "been completely rejected in scientifically advanced countries." Still, from the very beginning, the scientists adopted a political tone, warning that "certain interests are continuing a war against the secular system and free and modern education" and charging creationists with aiming to undermine the secular state.[52] TÜBA also formed a commission to publicly combat Yahya's creationism. However, discussions in the popular press quickly got lost in the culture war, with creationists and evolutionists alike making extravagant political accusations against one another. The TÜBA effort soon fizzled out; in the media battle, the creationists had a clear victory.

One reason scientists in Muslim countries have not been able to effectively oppose creationism is their relative weakness and disorganization compared to the Western scientific community. In Turkey, scientists have little time and few resources to devote to a demoralizing political fight. Moreover, to further complicate matters, there is plenty of creationism within Turkish universities, including among science faculty. Similar conditions hold throughout the Muslim world. A survey comparing biology faculty from Lebanon with Australian biologists, for example, found very significant skepticism about evolution.[53]

In Turkey and throughout most of the Muslim world, the life sciences typically have a more applied, often biomedical focus. This causes a further lack of emphasis on evolution in biology education. Indeed, most Muslim countries emphasize disciplines oriented toward technology and practical benefits—engineering is typically a much more prestigious area of study than physics or other natural sciences. And so, the culture of applied science affects the perception of evolution in Muslim universities. Applied scientists tend to downplay theory and are typically more religious than researchers in basic science. For example, a 2005 poll of American medical doctors found that 34 percent agreed more with intelligent design than with evolution. For the Muslim physicians in the sample this number rose to 73 percent.[54]

So Muslim academics can lend only weak support to evolution, whether as scientists or more liberal-minded theologians who accept guided evolution. They particularly have to be careful when their views become public. Soon after the TÜBA statement in Turkey was released, a prominent Islamist newspaper published the names of its signatories on its front page, suggesting that they had trespassed against Islam. This had overtones of an invitation to violence, especially since a number of secularist intellectuals singled out by radical Islamist newspapers have been assassinated. Recently in Egypt, Abdul Sabbur Chahine wrote a book arguing that Adam was preceded by other prehuman creatures who had evolved to reach a human shape, trying to reconcile science and religion by adopting a new interpretation of the relevant verses in the Quran. His work led to a huge public outcry and charges of apostasy.[55] It is hard to see the Muslim world becoming more hospitable to evolution any time soon.

MORAL NATURE

Muslim creationists clearly are deeply concerned about materialism. This is somewhat curious. After all, full-blown materialists—or naturalists, or physicalists, to use more current terms—are not common in the Muslim world. Conservative Muslims have opposed westernizers and secularists for a long time, but few westernizers have ever rejected all supernatural claims. Until recently, Marxism could have been one of the political alternatives in play, but the Marxists have either vanished or lost most of their influence. Many have converted to political Islam. But it is now, just when just about everyone claims that they are a good Muslim in their own fashion, that creationism has become most visible.

The creationists still perceive plenty of materialism around. To believers, Islam is not just a concrete set of religious practices and beliefs but also a symbol of all that is good. Anything that goes wrong—the decline of Muslim civilization, newer "Western" evils such as crime or sexual laxity—must be due to deviations from the straight path of Islam. There are problems, problems are caused by impiety, and the most extreme impiety is the materialist denial of any spiritual reality. "Materialism" is a symbolic enemy that has little to do with scientists and philosophers skeptical about gods and ghosts. Creationists lead a moral crusade; they aim to protect the community of the faithful from spiritual corruption.

The moral impetus behind creationism has much to do with the social circumstances of the creationist public. Traditionalist, old-fashioned believers, especially those with peasant backgrounds, are hardly aware of evolution and have little reason to support creationist pseudoscience. Harun Yahya finds a market among urban, modernizing Muslims—modern-minded believers such as those attracted to the Nur movement, including many who have become part of the professional classes. While pursuing material success, however, they also try to reproduce their religious convictions in a rapidly changing social environment. The modern world is both an opportunity and a threat—commerce and wealth and entertainment, but also temptation and cultural alienation. Creationists usually respect science, largely because technology is an important part of their lives. So they handle religiously uncomfortable aspects of modern science by declaring that "true science" actually supports their views—they put their trust in an alternative "creation science." The social environment in which Muslim creationism flourishes is very similar to the environment that supports Protestant creationism in the United States,[56] though Muslim creationism has an extra edge that comes from modernity being closely identified with the tempting but dangerous West.

Especially when adjusting to new circumstances, people can use advice. And Islamic traditions are well poised to offer advice.

Orthodox Islam is centered on questions of law, and Muslim efforts to understand sacred texts very often take mundane matters of everyday life as their point of departure. Practical questions and the need to validate answers with the authority of the sacred sources drive much of Muslim literature, whether in the historical development of the faith or among Islamist students in university campuses today.[57] And modern communication technologies have made religious advice available to believers who no longer enjoy a traditional community. Advice manuals, religious newspaper columns, and Web sites devoted to counsel from religious scholars have become very common. Almost all uphold traditional Islamic moral ideals, extrapolating from conservative legal principles to obtain rulings applicable to modern circumstances. They argue by presenting proof-texts: verses from the Quran or a hadith that they interpret to lead to concrete advice.

For most devout Muslims, the authoritative texts and their accepted interpretation settle the matter. The advice-givers work within the classical Islamic tradition honed through layers of commentaries upon commentaries; they take it for granted that an idealized orthodox Muslim culture in the classical mold is their God's will. Clarifying the divine commandments is all that is necessary. But since more westernized options for life have become available, many Muslim popular writers feel a need to explain and defend their prescriptions. Modern Muslims demand more from their faith-affirming literature than a laundry list of traditional proof-texts. They have become familiar with and work within a cultural world other than that of classical Islam—a world in which secular legitimation often comes through invoking science.

Islamic theology already had a concept that is very suitable for bridging the gap between text-based and ostensibly scientific forms of legitimation. This is the notion of *fitra*, or created nature.[58] According to Muslim tradition, everything in creation, especially humans, has an essential nature that determines its proper place and function. For example, popular Muslim writers often say that the created nature of humans is such that we are all born submitters to the One God and hence Muslim; it is only social indoctrination that turns many of us into adherents of other religions or of no religion. Many Western converts to Islam therefore describe themselves as "reverts," perceiving themselves as having reverted to the natural state of humankind. In more mystical and metaphysical currents of Islam, *fitra* often refers to a Platonic ideal, a primordial humanity associated with mystical notions of human perfection.[59] With all its variations, however, the central thrust of the *fitra* concept is that the created nature of humans is inscribed with specifically Muslim ideals. When asked about cosmetic surgery, religious scholars will typically answer that it is not permitted if it is a matter of frivolously interfering with God's creation, but it is permissible if it corrects a defect and thereby brings someone closer to the ideal state of the *fitra*. Created nature embodies a moral ideal, and so deviations from an ideal state are morally tainted. Within this context, Islamic thinkers are also able to accommodate the imperfections of human nature. Unbridled male sexuality, for example, is supposed to be a created weakness, but it can be turned into a strength when it finds its proper place in a strong Muslim family.

So a more modern audience that responds to claims made in the name of science as well as scripture can very easily use the concept of *fitra* to link the two approaches. For them, *fitra* easily comes to mean created nature as revealed by biology as well as religion. Humans and all living things, after all, are created by God, and they must have definite roles, a purpose in the divine scheme of things.

Evolution casts doubt on the whole notion of a fixed created nature, and so it threatens Muslim understandings of the nature of morality. Muslim creationists, like their Christian and Jewish counterparts, associate Darwinian evolution with social Darwinism, sexually "animalistic" behavior, and family breakdown, projecting a host of anxieties about modern life onto evolution. Their objections, however, run deeper. Harun Yahya, for example, claims that evolutionists are ideologically motivated, and says: "We can add [to racists, fascists, socialists, etc.] those homosexual ideologues who try to explain their sexual deviation by 'a genetic variation produced by the process of evolution.' These 'scientific' vanguards of the homosexual movement claim that homosexuality arose in a certain stage of the process of sexual evolution and contributed to the progress of this process. In doing so, they seek to legitimize their perversion."[60] Yahya is concerned with the *boundaries* within created nature; since nature embodies a moral order, violating natural boundaries in matters of sexuality is also a moral perversion. By reaffirming creation in the face of the fluidity and variation inherent in modern biological understandings of life, Yahya defends social boundaries inscribed into nature. After all, evolutionary theory does not describe species in terms of natural roles or Platonic essences. In modern biological thinking, variation is intrinsic to populations; it is not a deviation from an ideal form. Hence evolutionary thinking undermines conceptions of morality that emphasize created nature.

Darwinian evolution also makes it more difficult to think of morally higher or lower states in biology. Muslim tradition tends to conceive of nature hierarchically, so that plants and animals occupy lower levels in the grand scheme of reality. Therefore, when "humans, who have a rank in the order of reality that is not merely at the level of instinct, bring themselves down to such a level by their own hands, the result will be evil."[61] Suggesting that humans are animals is, naturally, unacceptable.

Muslim creationism, then, was almost inevitable. For many Muslims, modernization brings moral anxieties and a need to defend traditional morality—they can no longer assume that the modern social environment will affirm traditional roles as just the unquestioned, natural order of things. And in Darwinian evolution, devout Muslim intellectuals encounter an idea that is deeply offensive to how they conceive of the very nature of morality.

FITRA AND GENDER ROLES

The most prominent examples of how the concept of created nature is connected to biology in Muslim apologetics come from the debate about gender roles. Modernization has usually meant greater opportunities for women in the public sphere and more pressure for women to join industrialized economic production. The status of women is always a flash point in the political struggle between westernized and more conservative Muslims; women's dress is the most visible marker of difference between traditional and more modern people.

By and large, Muslims remain very patriarchal in outlook. This is not to say, however, that devout Muslims live according to the stereotype of secluded and veiled women. Even in medieval times, that was an ideal that was feasible only for the upper classes. The majority of women worked and were present in the public realm— though public space was sexually segregated and women were subordinated to men. Today, only ultraorthodox enclaves and certain rural areas can approximate the idealized traditional pattern of life. Even political Islamists and revival movements acknowledge a much more active role for women compared to traditional Muslim societies. In Iran, women are required to wear Islamic dress in public, but denying women the right to vote is not a serious option. Women work in modern occupations, though in ways minimizing male contact. In Turkey, Islamist movements have become the most dynamic new force in contemporary politics, mobilizing many women in their ranks.[62] "Islamic feminists" have appeared who both assert their piety and accuse men of misinterpreting the sacred sources so as to turn women into second-class Muslims.

Still, a more traditional ideal of gender roles continues to dominate Muslim societies. Even women who demand a larger public role often maintain that the sexes have separate spheres and that the primary responsibilities of women are in the home and family. Women have a role that is complementary to that of men. This role is no less honorable, even if it is clearly subordinate from a Western, liberal feminist point of view. Moreover, while relentlessly patriarchal, the conservative Muslim ideal is very family-centered. The security and strong family promised by the Muslim ideal appeals to many women in modern, fluid social environments. And even a subordinate role can allow considerable indirect power within the family.[63]

As always, among conservative Muslims, arguments supporting women's primarily domestic role mostly rely on proof-texts and little else. For example, 4 An-Nisa 34 says, "The men are supporters of the women, by what God has given one more than the other, and by what they provide from their property." Husbands must protect and provide for their wives, and if commentators give any reason, they say it is because God has made men stronger than women and so responsible for their protection.

But proof-texts are not always enough, and thus some writers try to strengthen their case by bringing in science and created nature. Abdal Hakim Murad, a Muslim intellectual based in Britain, says, "The Quran and our entire theological tradition are rooted in the awareness that the two sexes are part of the inherent polarity of the cosmos," and

> Islam's awareness that when human nature (fitra) is cultivated rather than suppressed, men and women will incline to different spheres of activity is of course one which provokes howls of protest from liberals: for them it is a classic case of blasphemy. But even in the primitive biological and utilitarian terms which are the liberals' reference, the case for absolute identity of vocation is highly problematic. However heavily society may brainwash women into seeking absolute parity, it cannot ignore the reality that they have babies, and have a tendency to enjoy looking after them. . . . The screaming fanatics who "out" bishops and demand a lowering of the "gay" age of consent are among the most bitter enemies of the fitra, that primordial norm which, for all the diversity of the human race, has consistently expressed itself in marriage as the natural context for the nurturing of the new generation. That which is against the fitra is by definition destructive: it is against humanity and against God.[64]

Nontraditional gender roles violate nature's law and the moral order laid down by the creator. In a popular Turkish advice manual on the family, Bekir Topaloğlu writes:

> In connection with physiology, there will of course be important differences in the area of psychology. In men, you cannot find the delicate emotions of women, or the behavior which adjusts to the ever changing needs of children. The created nature of man is such that he can withstand the ravages of the natural world, and the numberless difficulties of life. . . . The woman has some special properties due to her physiology. Heat, pulse, and breath is higher in women. Muscle power is stronger in men. This situation places woman in a position intermediate between children and men.[65]

It is interesting that Topaloğlu's references to physiology and psychology have little to do with today's state of knowledge. Instead, they echo concepts of women's nature current among Western scientists in the nineteenth century and even show similarities to much older medical ideas in the ancient Greek tradition. Indeed, ancient Aristotelian medical beliefs became part of the medieval Muslim sciences, and even today, the background of a classically educated religious scholar incorporates centuries-old philosophical traditions, including Muslim developments of Hellenistic ideas about human nature.[66]

An intriguing example comes from the writings of Süleyman Ateş, a leading Turkish theologian who has served as head of the national Directorate of Religious Affairs. In response to a series of publications critical of Islam, he wrote a number of books in the 1990s defending the faith and justifying the traditional place of women. Given his audience, Ateş had to do more than produce proof-texts or rely on a notion of *fitra* that needed no elaboration. In doing so, he drew on a conception of nature that incorporates ideas going back to the Greek philosophers. Defending 2 Al-Baqarah 228, which says of women that "men have a rank above them," Ateş says that "as a whole, the male sex has been created superior to the female. Even the sperm that carries the male sign is different from the female. The male-bearing sperm is more active, carrying light on its head, the female sperm is less active. The egg stays stationary, the sperm seeks her out, and endures a long and dangerous struggle in the process." This echoes Galen's notions about weaker, less perfect female seed. Ateş adds, "Generally in nature, all male animals are more complete, more superior compared to their females. For example, the cock compared to the hen, the ram to the ewe, the male lion to the lioness, is more beautiful and stronger,"[67] sounding much like an Aristotelian natural historian.

Though such examples are evidence for archaic biological ideas surviving in Muslim intellectual culture, they do not represent all popular literature on gender and *fitra*. Abdal Hakim Murad, for example, has a more modern way of suggesting that Islamic morality is reflected in nature. He uses pop-sociobiology:

> A further controversy in the Shari'a's nurturing of gender roles centres around the institution of plural marriage. This clearly is a primordial institution whose biological rationale is unanswerable: as Dawkins and others have observed, it is in the genetic interest of males to have a maximal number of females; while the reverse is never the case. Stephen Pinker notes somewhat obviously in his book *How the Mind Works*: 'The reproductive success of males depends on how many females they mate with, but the reproductive success of females does not depend on how many males they mate

with.' Islam's naturalism, its insistence on the fitra and our authentic belongingness to the natural order, has ensured the conservation of this creational norm within the moral context of the Shari'a.[68]

There is a long and controversial tradition within evolutionary biology of trying to explain female subordination as a biologically determined phenomenon. And even this can appear in Muslim *fitra* apologetics, regardless of the antievolutionary thrust of the created nature concept. As always, popular apologetics is disorganized and opportunistic. Such writings do not strive for any serious intellectual structure. Instead, popular writers throw together scientific-sounding material from a variety of sources, often without attribution or just citing other popular literature. They treat science as a list of "facts" to use selectively with little regard for the theories in which the facts are embedded.

Still, however opportunistic and superficial, the popular literature about science and created nature reveals powerful currents in Muslim thought about gender. As more Muslim women have found a public voice, even starting to give religious advice, they have found themselves constricted by the notion of *fitra*. Female authors writing for popular audiences defend a subordinate role for women, emphasizing familial and caregiving activities. In Islamic women's magazines in Turkey, the notion of *fitra* features prominently in discussions of gender roles. When debating women's position in society, politically active Islamist women have to engage the traditional vision of created nature. It has been very difficult for them to challenge assumptions of women's weakness with any success. Women Islamists have also invoked *fitra* to say that women are naturally self-sacrificing and community-minded, hoping to argue that society would benefit by allowing women a broader public role.[69] But in practice, such arguments have had little success. Most sources favored by devout urban Muslims assume that the divinely created order mandates female subordination.

Some Muslim feminists blame the Hellenic philosophical tradition's influence on the training of religious scholars for what they see as distorted, antiwoman interpretations of the sacred sources.[70] More egalitarian interpretations, however, show little sign of catching on, though they draw academic interest among scholars attracted by the liberatory rhetoric of Islamic feminism.[71] As Serpil Üşür puts it, classical Islam was always inclined to see social roles in created nature; "within the ideology of Islam, . . . the sexual division of labor becomes a fundamental principle, a divine and eternal natural law determined by God when creating the sexes."[72] Today, this tendency has altered very little; it has only been updated with some biological-sounding references suitable for an audience influenced by Western modernity.

HARMONY

The Muslim world is home to plenty of pseudoscience and opportunistic abuse of science in popular apologetics. Superficially, this can all look like just a crude effort to reconcile science with traditional interpretations of Islam. Popular Muslim ideas about biology in particular look very much like views current among conservative Christians. United States representative Marilyn Musgrave declared, in a speech against gay marriage, that "our rights exist within the context of God's created order. The self-evident differences and complementary design of men and women are part of that created order."[73] Most Muslims would heartily agree and base their position on a similar understanding of the divine "created order."

Still, conservative Christian ideas about created nature are less well developed and have limited appeal outside a fundamentalist subculture. In contrast, many Muslim thinkers with broad influence on their culture are committed to strongly non-Darwinian views and insist that Muslim morality is reflected in created nature. God's creation must be harmonious at all levels: scripture, nature as revealed by science, and Muslim metaphysical thinking must all smoothly fit together in a God-centered picture of reality. Science-in-the-Quran apologetics, creationism, and *fitra*-based arguments all gesture toward making this underlying harmony clear. Although conservative Protestants also have strong convictions that nature and scripture must be in harmony, their views about created nature lack the depth of the Muslim concept.

Devout Muslims believe in harmony. But they also believe that harmony is *obvious*. Humans are forgetful—our main failing—so we might not always pay attention to the exquisite harmony and design of the natural world. Apologetics, however, needs only to remind us of this purposeful harmony. Once we are reminded, the divine design underlying nature is blindingly clear. Countless Thursday-night devotional television programs start with images of galaxies or of butterflies and birds, overlaying what look like clips from nature documentaries with religious music. They remind viewers of nature's order and nature's author. Harun Yahya does not have to work hard to convince readers that nature is intelligently designed. He just presents the wondrous interlocking complexity of nature, and the conclusion becomes obvious.

Leading Muslim thinkers from various backgrounds take this harmony for granted. Said Nursi emphasizes the harmonious relationships within the universe and between the universe and humans, who are the crown of creation and the center of the universe. So harmonious is the universe that "in no way could confused chance, blind force, aimless, anarchic, unconscious nature interfere in that wise, percipient particular balance and most sensitive order. If they had interfered, some traces of confusion would certainly be apparent. Whereas no disorder is to be seen anywhere."[74] Order and purpose are easily visible, and this is a better way to remind a reader of the single Creator than all the demonstrations of philosophical theology. Sayyid Abul A'la Maududi follows tradition and says that unbelief is but ignorance, wondering that "a man observes the vast panorama of nature, the superb mechanism that is ceaselessly working, the grand design that is manifest in every nook and corner of the creation—he observes this vast machine, but he does not know who is its Maker and Director. . . . He sees great beauty and harmony in its working—but not the Creator of this all." Though not perceiving the divine Engineer is ignorance, this lack of illumination is a moral darkness as well. All of the universe obeys the creator—even the sun and moon are Muslims in the sense that they submit to and obey God—but an unbeliever misuses free will and opposes the moral order inherent in the design of the universe. He "perpetrates the greatest injustice, for he uses all these powers of body and mind to rebel against the course of nature and becomes an unwilling instrument in the drama of disobedience."[75]

Many attempts to Islamize knowledge and revitalize Muslim culture draw further on concepts of harmony rooted in the classical Muslim perception of reality, emphasizing an organic view of nature. As the International Institute of Islamic Thought puts it:

> All things in creation serve a purpose and all purposes are interrelated, as a means and an end to one another. This makes the world one telic system, vibrant and alive, full of meaning. The birds in the sky, the stars in the firmament, the fishes in the depths of the ocean, the plants and the elements—all constitute integral parts of the system. No part of it is inert or evil, since every being has a function and a role in the life of the whole. Together, they make an organic body whose members and organs are interrelated.[76]

Sayyid Qutb, a leading Islamist theorist, also perceives the universe as an organic machine characterized by harmony and balance, where Islamic law is analogous to physical laws in being part of the universal divine law structuring all reality.[77]

As with most deeply held Muslim beliefs, the idea of harmony finds support in the Quran. The Quran addresses an audience who already believes in God and concentrates on reminding them of God and asserting the peerless unity of God. Still, the Quran also gestures toward reasons to believe there is a God. After all, God has given plenty of obvious "signs" in nature. 13 Ar-Rad 2–3 says, "God is the one who raised the heavens without pillars you can see, then mounted the throne and subjected the sun and the moon: each runs for a determined period. God arranges the order and elucidates the signs, so you may be certain of meeting your Lord. And God it is who spread out the earth, and placed on it mountains and rivers, and made mated pairs of all fruits; and causes the night to cover the day. Therein are signs for people who reflect." 30 Ar-Rum 20–27 lists more signs: creating humans from dust, creating mates, the constitution of the heavens and Earth, linguistic and ethnic diversity, sleep, lightning, rain, and the very existence of the sky and the earth. All have a single creator, all are united by a divine purpose.

This is not to say that Muslim ideas about harmony proceed directly out of the Quran. The Quran is a disorganized book with ambiguous meanings; Muslims can emphasize or downplay different parts. Tradition, however, has emphasized plainer readings that support a purposeful, harmonious nature immediately created by God. The intellectual culture of Islam has done the same. Early Muslim philosophers adopted "proofs" of God from Greek and Christian philosophy. Compared to the more abstruse metaphysical proofs, however, the argument from design ended up carrying the most weight outside of a narrow circle influenced by philosophy. The harmony of the complex world we live in meant that it all had to have been designed and created by God. In a more modern environment, where people are more conscious of science as a means of validating fact claims, the design argument gains even more emphasis. Today's Islamic movements work to reinforce the traditional perception of design and harmony in nature.

So the Muslim perception of harmony runs deep, from popular apologetics to more substantial reflections on an Islamic view of nature. In fact, devout Muslims are typically surprised that anyone can think there is no divine intelligence that directly orders nature. Darwinian evolution seems an especially odd concept, on top of the intrinsically counterintuitive nature of the theory.

Among the theories of modern science, Darwinian evolution most visibly disrupts the picture of harmony. Evolutionary biology makes it more difficult to seek rigid boundaries in life that carry moral meaning. Human differences are real—there is, for example, evidence that certain patterns of human sexual behavior are closely connected to our biology—but these are never separate from culture and environment, and they never have any clear transcendent purpose or moral implication. In fact, the development of biotechnology opens up possibilities for greater fluidity. We can consciously modify human nature or its consequences; indeed, we have already done so, with technologies such as the birth control pill.

Moreover, trends in evolutionary science today make it increasingly difficult to bridge the gap between natural science and the Muslim conception of a harmonious, morality-infused nature. Evolutionary explanations of human behavior, including moral and religious behavior, portray morality and spiritual beliefs as emerging within nature, rather than being handed down from above. Moral perceptions, it appears, are built upon a set of evolved skills that help humans negotiate the social realm. Religious and supernatural beliefs themselves appear as by-products of how human cognitive systems have evolved. Moreover, if such views are correct, it becomes increasingly difficult to think of absolute moral rules binding for everyone in every circumstance. We end up with a "moral ecology," where human societies can harbor groups with different stable configurations of interests and where different moral perceptions attend different interests.[78] None of these ideas are even remotely acceptable to the vast majority of Muslims. They can only reinforce the common Muslim conviction that Western science, having lost its anchor in faith, inevitably becomes a threat to morality.

And so Muslims come to look at Western science and they perceive a moral void. They ask what an Islamic science might look like, what Islam might contribute that is missing, and they find that their answers involve morality and spirituality. A science illuminated by Islam would have a moral center. It would not destroy the environment. It would not be driven to produce the technologies of oppression and alienation. It would approach the biology of the sexes in a framework of dignity and respect for complementarity. It would, most radically, counter the Enlightenment myth that science is value-free.[79] And an Islamic approach to science would accomplish all this because it would recognize the divine truth at the center of all the partial truths gathered by science.

Such a vision has undeniable appeal. Not a few non-Muslims would agree that Western technological civilization is seriously out of balance. Scientists might like to pursue questions brought forth by their curiosity, but science is expensive. In the technologically advanced West, scientific institutions receive support primarily because the knowledge they produce serves powerful commercial and military interests. And Western commercial and military superiority—a destructive superiority—is exactly the context in which Muslims encountered modern science. It was soon clear that they needed the power of science, but for many, the West and its science was still a soulless, mechanical monstrosity. Muslims conceived of science as a pragmatic enterprise, the handmaiden of technology. Western civilization, however, used technology destructively. Materialist science served material greed, investigating physics in order to build bombs, probing chemistry to make unnecessary plastics destined for ever-swelling landfills.

So, many Muslim thinkers about natural science try to resist this path. Some claim that all that is true in science was already anticipated by the Quran, that Islam is literally a scientific religion. Some see that a modern version of Islam needs to do more: to provide an alternative, a replacement for unacceptable theories such as Darwinian evolution. Others insist that an Islamic science is a moral science, and that Muslims must practice science differently. But the most ambitious thinkers think that Islam's response to science must equal the magnitude of the crisis in Muslim intellectual life. The crisis goes to the roots, the fundamentals. Resisting materialist theories in science and immoral impulses in technology is vital but not enough; Muslims must respond at the level of basic metaphysical assumptions. They must reconstruct science around an Islamic vision. They must discipline science, constraining inquiry by the higher truths of revelation. At the very least, they must excise the materialist philosophy that appears in the guise of scientific fact.

So Osman Bakar, for example, calls for an Islamic approach that is distinctly different than secular modern science. Islamic science is supposed to work with different methods, a different philosophy of science. Contemporary naturalism presents a bottom-up view of the world, where complex processes such as those that make up life are assembled out of simpler physical processes. Bakar inverts this bottom-up approach and proposes to restore the top-down view of the world favored by religious traditions:

> There is an hierarchy of universality of laws of creation corresponding to the hierarchy of the created order. For example, biological laws are more fundamental and universal than physical or chemical laws since the former laws concern the biological domain which possesses a higher ontological reality than the physical domain which gives rise to the latter kind of laws. But the biological laws themselves are subject to a higher set of cosmic laws which are spiritual in nature. If the attempt to unify all the known existing laws in physics and biology is progressively pursued and in an objective manner, then a point is reached whereby the higher, nonphysical orders of reality would have to be seriously considered and examined.[80]

These are interesting claims—if they are not just metaphysical hand waving or an attempt to make too much of the way certain universal properties of complex systems can be realized on very different physical substrates. And clearly Bakar is looking for something substantial: at the very least, he is trying to claim that phenomena such as life and mind are not reducible to physical processes. But that is where it ends. Bakar gives his readers no real evidence to support his views. He never gives an example of what the "biological laws" he mentions might be, nor does he argue in detail that his higher levels of reality are not physically realized, let alone show how they are more fundamental. Indeed, the main advantage of Bakar's philosophy of science appears to be that compared to more familiar Western views, it is much more consonant with a classical Muslim picture of reality. As is always the case with proposals to Islamize science, his philosophical ambitions and grandiose plans for reconstruction strongly contrast with the complete lack of actual scientific productivity that results.

And in the end, it is scientific results—interesting experiments, better theories with more explanatory power—that matter. After all, Muslims feel they have to adopt science because of its real-world success. Muslim proposals to improve science by injecting morality or higher levels of being into its structure are easy to come by, but none of these proposals lead to any concrete reason that would help overturn the naturalism that so bothers Muslim sensibilities. There is nothing really new in Bakar-style ideas; they are variations on a theme of reviving the classical Islamic view of knowledge, of restoring obvious harmony to the universe. That appears to be a dead end, as are postmodern complaints about science not being value-free. It is unfortunate that so much of the effort of Western physicists goes into weapons research, but their bombs really do work. Science needs institutional values that promote learning about the world, but moral constraints on the scientific enterprise are up to social negotiations, not anything intrinsic to science as a form of inquiry.

So, too much of Muslim thinking about natural science continues to be caught between irrelevance and outright falsehood. Some Muslims think they should constantly add "because God wills it" to any naturalistic account, to remind themselves that God is the only true cause and that natural patterns exist only at the sufferance of the divine will. If this is an irrelevant metaphysical gloss, it might only impede communication with non-Muslim scientists. No

22. *Acts & Facts*, December 1992.

23. Adem Tatlı, *Evrim, İflas Eden Teori* (İstanbul, Turkey: Bedir Yayınevi, 1990).

24. Şükrü Günbulut, *Ortadoğu Din Kültürü* (İstanbul, Turkey: Kaynak Yayınları, 1996), p. 268.

25. Dorian Jones, "Debate over Creationism in Turkey: Evolution under Pressure," *Qantara.de*, August 1, 2006, http://www.qantara.de/webcom/show_article.php/_c-478/_nr-478/i.html (accessed December 3, 2006).

26. İrfan Yılmaz and Selim Uzunoğlu, *Alternatif Biyolojiye Doğru* (İzmir, Turkey: TÖV, 1995).

27. Taner Edis, "Cloning Creationism in Turkey," *Reports of the National Center for Science Education* 19, no. 6 (1999): 30–35. I reused some of the material in this paper in this chapter.

28. See http://www.harunyahya.com for the English-language version.

29. Taner Edis, "Harun Yahya and Islamic Creationism," in *Darwin Day Collection One*, ed. Amanda Chesworth et al. (Albuquerque, NM: Tangled Bank, 2003); Taner Edis, "A World Designed by God: Science and Creationism in Contemporary Islam," in *Science and Religion: Are They Compatible?* ed. Paul Kurtz (Amherst, NY: Prometheus Books, 2003). I reused some of the material from these articles in this chapter.

30. John D. Morris, "Creationist Evangelism in Turkey," *Acts & Facts* 27 (1998): 9.

31. Harun Yahya, *Evrim Aldatmacası: Evrim Teorisi'nin Bilimsel Çöküşü ve Teorinin İdeolojik Arka Planı* (İstanbul, Turkey: Vural Yayıncılık, 1997).

32. Harun Yahya, *Fascism: The Bloody Ideology of Darwinism* (İstanbul, Turkey: Kültür Yayınları, 2002).

33. Harun Yahya, *Islam Denounces Terrorism*, 3rd ed. (Bristol, UK: Amal Press, 2002), p. 147.

34. Yahiya Emerick, *The Complete Idiot's Guide to Understanding Islam* (Indianapolis, IN: Alpha Books, 2002), p. 81.

35. For example, Mehmet S. Aydın, *İslam'ın Evrenselliği* (İstanbul, Turkey: Ufuk Kitapları, 2000), p. 57.

36. Osman Bakar, *Critique of Evolutionary Theory: A Collection of Essays* (Kuala Lumpur, Malaysia: Islamic Academy of Science, 1987); "The Nature and Extent of Criticism of Evolutionary Theory," in *Science and the Myth of Progress*, ed. Mehrdad M. Zarandi (Bloomington, IN: World Wisdom, 2003).

37. Seyyed Hossein Nasr, *Knowledge and the Sacred* (Albany: State University of New York Press, 1987), pp. 237–39. Nasr's biography states that

his educational background includes physics, but this is hard to see in his writing.

38. Osman Bakar, *The History and Philosophy of Islamic Science* (Cambridge, UK: Islamic Texts Society, 1999).

39. Nasr, *Knowledge and the Sacred*, pp. 169–70.

40. For example, 'Adi Setia, "*Taskhir*, Fine-Tuning, Intelligent Design, and the Scientific Appreciation of Nature," *Islam and Science* 2, no. 1 (2004): 7–32.

41. Mustafa Akyol, "Intelligent Design Could Be a Bridge between Civilizations," *National Review Online*, December 2, 2005, http://www.national review.com/comment/akyol200512020813.asp (accessed December 3, 2006). Akyol has also been writing the first Turkish ID book, expected to appear in 2006 or 2007 (personal communication).

42. J. P. Moreland, "Theistic Science and Methodological Naturalism," in *The Creation Hypothesis: Scientific Evidence for an Intelligent Designer*, ed. J. P. Moreland (Downer's Grove, IL: InterVarsity Press, 1994); Alvin Plantinga, "When Faith and Reason Clash: Evolution and the Bible," *Christian Scholar's Review* 21, no. 1 (1991): 8–32.

43. Harun Yahya, *Why Darwinism Is Incompatible with the Qur'an*, trans. Carl Rossini, ed. Jay Willoughby (İstanbul, Turkey: Global Publishing, 2003).

44. Seyyed Hossein Nasr, *A Young Muslim's Guide to the Modern World*, 2nd ed. (Chicago: KAZI Publications, 1994), pp. 185–86.

45. Kirschner and Gerhart, *The Plausibility of Life*; Sean B. Carroll, *Endless Forms Most Beautiful: The New Science of Evo Devo* (New York: Norton, 2005).

46. Taner Edis, *The Ghost in the Universe: God in Light of Modern Science* (Amherst, NY: Prometheus Books, 2002), chap. 2.

47. Mohamed Mahmoud, "Mahmud Muhammad Taha's Second Message of Islam and His Modernist Project," in *Islam and Modernity: Muslim Intellectuals Respond*, ed. John Cooper, Ronald Nettler, and Mohamed Mahmoud (London and New York: I. B. Tauris, 2000), p. 122.

48. Muhammet Altaytaş, *Hangi Din?* (İstanbul, Turkey: Eylül Yayınları, 2001), p. 82.

49. Mehmet Bayrakdar, *İslam'da Evrimci Yaradılış Teorisi* (İstanbul, Turkey: İnsan Yayınları, 1987).

50. See contributions in William A. Dembski and Michael Ruse, eds., *Debating Design: From Darwin to DNA* (Cambridge: Cambridge University Press, 2004); and my review, Taner Edis, "The Return of the Design Argument," *Philosophy Now* 50 (2005): 42.

51. For example, essays included under the cover theme "there can be

no science without the theory of evolution" in the monthly low-circulation science magazine *Bilim ve Gelecek*, August 2004.

52. *TÜBA Bülteni* 10 (1999): 2. Ümit Sayın and Aykut Kence, "Islamic Scientific Creationism," *Reports of the National Center for Science Education* 19, no. 6 (1999): 18.

53. Barend Vlaardingerbroek and Yasmine Hachem El-Masri, "The Status of Evolutionary Theory in Undergraduate Biology Programmes at Lebanese Universities: A Comparative Study," *International Journal of Educational Reform* 15, no. 2 (2006): 150–63.

54. Poll by the Louis Finkelstein Institute for Social and Religious Research, http://www.hcdi.net/polls/J5776/ (accessed December 3, 2006). N = 1,482, with 40 of them Muslims—too low a number of Muslims to draw anything but suggestive conclusions.

55. Raymond William Baker, *Islam without Fear: Egypt and the New Islamists* (Cambridge, MA: Harvard University Press, 2003), pp. 262–64.

56. Raymond A. Eve and Francis B. Harrold, *The Creationist Movement in Modern America* (Boston: Twayne, 1991).

57. Richard W. Bulliet, *Islam: The View from the Edge* (New York: Columbia University Press, 1993), pp. 195–200.

58. Taner Edis and Amy Sue Bix, "Biology and 'Created Nature': Gender and the Body in Popular Islamic Literature from Modern Turkey and the West," *Arab Studies Journal* 12, no. 2; 13, no. 1 (2005): 140–58. I reused some material from this paper in this chapter.

59. Seyyed Hossein Nasr, *Traditional Islam in the Modern World* (London and New York: Kegan Paul, 1987), p. 50.

60. Yahya, *Evrim Aldatmacası*, p. 307.

61. Aydın, *İslam'ın Evrenselliği*, p. 118.

62. Ayşe Saktanber, *Living Islam: Women, Religion and the Politicization of Culture in Turkey* (London: I. B. Tauris, 2002); Jenny B. White, *Islamist Mobilization in Turkey: A Study in Vernacular Politics* (Seattle and London: University of Washington Press, 2002).

63. Jane I. Smith, *Islam in America* (New York: Columbia University Press, 1999), chap. 5.

64. Abdal Hakim Murad, "The Fall of the Family," (n.d.), http://www.islamfortoday.com/murad08.htm (accessed December 3, 2006). See also Abdal Hakim Murad, "Islam, Irigaray, and the Retrieval of Gender," 1999, http://www.admin.muslimsonline.com/bicnews/Articles/gender .htm (accessed December 3, 2006); Mahmoud Abu Saud, "Sex Roles in Muslim Families in the U.S.," in *Sex Education: An Islamic Perspective*, ed. Shahid Athar (Chicago: KAZI Publications, 1995), pp. 43–44.

65. Bekir Topaloğlu, *İslam'da Kadın* (İstanbul, Turkey: Rağbet Yayınları, 2001), p. 77.

66. Edis and Bix, "Biology and 'Created Nature.'"

67. Süleyman Ateş, *Gerçek Din Bu*, vol. 1 (İstanbul, Turkey: Yeni Ufuklar Neşriyat, 1991), pp. 36–37.

68. Murad, "The Fall of the Family."

69. Hülya Demir, *İslamcı Kadının Aynadaki Sureti* (İstanbul, Turkey: Sel Yayıncılık, 1998).

70. For example, Zahra Seif-Amirhosseini, "A Change in the Conception of Muslim Women," *Islam21* 20 (1999): 15, 18.

71. For a critique, see Haideh Moghissi, *Feminism and Islamic Fundamentalism: The Limits of Postmodern Analysis* (London: Zed Books, 1999).

72. Serpil Üşür, "Islamcı Kadınların Yaşam Alanı: Tepkisel İndirgemecilik mi?" in *Türkiye'de Kadın Olgusu*, ed. Necla Arat (İstanbul, Turkey: Say Yayınları, 1992), p. 135.

73. Quoted in Marci A. Hamilton, *God vs. the Gavel: Religion and the Rule of Law* (New York: Cambridge University Press, 2005), p. 52.

74. Quoted in Şükran Vahide, "Toward an Intellectual Biography of Said Nursi," in Abu-Rabi', *Islam at the Crossroads*, p. 17.

75. Sayyid Abul A'la Maududi, *Towards Understanding Islam*, trans. and ed. Khurshid Ahmad (Indianapolis, IN: Islamic Teaching Center, 1977), pp. 5–6.

76. 'AbdulHamid AbuSulayman, ed., *Islamization of Knowledge: General Principles and Work Plan*, 2nd ed. (Herndon, VA: International Institute of Islamic Thought), p. 37.

77. Roxanne L. Euben, *Enemy in the Mirror: Islamic Fundamentalism and the Limits of Modern Rationalism* (Princeton, NJ: Princeton University Press, 1999), p. 76.

78. Edis, *Science and Nonbelief*, chaps. 6 and 7.

79. Ziauddin Sardar, ed., *The Touch of Midas: Science, Values and Environment in Islam and the West* (Manchester, UK: Manchester University Press, 1984).

80. Bakar, *The History and Philosophy of Islamic Science*, p. 72.

CHAPTER 5

REDEEMING THE HUMAN SCIENCES

MAKING IDEOLOGY

Most scientific work is routine. Physicists make measurements, build devices, and do calculations to see how well-established theories apply to little-explored phenomena. Scientists in Muslim lands do plenty of such research, within the constraints of the often meager resources they can devote to their work. Especially in applied science, and in incremental, narrowly focused investigations in basic science, Muslim ingenuity is not hard to come by. For example, in 2005, an Iranian electrical engineer published some noteworthy research on a soliton transistor, which promises to find useful applications in supercomputing.[1] Such work is not very unusual. And researchers in the international community of applied physics do not care if the Iranians involved are religiously liberal or conservative, if they object to evolution, or if they have any interest in Islamizing science. All of that is irrelevant to the transistor.

Most routine science done in the advanced West also has nothing to do with religious concerns. For example, a small percentage of American biologists do not accept evolution. It is not impossible to run into devoutly Christian cell biologists who do solid work in their labs but resist the overall theoretical framework provided by evolution. Modern science is much more than collecting facts like stamps, but in routine research, many scientists can be successful doing little but stamp collecting.

So if there is any friction between science and Islam, it has little to do with the ability of devout Muslims to practice routine natural science. The relationship gets shakier only where broader theoretical thinking and innovation are concerned. Research agendas in the natural sciences are set by the Western-based scientific community; Muslims contribute as peripheral participants rather than deciding what the interesting questions are. And when conservative Muslims perceive some science to be relevant to religious matters, the wheels begin to come off. By the time religiously sensitive issues get public attention, Muslim views are often swamped by completely pseudo-scientific ideas. Evolution is the most prominent example, but other areas also have a potential for flare-ups. Current developments in cognitive neuroscience, for example, are religiously disturbing—they move toward explaining human perception, intelligence, and consciousness in a materialist fashion, threatening the religiously important concept of an immaterial soul.[2] Neuroscience has not attracted any significant Muslim attention yet, but it is not hard to imagine Muslim thinkers lining up to insist that the soul is real, no matter what Western materialist scientists may say.

There is, however, another current example of an area in which many Muslim thinkers are disturbed by the Western forms of inquiry and established knowledge. The human sciences—sociology, economics, history, and so on—clearly touch on religious concerns. These sciences, just like the natural sciences, have been imported from the West. And Western social scientists typically approach questions regarding social order, political systems, and economic prosperity from a nonreligious perspective. Worse, many Western social scientists and historians treat religion itself as a social phenomenon to be studied in analytical rather than reverential terms. Unlike the very recent developments in cognitive neuroscience, Muslims have been exposed to Western social thought since they began to be aware of being overtaken by the West. Muslims have produced an extensive literature on adapting the human sciences to Islamic circumstances or rejecting them in favor of Islamic alternatives.[3]

The Muslim response to the human sciences has been similar to how Muslims have dealt with natural science. Today, academic institutions and government agencies in Muslim lands do competent empirical work: demographic studies, surveys, economic statistics, and so forth. Moreover, they use their familiarity with their own societies to good advantage. Turkish historians wade through Ottoman archives or try to trace the development of heterodox sects from Central Asia through Turkish migrations into Anatolia, producing solid historical work. Political scientists examine the voting patterns of devout Muslim women, sociologists ponder the effects of mass migration to cities. The tools of social science also find use in business and politics. Corporations supporting conservative Muslim cultural politics rely on market research as much as their competitors do. Moderate Islamist political parties employ sophisticated polling data. They often use polling to manipulate public opinion rather than study it, but then that is true for politics all over the world.

The Muslim world also provides many examples of dubious social science, especially where less routine work is concerned. Even more obviously than is the case with natural science, the human sciences are everywhere entangled with political and moral points of view, and therefore social science tends to include different interpretations and emphases. Reasons to do sociology can include, for example, a desire to find out how to produce certain kinds of social change. This need not be any more problematic than some physicists being interested in physics because they want to build electronic devices. But in places such as Turkey today, the human sciences too often get subordinated to ideology, especially if there are any broad public concerns at stake. For example, in Middle Eastern countries archaeology is often treated as a political football. Nationalistic regimes such as Turkey under military secularism and Iran before the Islamic revolution favored research into pre-Islamic civilizations since they tried to derive legitimacy from territory-based national identities. If the nation could be presented as heirs to a glorious past, so much the better. Islamists are, in contrast, cool toward archaeology. For them, the history that matters begins with Islam; national identity, if it is even proper to speak of separate nations within the *umma*, is inextricably linked with Islam. Western archaeology has never lacked for political entanglements; even today, so-called biblical archaeology suffers due to the religious or Israeli nationalist framework in which it is so often practiced. In Turkey, however, archaeology starts with a further handicap: in a poor country, it is hardly a high priority. Without funding from European and American sources, Turkish archaeologists would be out of work.

Many of the problems faced by the human sciences in Muslim lands are due to institutional weakness, which makes political interference all the more damaging. Consider history. Republican Turkey promoted a nationalist ideology that included an official version of history that tended to legitimize the regime. Today, a more open climate prevails. Turks have become more interested in history, and intellectuals have heated debates over different interpretations of past events. Still, relative openness does not always mean better scholarship, as oppositional history writing can be just as ideologically blinkered as the official version. Public historical discussion threatens to become a collection of the self-serving stories of various groups. And again, at a popular level, all sorts of weirdness takes the stage. In Turkey, as throughout the Islamic world, conspiracy theories are very popular; among political Islamists, these often take on an anti-Semitic color, extending to Holocaust denial. And the past always appears to reflect the present. The European Crusades had only a limited effect on Muslim lands; while they were devastating to local populations invaded by the Christian forces, they did not greatly challenge any major Muslim powers of the day. Hence chroniclers based in the major empires did not treat the Crusades as an exceptionally significant clash with infidels. But today, the Crusades have become symbols of Western hostility, helping frame all conflicts with the West as Muslims defending themselves against aggressors. So the Crusades have begun to occupy a disproportionally large role in today's Muslim perception of history.

In preferring historical myth to the ambiguities of serious social and historical thought, Muslims are not very different from people in other cultures. But the constant political upheavals and cultural transformations of recent Muslim history give an intensely ideological edge to the questions studied by the human sciences. Even academic work is affected. And today, as political Islamists fashion an ideology for modern mass society out of a centuries-old religious tradition, social science becomes even more ideologically loaded.

In such an environment, many thinkers look for a more Islamic understanding of human society. They reason that if the human sciences are inescapably political, then it must be legitimate to seek a more authentic, more locally rooted form of social knowledge. Indeed, Muslim thinkers who propose to Islamize knowledge pay special attention to the social sciences and humanities. The International Institute of Islamic Thought emphasizes "the contradiction of Western knowledge with the vision of Islam," adding that "the spiritual torture this conflict has inflicted upon us caused us to wake up in panic, fully aware of the rape of the Islamic soul taking place before our very eyes in the Muslim universities."[4] Since the human sciences "determine the definition of man, his ideals, his purpose in life, and his final goal,"[5] they are serious rivals to revealed religion and have to be cast in an Islamic mold if they are to serve a God-centered perception of reality. Just as the early Muslims in the beginning of their empire absorbed and reshaped the knowledge they inherited from the Greeks, Indians, and Persians, Muslims today must radically reimagine Western social knowledge.

So much of today's Islamic thought about social science includes declarations that Western science is not as objective as it pretends to be, hopes for Muslims to be able to define themselves in their own terms, and grandiose plans for rebuilding social thought on a revealed foundation. Muslim creationists borrow from Christians, but in doing so, they rely on a disreputable fringe of Western natural science. Muslims who want to Islamize social science also import Western ideas, drawing on postmodern social thought. But now there is a difference. Islamic thinking about a new direction for the human sciences finds encouragement from ideas that have become influential, almost mainstream, in Western intellectual life.

POSTMODERN ISLAM

For a long time now, Muslims have been trying to catch up with the modern world. Westernizers have not only imported scientific and technological knowledge but also versions of Western institutions, social structures, and cultural elements that promised to support technical innovation. They have usually been convinced that a strong territorial state was necessary. The tight, intensely religious communities of tradition-minded populations would have to be shaken; modern Muslims would become primarily citizens of their states, organizing their identities around national allegiances. Local ethnic and religious identities would not disappear, but they would be subordinated to national citizenship. Radical republicans in Turkey thought that just as there was but one physics that was correct for everyone, there was one true civilization, one best path to development, one main way of being modern. The rest was a matter of private concern rather than public policy.

While Muslim westernizers struggled to achieve modernity, however, many observers began to think that the advanced Western countries had already moved on to a postmodern condition. Today, it seems like the social fragmentation of modern life has reached a point that strains national allegiances. Late modern societies harbor many overlapping forms of life; especially in conditions of increased immigration, it has become harder to sustain homogeneous national cultures. Meanwhile, the narrowly focused economic rationality that has guided modern social organization has culminated in a global consumer culture. Indeed, culture is now conveyed by a pervasive international media. In these circumstances, local allegiances and tight community identities reassert themselves. The local gains force at the expense of the national; popular culture eclipses elite knowledge and expertise. Most everyone is more aware of other groups of people, and it becomes more difficult to say that any one way of life is the one correct way for all. Yet the very relativism of postmodern consumer culture also motivates individuals to embrace community identities, even if they are imaginary, "virtual" communities constructed through the media. Followers of the European Enlightenment held up an ideal of progress: through human effort and human reason, we would improve in knowledge, advance in ethics, and human cultures everywhere would converge upon a universal civilization. But today, moral and social diversity is the reality of everyday life. As it becomes harder to talk about "progress" without irony, religious faith becomes more attractive, not just as a private belief but as a principle of community.[6]

Such a postmodern condition affects Muslims as well. The irony and playfulness associated with postmodernity may provoke distaste in pious Muslims who take their faith very seriously; its relativism may clash with their certainty about revelation. Nevertheless, Muslim populations are also media consumers and part of the global economy, so they are affected by and respond to postmodern conditions. And there is much in a postmodern mood that Muslims find positive. Many immigrants to Western lands appreciate the present Western emphasis on tolerance and letting different communities define their own realities. And Muslims often respond to the antielitist, populist thrust of postmodernity and the way it legitimizes religious faith against criticism originating in elite forms of knowledge. As anthropologist Akbar S. Ahmed describes it, Muslims have a distinct form of postmodernity: "In Muslim society postmodernism means . . . a shift to ethnic or Islamic identity (not necessarily the same thing and at times opposed to each other) as against an imported foreign or Western one; a rejection of modernity; the emergence of a young, faceless, discontented leadership; cultural schizophrenia; a sense of entering an apocalyptic moment in history; above all, a numbing awareness of the power and pervasive nature of the Western media which are perceived as hostile."[7]

Ordinary Muslims have encountered science as an elite-oriented, Western form of knowledge. So postmodern populism and distrust of elites affect how Muslims respond to science. Moreover, a postmodern current of thinking has taken hold within the humanities and social sciences in Western academic circles. Academic postmodernists distrust the grand narratives and universalist ambitions of modern social thought and extend their skepticism to natural science as well. Many postmodern thinkers see science as a limited and pragmatic enterprise—a powerful tool, perhaps, but no more. They treat science's more abstract theories and ambitions to describe how the world works as unwarranted extrapolations. Enlightenment rationalists have thought of scientific theories as rational responses to evidence; in a postmodern view, these theories become more like ideological schemes imposed by the politically powerful. The European Enlightenment has, many postmodernists think, promised to liberate people but instead has resulted in a moral disaster, forcing the diversity of humanity into one form of civilization. Scientific claims to universal truth sound uncomfortably similar to claims that there is only one form of economic rationality or a single political model that everyone must adopt.

Now, postmodernism has hardly taken over the Western academy; indeed, it appears to have passed its peak. And postmodernism never caught on in the natural sciences—scientists find it hard to take its cognitive relativism seriously.[8] It is pretty obvious that physical science leads to devices like transistors and that the theories of physics provide an excellent understanding of such physical systems. Our theories are often approximate and always fallible, and the scientific community is composed of people with political interests who are never completely isolated from wider social influences. But most natural scientists see this as a reason to re-emphasize that science does not produce absolute certainty and to highlight how even the most solid conclusions are always subject to further criticism. Science is a social activity, but it also seems that the social arrangements within the scientific community help produce some very reliable knowledge. Declaring all knowledge to be tainted by power and ideology is perverse.[9]

Still, in philosophy, the humanities, and social science, postmodernism is an enduring influence. In part, this is for good reason. Areas of inquiry that focus on complex matters, especially anything relating to human and social concerns, are more susceptible to ideological distortions. And the postmodern emphasis on social causes behind scientific as well as other types of community beliefs can be useful in highlighting possible problems in science. For example, a century ago, much in Western science was racist and sexist by today's standards. The inferiority of just about everyone to males of European descent was considered an obvious fact to be explained rather than a belief to be critically examined. Not just social thought but natural science was affected. Early evolutionary biologists considered nonwhite races to be inferior varieties of the human species; Muslim creationists such as Harun Yahya eagerly point out how Charles Darwin referred to Turks as a lower race in his private letters.[10] And since thinkers who embraced evolution tended to portray evolution as a story of progress, it was all the easier to think of life as ascending up a ladder, going through inferior stages until it culminated in the men who led Western Christian civilization.

Today, all of this looks like bad biology and social science that uncritically affirmed the conventional wisdom of the time. More scientists have become aware of how their social and political context affect their work and think this awareness can improve how science is practiced. Postmodernists, however, continue to raise questions about the ideal of scientific objectivity. That is legitimate enough— if science is fallible and subject to criticism, it can always be challenged. But many postmodernists raise questions and then immediately jump to the conclusion that science is thereby exposed as a modern myth. They embrace "other ways of knowing," including intuition, religious faith, and no end of pseudoscientific practices. Even some defenses of creationism make use of postmodern, cognitive relativist themes.[11] Since postmodernists emphasize the "Other" that has been excluded by elite knowledge, they promote populist and non-Western claims to knowledge. This postmodernist approach also ties in with more traditional antiscientific currents within the humanities. Scholars based in the humanities are often wary of the reductionist tendency of natural science, and think that when it comes to human thought and human communities, the task of a scholar is not to explain phenomena but to achieve a sympathetic understanding. The humanities are concerned with *meaning,* and many scholars believe that the meaning of something like a life of religious commitment can only be grasped from the inside, by living such a life.

Many Muslim thinkers are attracted to such postmodern themes. After all, if the idea of progress derived from the European Enlightenment is an ethnocentric concept that has lived out its day, then progress cannot be equated to westernization. Muslims are free to seek their own version of cultural development, rooted in their particular faith. Devout Muslim thinkers, always more sympathetic to the idealist and hermeneutical strains in Western social thought, can reflect on social matters while protecting their religion—their source of transcendent meaning—from criticism. As Egyptian sociologist Hassan Hanafi puts it, since Western social science expresses a secular European worldview, and since its claims of objectivity, neutrality, and universality are mere myths, the path is clear to make a "new social science" suitable for Muslims.[12]

Western social scientists and historians have long studied

Muslim cultures, and this work is a particular target for postmodern Muslim social thinkers. Orientalism—their term for most Western research on Islam and Muslim societies—is, they say, an extension of colonialism. It is not so much a scholarly enterprise as an exercise of power. Westerners, enjoying military and commercial power, constructed an image of the Oriental as an "Other" that let Europeans define their self-images as everything the Oriental was not. Even in today's Western social scientific literature about Islam, it is common to find declarations that Edward Said's *Orientalism*, like the work of postmodern icon Michel Foucault, exposes how "knowledge" is really an expression of power.[13] And so it is hardly surprising that Muslim intellectuals can produce apologetics for the Nur movement using similar language. Sociologist Mücahit Bilici says that

> the discourse of Westernization legitimates a cultural 'panopticon.' Its gaze claims the power to see and to represent other cultures, but escapes from representation. Most of the assumptions made for Western notions of rationalism and secularism render many dimensions of non-Western cultures incomprehensible. These unequal translations within the webs of knowledge and power forge the space of representation. Only the postmodern turn and the crisis of representation have made it possible to discuss Nursi on equal terms with Gramsci.[14]

Such postmodern jargon does not express the unexceptionable observations that Western descriptions of Islam and the Muslim social world have often overreached, that they have incorporated mistakes, and that the colonialist perspective has been a potent source of such mistakes. Instead, Bilici and other postmodernists suggest that the scientific strain within Western social thought is completely tainted and that only an insider's perspective can be trusted. According to this view, Western rationalist scholarship has been blinded by power. Orientalism says much more about Europe than about Islam; the oppressed "Other" enjoys a more authentic self-knowledge.

Perhaps. But it is hard not to notice that when applied to natural science, such conclusions are very implausible. Western science is hardly perfect, but the advanced Western societies have been much better equipped to produce knowledge—reliable knowledge that is not entirely swamped by cultural apologetics. Oppressed people do not have either the intellectual or the material resources to build particle accelerators or develop quantum mechanics. Western societies have, to a large extent, sustained their power and privilege by using knowledge, and they have used some of their power to keep producing new knowledge. In natural science as it has developed in the West, increased power has also meant increased capabilities for investigation and learning.

Such a mutually supportive relationship between power and knowledge might not apply in the human sciences. Here, it is more tempting to say a Western perspective is too limited. But the scientific, explanation-oriented strain in Western social thought is continuous with natural science, and an advantage in power could improve social knowledge as well. Even if motives such as effective colonial administration affected how Western social thinkers and historians inquired into Muslim societies, these motives do not automatically invalidate the Western perspective. After all, the colonialists needed accurate knowledge to do their job. And focusing on imperial designs overlooks how many Western orientalists and social scientists have also been motivated by curiosity, have sincerely appreciated Muslim civilization, and, most importantly, have worked in a critical scholarly environment.

Still, Muslim responses to Western scholarship continue to be strongly affected by politics. For example, Bernard Lewis, a historian close to the orientalist tradition, has drawn much fire from Muslims. Indeed, in some of his writings for a popular audience, Lewis is not only critical of some broad features of Islam but often echoes unimaginative political positions taken for granted among Western conservatives.[15] Nevertheless, Lewis is an undoubted expert on late Ottoman history, and anyone doing serious work on that critical period when westernization began has to engage Lewis's research rather than automatically dismiss it as a product of an orientalist imagination. Otherwise, judging scholarship according to politics leads to a sealed-off, inward-looking intellectual culture. Intellectual life in Muslim lands already has a tendency toward putting group and ideological loyalty first. The postmodern turn only exacerbates this tendency.

In fact, much Muslim use of postmodernism is similar to the

way Muslim creationists borrow from their Christian counterparts. Muslims use postmodernism selectively, even opportunistically. Postmodernism declares a crisis of confidence in Western rationality; Muslim thinkers propose to overcome the crisis by introducing an Islamically colored metaphysics that will fundamentally change how scientists construct knowledge. Postmodernism helps with the negative task of rejecting Western viewpoints, but this only clears the way for an Islamic reconstruction project.

For example, Merryl Wyn Davies, a British anthropologist who has converted to Islam, proposes a radical rejection of Western anthropology, which she considers to be too integral a part of the Western worldview and Western social system to salvage. Muslims will have to rediscover their own authentic ways of thinking about social questions, ways that have been suppressed for centuries by the dominant Western paradigms.[16] Turkish sociologist Recep Şentürk observes that though the Western social science paradigm has been gaining in influence in the Muslim world, the traditional Islamic science of *fiqh*, the interpretation of Islamic law, can be seen as an alternative Islamic paradigm. Invoking philosopher of science Thomas Kuhn, Şentürk argues that these paradigms are incommensurable. From either perspective, the other seems "unscientific"—they can be compared, but there is no independent standpoint that can decide which is really correct. If, for example, Western social science considers monetary interest to be vital to a modern economy, and Muslim *fiqh* declares all interest to be economically harmful instead, there is no sense in asking which view is more accurate. Şentürk thinks that the most comprehensive paradigms of social thought, such as Western "positivist" social science and Muslim *fiqh*, are derived from different basic metaphysical assumptions that frame their worldviews and make different social theories plausible.[17] Mevlüt Uyanık, a Turkish philosopher and theologian, argues similarly. He says that since knowledge is socially constructed, and Muslim and Western civilizations construct their worldviews upon different basic assumptions, they cannot agree on a common definition of truth. Western positivism, deeply connected to the colonial project, arbitrarily denies validity to revelation, while Muslims hold their revelation to be infallible. So Muslims, naturally, will have to think differently about social matters.[18]

Few such writers endorse postmodern relativism to the extent of allowing doubts about revelation or to suggest that communities other than those endorsing an Abrahamic theism have an equal standing. Postmodernism is useful because of its anti-Enlightenment stand, not its pervasive doubt or its ironic detachment. Still, it is interesting to ask if an Islamic alternative to Western social science is becoming more feasible, once postmodernism has cleared the. way. After all, for all their flaws and failings—not entirely surprising, given the overwhelming complexity of human social systems—the human sciences in the West can claim to have produced some reliable knowledge. How do the Muslim alternatives compare? They may not have had time to develop fully, but do they even show much promise?

ISLAMIZING SOCIAL SCIENCE

Most academic social scientists in Muslim lands have little interest in Islamizing the human sciences. Nevertheless, attempts to construct a more Islamic social science have attracted much attention. According to its proponents, Islamic social science is supposed to affirm revelation. It should be centered on and inspired by the Quran. So, efforts to develop a distinctly Islamic sociology try to refer to the scriptures to find concepts useful for the analysis of Muslim and infidel societies and to describe ideal forms of social order. For example, Ali Shari'ati, a prerevolutionary Iranian sociologist who has had considerable influence on today's Muslim social thinkers, argued that he could draw on the Quran and Islamic tradition to obtain an Islamic sociology. Studying the Quran, he found "a whole series of new topics and themes relating to history, sociology, and the human sciences." Indeed, he came close to presenting a sociological version of science-in-the-Quran apologetics, except that he took a subtler approach and claimed that scripture inspired a basic framework for social thought: "The Qur'an itself, or Islam itself, was the source of ideas. A philosophical theory and scheme of sociology and history opened themselves up before me, and when I later checked them against history and sociology, I found them to be fully correct."[19]

Shari'ati finds that since migration is such an important theme in the Quran, it must also be a deep social principle, not just a singular historical event. He also declares that "Islam does not consider the fundamental factor in social change and development to be personality, or accident, or overwhelming and immutable laws." What he means is that all of these, together with "the people," are important. No serious social scientist would consider social history to be shaped by any single factor alone, but Shari'ati presents this triviality as a profound illumination revealed in the Quran.[20] Other sociologists also claim to derive a perspective on human societies from the Quran. Recep Şentürk observes that the Quran views human societies as creedally structured religious "nations." Non-Muslim societies are therefore understood according to their deviations from the Islamic ideal—their fundamental characteristic is that they lack knowledge about their creator. But Şentürk is content to leave this as an alternative paradigm based on revealed knowledge. Since different paradigms cannot be compared in terms of accuracy, no argument is necessary to show that a Quranic view provides a more accurate understanding of social life.[21]

By and large, attempts at Islamic sociology focus on the Muslim nation, the *umma*, as the central concept when posing questions about collective social life. Islamic social thought presents a vision of an ideal society: the Muslim *umma*, especially as it is imagined to have been constituted in the early days of Islam, when the example of Muhammad and his Companions was fresh in the minds of the faithful.[22] This ideal leads Muslims toward answers to the questions that have always been foremost for social thinkers: explaining and ensuring social order and understanding how social acts take on meaning. But since all of this takes place in the context of the revealed ideal, "Islamic sociology" is very goal-directed, even ideological. It points the way toward making the people better Muslims.[23] Indeed, all efforts toward the Islamization of knowledge share such a goal. Even in conditions where the government does not further Islam as it should, Islamizing knowledge helps create an Islamic ambience through education and the media, leading to a more Islamic society.[24]

Just having a notion of an ideal society and asking how to achieve such a society does not make Islamic social thought very distinctive. Every complex civilization boasts political philosophers who ask questions about social cohesion and strife and propose ideal social orders. Modern Western social science also does not limit itself to describing and explaining human societies. Social scientists apply their knowledge to try to achieve lower crime rates, faster economic growth, democratic political systems, and other outcomes they or their funding sources consider desirable. Islamic sociologists, however, desire to make morality much more central to their version of social science. In fact, Islamic sociology echoes pre-Enlightenment Christian social thought, when social questions were invariably addressed in a moral, theological context. This habit of letting moral convictions shape social knowledge did not immediately change with the European Enlightenment. European social thinkers thought of the emerging human sciences as the "moral sciences," and many hoped that social science would serve more secular social ideals. Still, no overall moral consensus dominated modern European societies—different social ideals were in play. Social scientists also hoped to be able to emulate the natural sciences by producing solid explanations for the phenomena they studied. Post-Enlightenment Europeans produced grandiose, ideological views of society and history, such as Marxism. But they also allowed for more modest ways of obtaining knowledge about social realities. Advocates of Islamic social science want to resist such secular developments, to reinstate a view where the interesting questions and the possible answers are constrained by a revealed ideal.

This affinity to pre-Enlightenment social thought is particularly clear in the work of Recep Şentürk and others who propose that *fiqh*, or Islamic jurisprudence, provides an authentic Islamic alternative to the Western sociological paradigm. Şentürk plausibly argues that the social and intellectual role that sociology plays in modern Western societies was filled by *fiqh* in classical Islamic civilization.[25] *Fiqh* nevertheless concentrates heavily on moral and ritual prescriptions and does not really attempt to explain social dynamics. Şentürk's postmodern talk about incommensurability only conceals how hard it is to think of *fiqh* as a science continuous with natural science. A more appropriate analogue to today's efforts to find an Islamic framework for social thought is not the kind of sociology that works at the level of empirical data and modest theories about social forces but the more sweeping, grandiose forms of social philosophy in the West. Indeed, Muslim social thinkers regularly compare and contrast their views with Marxism, liberalism, or free-market neoliberalism. They even see more modest sociological work as an extension of an ideological "positivism" that arbitrarily denies that revelation is a valid source of knowledge.

There is nothing wrong with seeking ambitious theories that could provide an overall framework for doing science. After all, such theories are vital for the success of the natural sciences. Now, this very success complicates the picture—if human societies are very complex physical systems, then we cannot expect to find the same sort of powerful framework theories when studying the social world. If sociology is continuous with physics, biology, and psychology, the complexity of its subject matter likely means that modest work, full of exceptions and qualifications even in the best of circumstances, must characterize sociology. Perhaps such a naturalistic view itself could be seen as an overall framework for sociology, though it is much less dogmatic than portrayed by its detractors. In any case, in a scientific setting, broad framework-theories become more persuasive when they inspire and make sense of more modest work. Any sociology worth the name must not have just some overall framework and some ability to generate raw data about societies, it also must fill in the middle ground of modest explanations of limited social phenomena. And Islamic sociology has no success occupying this middle ground.

Consider the sociology of religion, a topic of special interest to proponents of an Islamic sociology. They start with a critique of Western approaches, accusing Western sociology of reductionism. By reducing religion and religious belief to social forces, analyzed in this-worldly terms, Western sociologists illegitimately exclude the possibility that religion is a response to encounters with genuinely supernatural realities. There is some merit to such a worry; after all, social science has roots in the European Enlightenment and has inherited some of the Enlightenment's anticlerical politics and its distrust of revelation. Since social science emerged as a substitute for theological ways of thinking about society, many secular Western social thinkers have been attracted to the idea that religion was just another social phenomenon. None of this, however, means that reductionist views are incorrect. Scientists like to explain phenomena in as tidy and unified a manner as possible; *if* the human sciences can account for religion in psychological and social terms, that is a successful explanation rather than a mere philosophical prejudice. Moreover, social scientists can always try to partially explain religion. After all, it is clear that religious beliefs are shaped and reproduced through various social mechanisms regardless of whether these beliefs happen to be true or false. Churches, sects, and religious movements are social entities, whether or not they actually mediate contact with a supernatural realm. The social aspects of religion should be susceptible to sociological explanation.

Islamic social thinkers have also charged Western sociology with taking Christianity as the model for religion and hastily generalizing explanations derived from experience with Christianity to other religions. Again, there is more than a little truth here. Still, trying to make universal claims based on local experience is common scientific practice. If the claims fail, then scientists have to rethink their explanations. This seems to have happened—it is hard to accuse more recent scientific approaches to religion of being centered on Christianity. For example, some of the most promising recent research examines religion from the perspective of cognitive science. Belief in supernatural agents is universal in all human cultures, in complex societies and small groups alike. So it is interesting to see how such beliefs are enabled by common features of the human brain, shaped by its evolutionary history.[26] The universal human tendency toward believing in supernatural agents and making such belief central to social interactions is the basis for religion, but the details of each religion depend on the history of each society and how it organizes social forces to reproduce belief in particular doctrines. So while sociology alone cannot produce a comprehensive explanation of spiritual beliefs, it has plenty of scope to account for how social forces shape particular religious traditions.

Some sociologists apply an economic perspective to religion. The human demand for supernatural compensators for the shortcomings of life on Earth, they say, should remain roughly constant, since life is always imperfect.[27] The form of religion people adopt is a rational economic choice, much like decisions to buy consumer products. In that case, the religious landscape of a modern, complex society should be shaped by the supply side in what is in effect a market for religion. In places where the market is restricted, such as European countries with their established state churches, not all demand will be met, and public religiosity will be weaker. The United States, in contrast, maintains a diverse free market in religion, which can meet most varieties of demand. Therefore America is much more religious than most of Europe.[28]

Other sociologists disagree, arguing that Western-style modernization interferes with the mechanisms by which organized religions reproduce themselves. Defenders of the secularization thesis argue that Western Europe has gone further down the path of secularization, where even though diffuse supernatural beliefs linger, religion has a much diminished role in public life. They observe that public life in the United States has also become more secular, especially compared to the informally established Protestant piety of the nineteenth century.[29]

Among Western sociologists, the debate on questions such as secularization continues. It even has an ideological aspect. Rodney Stark, the leading proponent of the rational choice theory of religion, regularly charges the Western sociological tradition with an antireligious bias, is very favorable to Christianity in his writings, and even expresses skepticism about Darwinian evolution.[30] But all parties to the current debate agree that their explanations, if correct, are not universal: they have to do with the long-term tendencies of European cultures that have undergone the Western form of modernization. They cannot easily be generalized to Muslim lands. And even with the ideologically charged nature of the debate, the contending explanations are subject to reality tests. Rational choice theory, for example, might work in the very narrow context of American-style Protestantism, but it fails to account for much empirical data otherwise.[31] And the secularization thesis is challenged by the continuing strong religiosity of the United States.

Nothing in the work of those who attempt to Islamize sociology compares even to this unsettled debate in Western sociology of religion. Their views make no contact with biology and cognitive science. They assert that the created nature of humans inclines everyone to believe in one peerless God, unless their *fitra* is overshadowed by subsequent social conditioning. But none of this is of any help in answering questions about why only certain kinds of supernatural beliefs are found in the world's religions or how religious concepts are learned. The explicit supernaturalism of Islamic sociology—its insistent defense of traditional concepts of spirit, meaning, and revelation—hardly encourages learning from cognitive science or evolutionary psychology. The intellectual isolation of Islamic social thought continues where more directly sociological issues are concerned. Islamic sociologists talk about the unity of the *umma*, but they do not have any distinctly Islamic tools to address questions about secularization, why political Islam has intensified in recent times, or how religious revival ties in to rapid social change in Muslim lands. If they comment on such questions, they rely on arguments derived from Western social science.

In fact, there appears to be no such thing as a distinctly Islamic sociology apart from restatements of theological beliefs in a more modern idiom, mixed with elements of Western social thought that are congenial to traditional religion. And since Islamized sociology does little but affirm theology, it is not very useful even for Muslims. Christian churches occasionally fund social scientific research to try to find ways to grow their memberships or extend their political influence. It is hard to see Muslim groups using the services of Islamic sociologists to produce anything so practical. In the end, Recep Şentürk, though defending *fiqh* as an alternative social scientific paradigm, acknowledges that efforts to renew social science have not been productive. Looking back at the Egyptian experience and comparing it to Turkey, he says that "today, the formation of a 'new sociology' as envisioned by its vanguard seems like a very broad and distant ideal. On the other hand, it appears odd that Egyptian sociologists who have not been able to solve their own social problems should propose solutions for the West, whose imperialism they never fail to emphasize."[32] Even this is too optimistic. Today, there is no reason to think Islamic sociology has any prospects at all as a science, even as a distant ideal.

ISLAMIC ECONOMICS

Modern Muslim thinkers, even many who are skeptical about Islamizing sciences such as sociology, pay close attention to economic matters. After all, economics is vitally important for modern societies, and Muslims have a special interest in accelerating development and alleviating the relative poverty of their countries. Economics appears to be the most practically applicable among the social sciences. It is hard not to notice that economic advisers have become as indispensable to modern governments as the court astrologers of old. And any ideology or political philosophy, if it is to achieve real political power, has to present an economic vision of how it will bring prosperity to its constituencies. Therefore, any distinctly Islamic version of modernity must include an Islamic version of economics.

Islamic economic thinking includes views about how to integrate economics with Muslim social morality as well as ideas about how to put Islamic economics into practice. Economic activity, most devout Muslims think, should take place within the moral and legal limits set by Islamic law. But this is not supposed to be an artificial, external restriction. After all, Muhammad was a merchant, and classical Islamic civilization encouraged commerce. Islam can provide the cultural and moral background that can support prosperity without plunder, development without exploitation. Indeed, according to theologian Mehmet S. Aydın,

> The Western world is in dire need of a spiritually strong philosophy of development. The Islamic world must learn from the historical mistakes committed by the West in its concept of development. In the material development of the West, a large role was played by an insufficiently moral conception of production and consumption, exploitation of humans and nature for sinful gains, and therefore the blood and sweat of the oppressed. Having seen power and domination as the prime virtues, and having formulated many things such as rationality—especially economic rationality—according to these "virtues," the West has only recently started working on and thinking about "human and environment-centered development models."[33]

In an Islamic economy, profit seeking would be tempered by social justice. Indeed, Islamist writers who desire a more moral economy sometimes echo Western critics of neoliberal political and economic ideology. It is clear that the current IMF and World Bank model of development works to the advantage of a global investor class rather than ordinary working people. Indeed, while the currently dominant neoliberal approach to economics might do well in promoting short-term economic growth, it is notoriously inadequate in dealing with the social and environmental costs of economic activity. So an Islamic perspective can be a useful reminder that economics is not just a domain of narrow technical expertise but an inherently political enterprise. It is legitimate to ask questions about the overall social purpose of economic policies, and if Islam provides a different political option than Enlightenment-based ideologies, it will naturally lead to a somewhat different political economy.

To put their high-minded ideals into practice, Islamic economic thinkers need to propose ways to keep a modern economy within the bounds of Islamic law. They pay particular attention to the strict prohibition of usury, usually interpreted as a ban on all interest. Muslim apologetic literature is full of denunciations of interest taking as an evil, rewarding exploitation rather than honest production. Nevertheless, it is clear that interest-based banking is vital for capitalist development and integral to a modern economy. The common solution to the dilemma is Islamic banking. In other words, conservative Muslims cheat against Islamic law while following its letter. They deposit their money in banks that supposedly agree to share in the profit or loss resulting from the money's investment; in practice, the Islamic banks provide a safe rate of return that ends up equal to the prevailing interest rates offered by their secular competitors. Still, Islamic banking has become an established part of economic life in Muslim lands. Moderate political Islamists consider them a success, demonstrating the promise of an Islamic economics.[34] More secular critics find it hard to take interest-free banking seriously, because of the obvious cheating. But the Islamic banking phenomenon is also an example of flexibility in conservative Islam, of its ability to support institutions suitable to the modern world—as long as they are disguised to appear in full compliance with traditional Islamic law.

The banking example also shows, however, that Muslims have been more ingenious in adapting to modern economics than in producing a distinctly Islamic alternative. And economics is not just statistics about investment and growth, econometric models, or discussions of interest rates and the money supply. Economic thinkers also deal with more ambitious themes of rational behavior, markets as a general model for society, even human creativity and happiness. Naturally, this is risky. From the management fads and New-Agey inspirational literature of the business world to economists who act as if environmental science or the second law of thermodynamics are not relevant to the economic realm, the business and economic culture of the advanced West is a rich source of weirdness and outright pseudoscience. So it is no surprise that some of the strangest versions of Islamic social science are also linked to economics.

Many Muslim thinkers are attracted to the concept of *tawhid*—divine unity—as a way of conceiving of the unity of knowledge under God. According to Ali Shari'ati, "Existence is therefore a living being, possessing a single and harmonious order that is endowed with life, will, sensation and purpose, just like a vast and absolute man."[35] Masudul Alam Choudhury also takes *tawhid* to be manifest in all the laws of nature and all social reality. He presents a *tawhidi* view of social science, which is closely connected to the Islamization of economics that was put into practice in Malaysia as an alternative model of development.[36] He starts with some standard criticisms of liberal economic individualism as isolating divine laws from the social and economic realms, so that the social costs of policy become invisible to Western economic thought. Social morality, however, can be brought in through Islamic economics. Choudhury locates Islamic economics in a grandiose philosophical context that leads to rethinking natural as well as social science.

No truly ambitious reconfiguration of science is complete without a misunderstanding of modern physics. According to Choudhury, "With the intensifying interest in unification theory in theoretical physics, the anthropic principle of a universe that learns, and the interactive explanation of ecology, there suddenly appears to be a limitless horizon of potential for a unification epistemology of the natural, social and human sciences."[37] He adds some quantum mysticism, and then explains how *tawhidi* thinking can improve physics: "In Einstein's scientific theory construction, the axiomatic premise is changeable to the extent of anthropic differentiations that are caused by perceptual pluralism of the observer. . . . Thus differentiations in epistemologies become endemic to physics—as, for example, between an epistemology for classical mechanics, one for relativity physics, one for quantum mechanics and yet another for grand unified theories. . . . In the Islamic framework the axiomatic premise remains unchangeable. . . ."[38] It is hard to credit this even as a mistake, but it is still almost respectable compared to Choudhury's moral mathematics: "K´ [falsehood] primordially has a dimension (a topological measure) smaller in the scale of 10:1 [than K, divine goodness. K´ (falsehood) as the mathematical complementation of K is 'permitted' by the topology of K"]. This is a reference to the Qur'anic measure of goodness to evil in the scale of 10:1. Accordingly therefore 10 blessings for every goodness and one punishment for every evil."[39]

This is not from crank literature but an academically oriented book by a reputable Western publisher. Such ideas have apparently enjoyed some influence on policy in some corners of the Muslim world. And all of these pseudoscientific pronouncements serve only to set the stage for some very unoriginal fundamentalist Muslim positions concerning economics and social science. In the end, the superior morality and factual soundness of Islamic social thought is supposed to be guaranteed by its faithfulness to divine revelation. Still, even Choudhury has some doubts. On one hand he is confident: "All non-Shari'ah sciences or other studies—meaning all those that are not linked to objective attention to truth in God's unity and its externalisation toward understanding life in the midst of a consciously unifying universe—are bereft of inner coherence." On the other hand, "The question then is, why have these other sciences shown such prowess while the contemporary emergence of the Tawhidi sciences is nowhere to be seen?"[40] Choudhury tries to explain why, but his explanation involves more confusion about modern physics, complaints about controlled experiments being accessible only to the rich, and endorsements of medical superstitions such as homeopathy.

What, then, does Islamic economics amount to other than moral posturing, with or without abuse of natural science? Islamist economic policies have not performed any wonders in countries where they have been implemented, such as Pakistan, Malaysia, or Iran. Islamism may indirectly have had some positive effects, providing rapidly urbanizing populations with an alternative business network where shared religious beliefs serve to establish trust. Nevertheless, Islamic economics remains of dubious intellectual coherence and lacks in practical success.[41] In fact, a striking aspect of modern Islamic economic ideas is how elastic they are in practice. Muslim governments have often used Islamic rhetoric to endorse economies of plunder and patronage, whether in the guise of a Third-World version of state socialism or speculative free-market casino economies. No amount of talk about the moral qualities of Islamic economics has been able to propel Muslim populations to prosperity—all it does is lend cultural authenticity to economies entrenched in a subordinate position in the global marketplace.

Still, the emptiness of most Islamic economic rhetoric also means that some versions of modern Islam could promote economic success. If Muslim countries are to follow a capitalist path of development, they will have to grant economics more autonomy—from religion, from moral theology, from the politics of patronage. And yet, Islam remains essential to social solidarity and political legitimation. So the best solution may be to fake it, the way Islamic banks pretend not to deal in interest rates. In Turkey, the moderate Islamists who have recently enjoyed power follow mainstream economic policies and are even slightly less corrupt than more secular rivals. They use patronage politics to deliver services to their religiously conservative but poor constituents among recent urban immigrants, as well as to the rising class of devout provincial entrepreneurs. Islamic capitalism is gathering steam. If it works, this will be for reasons similar to those behind the economic success of early modern Protestants—not anything written by the intellectuals promoting Islamic economics.

History as Tradition

A Muslim perspective on history might have more intellectual substance than Islamic social science. After all, Muslim empires kept detailed records and supported a historiographical tradition long before the rise of European science. Moreover, while medieval Christians tried to place events in the context of the detailed salvation history imagined by their religious tradition, Muslims did not operate under such a constraint. Islam accepted the view of all Abrahamic religions that history stretched out between the creation and a possibly imminent divine judgment. Still, Muslims reading the Quran did not find any overall narrative of events. God sent prophets to various nations in the past, and these prophets delivered divine messages and acted as characters in some morality tales. But in the Quran, none of this takes place in any chronological or overall narrative context. Since the Quran lacks more than a weak sense of history, some Muslim scholars could study history for purposes related to the state, independent of religious interests.

Ordinary believers and most of the ulama did not care much about history: only a narrow segment of history, that concerning Muhammad and the generation who knew him, was relevant. That was when the religious ideals that guide the devout Muslim were made concrete. Before the time of the Prophet, or before the time a nation converted to Islam, there was only darkness, the Age of Ignorance. And afterward, there was keeping faith or being forgetful, or revivals that always hearkened back to the time of the Prophet. Muslim elites certainly accepted this framework, but they did not let themselves be limited by it. They created an extensive and sophisticated historical literature, especially when compared to medieval Christendom. For the officials of Muslim empires and those scholars interested in political and administrative questions, the deeds of dynasties and the examples of the past mattered greatly. Those ulama concerned with collecting accurate legal precedents carefully examined the past, even recording different versions of the same events and determining criteria for figuring out what kinds of accounts were trustworthy.[42]

Still, classical Muslim history writing did not follow modern critical standards. Especially in religious matters, the outlines of truth were already determined by a higher authority. And even elites did not depart far from the popular personalistic approach to knowledge, validating accuracy by the testimony of pious and therefore reliable opinion holders. Scholars carefully collected hadith reports and recorded their alleged chains of transmission, invalidating many hadith with inadequate testimonial support. But they never challenged the naive belief in the historical narratives of religious tradition. As a standard account of early Islamic history crystallized, it became the context for interpreting the sacred sources and came to be treated as an integral part of the faith. To most Muslims, this standard account is common knowledge—something known to be true rather than subject to debate.

None of this is unique to Islam. In the technologically advanced West, personalistic views of knowledge and uncritical trust in sacred representations of history continue to be widespread, especially among conservative Christians. The academic world, however, has long abandoned such views, and more liberal approaches to sacred history also enjoy some popular influence. In the Muslim world, scholars who publicly express significant doubt about the standard tale of early Muslim history risk unwelcome controversy, losing their jobs, or worse. Still, there are also some tentative steps toward more liberal views. For example, modernist Muslims have long presented their versions of the biography of Muhammad in order to advance their interpretation of the faith. These biographies are still historical myths, driven by a search for ethical and religious inspiration. Indeed, they are much like nineteenth-century liberal Christian accounts of early Christianity, which also tended to rationalize miracle stories and modernize ethical injunctions.[43] Their aim is not critical scholarship but to present revelation in a more credible light in modern times. And their method largely amounts to tendentious and selective reinterpretation. Nevertheless, they do make modern Muslims aware that there are alternatives to the traditional view of history.

The tendency to modernize also appears in work by religiously orthodox thinkers with nontraditional backgrounds. For example, Ahmed Yüksel Özemre, a Turkish nuclear engineer, proposes to solve conflicts between the hadith literature and modern science by declaring that all the traditions that contradict modern knowledge, such as those that indicate that the earth is only thousands of years old, must be excluded as inauthentic.[44] In effect, he wants to amend the traditional Islamic science of hadith criticism by including a new criterion. Since always resolving difficulties in favor of modern science risks putting science ahead of revelation, it is religiously dangerous. But again, undeniably pious thinkers such as Özemre can help promote changes in religious attitudes.

Another source of liberal views of Muslim religious history is the now sizable Muslim minority in the West. Many Western Muslims remain very conservative, but others take their distance from Muslim lands as an opportunity for religious experimentation and reform. They mostly follow the modernist formula: take the sacred sources at face value unless there are compelling reasons to do otherwise and interpret them according to today's moral sensibilities.[45] All the Muslim world is undergoing religious change, and views originating among Western Muslims can also influence the ongoing debates.

These developments create space for better historical scholarship and a better popular understanding of history in Muslim lands. Still, none of these steps toward retelling the story of early Islam come close to engaging critical history as practiced in the West. As history writing in Europe became more secularized, scholars increasingly began to understand the Bible as a collection of very human literary and historical documents. Today, in Western academic circles, it is commonly accepted that the Bible is primarily a collection of religious literature, that it cannot be taken at face value as historical reportage, and that it takes a very difficult process of textual criticism and comparison with independent sources of information such as archaeology to get even a brief glimpse of any events that may underlie the religious mythology. Much that is important is simply lost to history, and much that seems to be straightforward narration of events is religious propaganda. Having discovered that their own religious traditions could not be taken at face value, Westerners curious about Islam have begun to apply some of the techniques of biblical criticism to the Quran and traditions about early Muslim history. Naturally, such work has been far less extensive than the attention devoted to the Bible, and many scholars have remained content to trust traditional Muslim views and only take a very limited critical approach. But by and large, the emerging results have been similar to those concerning the Bible. The Muslim sources do not present the historian with a clear record but with an often fragmentary, tendentious collection of traditions that were assembled at a late date and in the context of legal, theological, and political struggles.[46]

This is not to say that Western historians of Islam discount the traditional outline of Muhammad's biography or the standard story of the emergence of Islam. With few alternatives, historians often can do little more than present a paraphrase that acknowledges the poor quality of the overall evidence and tries to figure out the most plausible course of events.[47] Some more radical historians have used

other evidence, such as contemporary Christian accounts of the first
Arab invasions, and proposed accounts according to which much of
Islam was invented after Muhammad, where the Quran was assembled from multiple sources in the century following the invasions,
and where the traditional story about Muhammad and early Islam
is largely a later fabrication.[48] There is also some very intriguing
philological evidence that much of the Quran is based on Syriac
Christian sources.[49] There is lively scholarly debate about such matters, though most historians remain dubious about the more radical
scenarios that shift too much of the religious creativity in the origins
of Islam to the early Arab Empire. There is no overall consensus, but
it is increasingly clear that the naive, pious version of events believed
in by almost all devout Muslims cannot survive critical scrutiny.

Much of this historical work is unacceptable to orthodox Muslims, because it challenges traditional beliefs about the origin of the
Quran. Almost all Muslims take the Quran to be the direct word of
God—unadulterated, inimitable, perfect in every detail. Nevertheless, to a critical historian, the Quran appears to have emerged in a
polemical environment. Religious rivals of early Muslims, such as
Christian scholars in the conquered lands, were quick to point out
that the Quran looked like a chaotic collection of story fragments
from Middle Eastern traditions, that many sources were used, and
that signs of sloppy editing were easy to detect. Some recent discoveries support this view; for example, from manuscripts found in
Sana'a it appears that passages in the present Quran starting with
"Say . . ." originally began with "He said, . . . ," suggesting that these
passages were taken from a list of Muhammad's sayings. Early Muslims responded to criticism by dogmatically asserting inimitability
and took signs of bad editing to be "positive rhetorical devices."
Awkward editing and contradictions became problems after the
present text was accepted as religiously authoritative, and some early
Muslim scholars began to write about these difficulties and the ways
to get around them.[50]

Today's Muslim scholars continue to try to dispose of such problems rather than acknowledge that the sacred sources are very
human works of religious literature. They continue to think that the
classical hadith collections are reliable; many even portray the
Islamic science of hadith anachronistically as a critical scientific

enterprise. And in the end, many fundamentally disagree with taking a critical attitude at all. Abdelwahab el-Affendi declares,

> There are those modern thinkers who believe that the reform of Islamic thought could be achieved through divorcing the 'reverential attitude' toward the texts from the sober evaluation of their import and the critique of traditional procedures and approaches. This is to miss the whole point of Islamic thought. For the Islamic sources are an inspiration only to those who view them with reverence. Otherwise, what is the point of seeking guidance in them? The ethical dimension has thus never been absent from the Islamic intellectual endeavor, even in its scientific part. The leaders of the main juristic schools did not attain influence solely on account of their erudition, but chiefly because of the public perception of their moral rectitude and verifiable commitment to Islamic values.[51]

Faith-based moral commitments permeate the ways Muslims are supposed to acquire knowledge. Accordingly, religious traditions are supported by traditions about the moral probity of hadith gatherers—true historical narratives are constructed by finding trustworthy testimony, as in Islamic legal practice. That the Quran might be a human construction is not even worthy of discussion.

Not every Muslim is so conservative, and some try to engage Western scholarship by presenting a more sophisticated view of the sacred sources, even moving toward a watered-down view of revelation similar to that of liberal Christianity. But even then, they usually engage in traditional forms of apologetics and cultural defense. Farid Esack, for example, acknowledges aspects of the Quran that might create an impression of incoherence or bad editing, but argues somewhat like early Muslim polemicists by saying that these are literary devices that only add to the beauty of the recited text.[52]

More disturbingly, there is a political undercurrent in debates between Muslim and Western scholars. Postmodern intellectual fashions have in some cases created an opening for the Western human sciences, as more sophisticated Muslims can make some gestures toward accepting critical scholarship while using postmodernist ways to protect their faith from criticism. But the postmodern turn also encourages politically based evaluations of scholarly work. So, in practice, Muslims readily accuse Western historians of orientalism. Indeed, in the early Western scholarship on Islam, colonialist or missionary aims were often intermingled with motives of intellectual curiosity. Even today, when Western funding of research on Islam is often connected with interests in oil, terrorism, or other motives of foreign policy, some caution is not a bad idea. But too often the Muslim response has been not to find a pattern of bad scholarship and suggest that political interests may have distorted the research, but to look for political motives and to take any suspect motives as a reason to discount scholarly conclusions.

This is unfortunate. Where religion is concerned, Western historians had to go through a long and painful process of discovering that their scriptures were earthly literature. But Western scholars were usually Christians themselves, and they were usually able to develop more liberal views of divine revelation as they cast doubt on beliefs that were culturally dear to them. For Muslims, skepticism about the sacred sources is a foreign import, not a native heresy that got out of control. Muslims taking small steps toward accepting the human element in the Quran also come closer to a Western, secular view—a perspective they typically see as hostile. This makes the whole process more difficult.

So among Muslims, critical historical approaches to religious matters are still virtually unknown. Some think this presents no problem, because historical criticism cannot challenge Islam. Ahmet Davutoğlu, for example, argues that since Muslims did not divinize history as did Christians, they treated history objectively to begin with and therefore have no difficulty acknowledging the historicity of their faith.[53] This is far from the truth. Almost all Muslims believe that their religion is founded on well-attested historical events. Not only do they have trouble perceiving the mythic nature of their beliefs, but they take great offense to any suggestion otherwise. As a result, some European scholars of Islam find it prudent to publish their research under pseudonyms, worried about Muslim reactions to work that challenges perceptions of the Quran as a pure divine communication.[54]

SEEKING AUTHENTICITY

The Islamic world has a long tradition of social thought, whether in elaborating on Muslim social ideals or in trying to solve social problems. For example, the fourteenth-century scholar Ibn Khaldun produced a noteworthy philosophy of history and is often considered a forerunner of sociology. And naturally, Muslims trying to understand their society in relation to the West drew first on the resources of their own intellectual tradition. Late Ottoman intellectuals who worried about the decline of their empire and were looking for sources of renewal often looked to Ibn Khaldun for understanding.[55]

As the Western style of modernization took hold, however, Western social thought began to dominate education and intellectual life. Muslim countries ended up half-modern; everything from clothing to government administration to television entertainment took on a Western veneer, while political and moral legitimation remained anchored to traditional Muslim thought. This halfway modernization, subordinate to the West it weakly echoed, satisfied few beyond a narrow segment of elites. At a personal level, most people wanted to maintain an authentic Islamic identity in the face of all the superficial changes. And at a wider social level, many devout intellectuals continued to look for more Islamic ways of organizing social life. They wanted, and continue to want, an Islamic modernity that preserves the deeply held values of the past and takes an alternative path of development that is creative in its own right. Westernizing too often means imitating the West in all things, turning Muslim societies into bad copies of Western originals. Another way should be possible, and new, authentically Islamic but modern forms of the human sciences could help blaze this path.

These are genuinely attractive ideas. Indeed, they resonate among more secular and nationalist intellectuals as well. After all, it is natural that in the process of secularizing and joining the West on equal terms, Turks, Arabs, Iranians, and other Muslims should want to contribute something unique of their own to the modern world. Global consumer culture, unfortunately, has a way of flattening everything, turning cultures into interesting flavors to buy in order to spice up after-work experience. And at work, where it really counts, everybody ends up immersed in the same corporate mindset. Anyone with intellectual interests and social awareness must be bothered by the lack of depth of late modern consumer life.

So it must be a profound disappointment that Islamic attempts to refashion social thought have invariably ended up as sterile reaffirmations of tradition. The religious change and vigorous experimentation going on among ordinary Muslims has inspired little creativity among conservative Muslim intellectuals, who seem to be most comfortable referring back to traditional doctrine. Even change, it seems, can only be legitimated by dressing it up as a return to a purer faith. Meanwhile, more liberal-minded Muslims do plenty of high-quality social scientific research in the Western mold, but they do not further ambitions for a distinctly Muslim approach.

At their best, the explanations put forth by the human sciences also point out new social possibilities, which is one reason they stand closer to ethical concerns than the natural sciences. Indeed, a critical, genuinely scientific approach to human societies is an indispensable aid to the moral imagination. And yet, too many Muslims, by the way they put moral convictions guaranteed by revelation in the center of their social thought, try to shut down moral debate rather than bring up options to think about. Even though radical posturing has become very prevalent among modern Islamists, the result is really a disguised and fearful conservatism. The different historical and social experience of Muslims raises the possibility that their different perspective can help advance social knowledge. Instead, today there is little to note in conservative Muslim approaches to the human sciences but a failure of imagination.

NOTES

1. Farshid Raissi, "Soliton Transistor," *Applied Physics Letters* 86 (2005): 263503–505.

2. Taner Edis, *Science and Nonbelief* (Westport, CT: Greenwood Press, 2006), chap. 4.

3. Recep Şentürk, *İslam Dünyasında Modernleşme ve Toplumbilim: Türkiye ve Mısır Örneği* (İstanbul, Turkey: İz Yayıncılık, 1996).

4. 'AbdulHamid AbuSulayman, ed., *Islamization of Knowledge: General Principles and Work Plan*, 2nd ed. (Herndon, VA: International Institute of Islamic Thought, 1989), p. 19.

5. Ibid., p. 73.

6. Ali Yaşar Sarıbay, *Postmodernite, Sivil Toplum ve İslam* (Bursa and İstanbul, Turkey: Alfa Yayınları, 2001), pp. 42–46.

7. Akbar S. Ahmed, *Postmodernism and Islam: Predicament and Promise* (London and New York: Routledge, 1992), p. 32.

8. Keith M. Parsons, ed., *The Science Wars: Debating Scientific Knowledge and Technology* (Amherst, NY: Prometheus Books, 2003); Paul R. Gross, Norman Levitt, and Martin W. Lewis, eds., The Flight from Science and Reason (New York: New York Academy of Sciences, 1996).

9. Taner Edis, *The Ghost in the Universe: God in Light of Modern Science* (Amherst, NY: Prometheus Books, 2002), chap. 8.

10. Harun Yahya, *The Disasters Darwin Brought to Humanity*, http://www.harunyahya.com/disasters03.php (accessed December 4, 2006).

11. Taner Edis, "Relativist Apologetics: The Future of Creationism," *Reports of the National Center for Science Education* 17, no. 1 (1997): 17–19, 22–24.

12. Hassan Hanafi, "New Social Science: Some Reflections," 1987, appendix in Şentürk, *İslam Dünyasında Modernleşme ve Toplumbilim.*

13. A particularly frustrating example is Roxanne L. Euben, *Enemy in the Mirror: Islamic Fundamentalism and the Limits of Modern Rationalism* (Princeton, NJ: Princeton University Press, 1999), p. 22. Much of the book is quite valuable; it continually tries to unsay what it says with the overblown postmodern rhetoric at the beginning.

14. Mücahit Bilici, "Forgetting Gramsci and Remembering Said Nursi: Parallel Theories of Gramsci and Said Nursi in the Space of Eurocentrism," in *Islam at the Crossroads: On the Life and Thought of Bediuzzaman Said Nursi*, ed. Ibrahim M. Abu-Rabi' (Albany: State University of New York Press, 2003), p. 176.

15. Bernard Lewis, *The Crisis of Islam: Holy War and Unholy Terror* (New York: Random House, 2004).

16. Merryl Wyn Davies, *Knowing One Another: Shaping an Islamic Anthropology* (London and New York: Mansell, 1988).

17. Şentürk, *İslam Dünyasında Modernleşme ve Toplumbilim*, pp. 19, 55–56, 106.

18. Mevlüt Uyanık, *Bilginin İslamileştirilmesi ve Çağdaş İslam Düşüncesi* (Ankara, Turkey: Ankara Okulu Yayınları, 2001), pp. 63, 70–72, 86.

19. Ali Shari'ati, *On the Sociology of Islam: Lectures by Ali Shari'ati*, trans. Hamid Algar (Berkeley, CA: Mizan Press, 1979), p. 43.

20. Ibid., pp. 43–44, 48–50.

21. Şentürk, *İslam Dünyasında Modernleşme ve Toplumbilim*, pp. 95–98.

22. Adil Şahin, *İslam ve Sosyoloji Açısından İlim ve Din Bütünlüğü* (İstanbul, Turkey: Bilge Yayıncılık, 2001), p. 33.

23. Sarıbay, *Postmodernite, Sivil Toplum ve İslam*, pp. 48–49.

24. Larry Poston, *Islamic Da'wah in the West: Muslim Missionary Activity and the Dynamics of Conversion to Islam* (New York: Oxford University Press, 1992), pp. 54–55.

25. Şentürk, *İslam Dünyasında Modernleşme ve Toplumbilim*.

26. Scott Atran, *In Gods We Trust: The Evolutionary Landscape of Religion* (New York: Oxford University Press, 2002); Pascal Boyer, *Religion Explained: The Evolutionary Origins of Religious Thought* (New York: Basic Books, 2001).

27. William Sims Bainbridge, *The Sociology of Religious Movements* (New York: Routledge, 1997).

28. Rodney Stark and Roger Finke, *Acts of Faith: Explaining the Human Side of Religion* (Berkeley: University of California Press, 2000).

29. Steve Bruce, *Religion in the Modern World: From Cathedrals to Cults* (Oxford: Oxford University Press, 1996); Steve Bruce, *God Is Dead: Secularization in the West* (Oxford: Blackwell, 2002).

30. Rodney Stark, "Fact or Fable? Digging up the Truth in the Evolution Debate," *American Enterprise* 15, no. 6 (2004): 40–44.

31. Steve Bruce, *Choice and Religion: A Critique of Rational Choice Theory* (Oxford: Oxford University Press, 1999).

32. Şentürk, *İslam Dünyasında Modernleşme ve Toplumbilim*, p. 274.

33. Mehmet S. Aydın, *İslâmın Evrenselliği* (İstanbul, Turkey: Ufuk Kitapları, 2000), p. 49. For a survey of responses to capitalism by Islamic thinkers, see Charles Tripp, *Islam and the Moral Economy: The Challenge of Capitalism* (New York: Cambridge University Press, 2006).

34. Raymond William Baker, *Islam without Fear: Egypt and the New Islamists* (Cambridge, MA: Harvard University Press, 2003), chap. 4.

35. Shari'ati, *On the Sociology of Islam*, p. 82.

36. For further context about this project, see Mona Abaza, *Debates on Islam and Knowledge in Malaysia and Egypt: Shifting Worlds* (London: Routledge Curzon, 2002).

37. Masudul Alam Choudhury, *Studies in Islamic Social Sciences* (New York: St. Martin's, 1998), p. 31.

38. Ibid., p. 41.

39. Ibid., p. 35.

40. Ibid., pp. 162–63.

41. Timur Kuran, *Islam and Mammon: The Economic Predicaments of Islamism* (Princeton, NJ: Princeton University Press, 2004).

42. Bernard Lewis, *From Babel to Dragomans: Interpreting the Middle East* (New York: Oxford University Press, 2004), pp. 406–409.

43. Andrew Rippin, *Muslims: Their Religious Beliefs and Practices* (New York: Routledge, 2001), chap. 13.

44. Ahmed Yüksel Özemre, *Din, İlim, Medeniyet (Düşünceler)* (İstanbul, Turkey: Pınar Yayınları, 2002), pp. 99–127.

45. For example, Reza Aslan, *No god but God: The Origins, Evolution, and Future of Islam* (New York: Random House, 2005).

46. Edis, *The Ghost in the Universe*, chap. 4.

47. For example, F. E. Peters, *Muhammad and the Origins of Islam* (Albany: State University of New York Press, 1994).

48. Some examples are included in Ibn Warraq, ed., *The Quest for the Historical Muhammad* (Amherst, NY: Prometheus Books, 2000).

49. Christoph Luxenberg, *Die Syro-aramäische Lesart des Koran: Ein Beitrag zur Entschlüsselung der Koransprache* (Berlin: Das Arabische Buch, 2000).

50. Rippin, *Muslims*, pp. 30–35.

51. Abdelwahab El-Affendi, "Rationality of Politics and Politics of Rationality: Democratisation and the Influence of Islamic Religious Tradition," in *Islam and Secularism in the Middle East*, ed. Azzam Tamimi and John L. Esposito (New York: New York University Press, 2000), p. 164.

52. Farid Esack, *The Qur'an: A Short Introduction* (Oxford, UK: Oneworld, 2002), pp. 73–75.

53. Ahmet Davutoğlu, "Philosophical and Institutional Dimensions of Secularization," in Tamimi and Esposito, *Islam and Secularism in the Middle East*.

54. For example, the groundbreaking work of Christoph Luxenberg, *Die Syro-aramäische Lesart des Koran*, is pseudonymous.

55. Bernard Lewis, *Islam in History: Ideas, People, and Events in the Middle East*, rev. ed. (Chicago and LaSalle, IL: Open Court, 1993), chap. 18.

CHAPTER 6

A LIBERAL FAITH?

A LIBERAL ALTERNATIVE

Modern science and conservative versions of Islam do not sit well together. Muslims think of the Quran as a revealed, infallible text. Moreover, that text presents a mostly straightforward message that is captured fairly well in the context of the hadith and the interpretations of traditional scholars. Devout Muslims perceive the world as an obvious manifestation of divine design, a place where supernatural influences may be subtle but are nonetheless visible to those who look. In the human realm and even beyond, the world turns according to Islamic morality; personal conduct and social interactions are measured according to a divine standard of justice. And so, when the natural sciences fail to recognize any sign of design in the universe and do not refer to any supernatural agent in their explanations, Muslims often think that science is at least incomplete, if not wrong.

Muslim efforts to correct modern science, however, have been unimpressive. When confronting the natural sciences, too many Muslims veer off into pseudosciences such as creationism. And attempts to construct a distinctly Muslim form of the human sciences have not amounted to much more than obscurantist cultural apologetics. Either as critics or as contributors, devout Muslims have not had much effect on the modern scientific enterprise.

This is not to say that Muslims are stuck in medieval times. Not at all. If Muslims anywhere lag in use of cell phones, television, or the Internet, this is largely because of poverty, not any rejection of modern technology. Some tight-knit groups, such as the Ismaili Bohra community centered in India, have recently carried out a program of increased orthodoxy and clerical control while also embracing advanced technologies.[1] The Nur movement in Turkey is well known for its support of early modern Protestant-style capitalist enterprise. It is easy to find pious Muslims working and thriving in technology-intensive businesses. In fact, Muslims who are intimate with modern technology and capitalism are the creators of and the strongest constituency for most Islamic-colored pseudoscience. The problem, as ever, is that Muslims have not been able to become truly productive in basic science. Muslim intellectuals have certainly put much effort into defending their faith from criticism. They have not, however, been able to construct compelling explanations of the world that can compete with the naturalism that has become entrenched in modern science. For all the continual declarations of harmony, the relationship between modern science and most popular currents of Islam is not always friendly.

In that case, just as Muslims import science and technology, perhaps they should also look to the West for a model of an amicable relationship between science and religion. After all, though theologically conservative versions of Judaism and Christianity remain strong and continue to invite friction with science, the Western world also harbors liberal religions that actively avoid interfering with science. Indeed, a very popular Western conception of science and religion is that these belong in separate spheres. Science is supposed to be concerned with the natural causes of natural phenomena, while religion addresses the realm of spirit, morality, and meaning. Science, therefore, is useful but limited. While our various religions affirm supernatural realities such as a divine spirit guiding the universe, these are ultimate causes that do not touch on the scientists' daily work of finding mundane, proximate causes for physical phenomena.

Whatever the intellectual merit of such a clean separation of domains, it is clear that as *institutions*, liberal religion and modern science coexist well. The scientific community is notoriously secular, and most elite scientists such as the members of the US National Academy of Sciences reject traditional religious beliefs such as a personal God.[2] Nevertheless, large numbers of scientists, especially applied scientists, remain religious believers: their convictions about spiritual realities do not interfere with their work in the laboratory, and their scientific knowledge does not challenge their interpretation of their religion.[3] Indeed, scientists and liberal religious leaders often meet on political common ground. In the United States, scientists hoping to counter creationist attacks on science education work closely with allies among liberal clergy, reassuring the public that nothing in science threatens core religious convictions. The availability of liberal religious options has been very important in smoothing out conflicts of interest between scientific and religious institutions.

So the best way to achieve Muslim harmony with science might be to promote liberal tendencies within Islam. Today, the possibilities for moderate and liberal Islam attract interest primarily because of their political implications. In the Western media, Islam is very often associated with terrorism and other violence, the subordination of women, or immigrant groups who have difficulty integrating into their host societies. Bringing forth a more liberal face of Islam has become important to prevent a clash of civilizations. And there are plenty of liberal-minded Muslims to showcase. Many moderate Muslim intellectuals are deeply concerned about the violent and repressive elements who claim to represent their faith. They think of Islam as a godly and yet sophisticated civilization rather than a rigid set of divinely ordained rules of conduct. Indeed, they are appalled by the puritan extremists whom they perceive to be hijacking a religion that represents the best in humanity.[4] Islam, many say, is a religion of balance, of the middle path: not the fanaticism and superficial rule-observance that leads to banning music and chopping off the hands of thieves. Surely the Islam that stands for a deeply rooted civilization can sustain scientific inquiry as well as its Christian and Jewish cousins.

Intellectually, a more liberal Islam could also claim its own separate sphere and stand aloof from scientific matters. Philosophy, in fact, can be a help rather than a hindrance in this task: philosophical theology often tries to limit the scope of science and stake out an intellectual space where religious faith is protected from criticism. Many Christians, for example, minimize friction with science by trying to establish a specifically religious domain within intellectual life. They read the supernatural fact claims of their tradition in a more metaphysical sense, rather than making concrete claims that invite direct scientific investigation. They concentrate on their deep moral convictions, expecting that science cannot say much about how we ought to live. God becomes real to them through the life of faith and through religious experience. They perceive a meaning in the universe that transcends mere material goings-on without contradicting scientific statements about subatomic particles or the evolution of frogs. Theological liberals lay claim to considerable intellectual sophistication, including the heritage of the Western philosophical tradition. They say they have a better way to achieve harmony between faith, philosophy, and the scientific enterprise.

Naturally, such views help support an environment where scientific and religious institutions coexist amicably. And in turn, liberal views appear most plausible in such an environment. So it might seem that this is just what the Muslim world needs. After all, the liberal Christian formula is a proven success. And there is no deep reason that more liberal developments cannot take place within Islam. The question, as always, is not about some mythical "essential nature" of Islam but about whether more liberal approaches are realistically available within the Muslim world today.

PROTECTING REVELATION

Liberalizing Islam is an attractive idea. It can, however, easily be perceived as yet another demand for westernization in a time when Muslim intellectuals are more concerned to reassert an Islamic identity. Many Muslims desire change, but they typically present religious reform as a way to defend what is most essential about the Islamic revelation. A more accommodating view of science would most easily take hold if it were advertised as part of a more authentic approach to a timeless faith. And here, conservative thinkers have an advantage. After all, they also claim to allow science to flourish within its proper sphere. Conservatives say that they put Islam first: not only is their version of faith more compellingly rooted in tradition but they can better set the bounds of modern science, subordinating science to an overall Islamic view of the world.

Many Muslims grant some independence to science while also being clear about setting limits. Metin Karabaşoğlu, for example, expresses the Nur movement's view, that science can be a valuable resource for Islam:

> The Qur'an and the universe form an inseparable whole. The Qur'an is the guide that demonstrates the right way of seeing the universe, and the universe is the evidence and witness of the rightness of the truths preached by the Qur'an. Contemplating revelation without taking the universe into consideration gives rise to an imitative submission to the revealed truths, while looking at the universe without the Qur'an leads only to surmise and conjecture. When the Qur'an and universe are seen to correspond, both questions can be resolved. Nursi's emphasis on the compatibility of the religious sciences as the light (*dhiya*) of the conscience with the 'modern sciences' as the light (*Nur*) of reason must be seen in this context.[5]

If science were not at least partially independent of revealed religion, it could not do its part in the Nurcu scheme of faith. Nevertheless, Said Nursi and his followers are also aware that science and reason can, if left alone, drift away from God. So they insist that reason should be subordinated to a traditionally conceived idea of revelation.

This is a common sentiment among Muslim thinkers. Seyyed Hossein Nasr is more direct about the limitations of science, declaring that

> modern science can be conceived as a legitimate way of knowing certain aspects of the natural world, a way which is able to discover some of the characteristics of the natural or physical world but not all of that world. If its limited range of vision could be accepted, it

could be integrated into a more general scheme or hierarchy of knowledge in which higher forms of knowledge would dominate over but not necessarily obliterate the knowledge of the quantitative aspect of nature gained by modern scientific methods.[6]

Like many Christian and Jewish thinkers, Nasr is bothered by "scientism," where what starts as a legitimate empirical investigation oversteps its bounds and becomes a more ambitious philosophy that challenges a spiritual view of the world. Sayyid Qutb, a well-known Islamist theorist who represents a significantly different approach to Islam than Nasr, expresses a similar concern. Bringing up what has become a very common theme in Muslim writings on science, Qutb argues that science is fine as long as it does not overstep its boundaries and depart from immediate, experimentally verified facts.[7]

Clearly, however, such views are too conservative to allow science much independence or even breathing space. They invariably try to restrict science to a stamp-collecting enterprise, frowning on the theoretical work that is integral to modern science. And the charge that science has overextended itself and become harnessed to a disguised antireligious philosophy is often made by religious thinkers who have not made their peace with science—it is, for example, a common feature of antievolutionary literature among conservative Christians as well as Muslims.

Still, many conservative Muslim thinkers at least rhetorically allow science *some* room to operate independently. Efforts to liberalize Muslim views of science could try to expand the perceived limits of science. More liberal Muslims want to avoid explicit claims that may end up conflicting with physics or biology, and grant more legitimacy to the theoretical aspect of natural science. But they also share much common ground with conservatives in their concern over delineating the proper spheres of scientific and religious thought. So, liberally inclined Muslims might be able to persuade their coreligionists that a less rigid view could promote Muslim development while still protecting the core of the faith from science-inspired criticism.

In the United States, the political controversy over intelligent design and evolution in public education pits religious conservatives against religious liberals. The liberals want to exclude explicitly supernaturalistic views from science education, and they do so by arguing that there is a sharp separation between scientific and religious ideas. Science, they say, is concerned with natural explanations of natural phenomena. By definition, science is restricted to investigating naturalistic possibilities. So ideas such as design by a supernatural intelligence have no place in science and are therefore out of bounds to science education. Religious conservatives who believe their scriptures make concrete claims about how their God acts on nature usually do not respond well to this exclusion by definition.[8] Liberals try to reassure them, however, by pointing out how this same sharp separation protects the supernatural from scientific criticism. If science cannot say anything about the supernatural one way or the other, the dreaded secular humanist who might argue that evolution supports a godless universe is also being unscientific. Disconnecting science and religious—supernatural and metaphysical—claims allows science room to operate and at the same time protects religion from evidence-based criticism.

This suggests that liberal versions of Islam could also draw on philosophical conceptions of science that allow scientific investigation wide latitude but also firmly block scientific intrusions on religious territory. Again, more tradition-minded thinkers already claim to accomplish this, so liberalization can begin by tinkering with conservative ideas.

Unfortunately, there is not much agreement among conservatives who have thought about how to fit science into a distinctly Muslim view of knowledge. Seyyed Hossein Nasr wants to subordinate science to a metaphysical scheme of knowledge derived from traditional Muslim conceptions. And similar themes of reviving the Muslim religious sciences and locating modern science within a metaphysical scheme derived from classical Islam continue to be attractive. But thinkers who propose to Islamize science, though they have broadly similar aims, typically resist the speculative metaphysical tradition in Islam, especially when it has too obvious links to Sufi or Shiite mysticism. Standing closer to the Wahhabi strain of reformist Islam, they blame medieval mystical and metaphysical thinking for the stagnation of Islamic science. So Islamizers emphasize "the importance of purifying Islamic knowledge from the pitfalls of sophistry and alien metaphysical concepts that corrupted

Islamic methodology of thought and education."[9] In response, Nasr and other critics of the Islamization of knowledge charge the Islamizers with trying to create an incoherent hybrid and with failing to challenge the modern Western metaphysical assumptions that remain implicit in their conceptions of knowledge.

Many thinkers would like to develop a devoutly Muslim view of science, but beyond some broad sentiments that most Muslims affirm, they have a hard time agreeing on details. Views that emphasize a theology of mystical illumination and those that prefer a more concrete and practical approach are especially hard to reconcile. And much of this disagreement has to do with divergent views about the essence of Islam, even when all think that true science should not trespass on core religious commitments.

Moreover, the demand for a specifically Islamic framework for science—whether through an effort to Islamize specific sciences or through a revival of medieval views of knowledge—can easily lead to a philosophy that constructs a straightjacket for scientific inquiry rather than allowing science any real independence. Consider the views of Mevlüt Uyanık, a Turkish theologian who is a sympathetic critic of calls for the Islamization of knowledge.[10] Uyanık thinks that metaphysics is fundamental, in the sense that everything important proceeds out of prior metaphysical convictions concerning knowledge. Since metaphysical assumptions guide and constrain all attempts at knowledge, conflicts between Western varieties of knowledge and Islam are only to be expected. After all, they derive from different fundamental presuppositions, particularly where revelation is concerned. Muslims take the Quranic revelation to be absolutely trustworthy, unmediated knowledge from God, beyond rational testing and critical scrutiny. Therefore, the task facing Muslims is to de-westernize their philosophy and return to the Muslim revelation, which includes all the resources needed to be successful in practical technology and applied science.

It is unlikely that any approach such as that promoted by Uyanık can do more than serve as an apologetic device in defense of a rigid conservatism. Such an approach proclaims that revelation, including those aspects of revelation that appear to make ordinary fact claims, is immune to criticism. So while it protects religion from science, it does so in altogether too heavy-handed a fashion. For liberals, there is a problem in that not only are many Muslim thinkers attracted to such views, but these views are close to cultural norms as expressed in legal thinking. For example, law professor Mohammad Hashim Kamali, in his exploration of the freedom of expression according to Islamic law, says that Islam allows the widest possible scope for "rational enquiry and the quest for truth . . . even in the face of hostility from the masses." But this openness can be very limited where religious matters are concerned, since "no intellectual enquiry may begin on the premise of denying the fundamental truth of monotheism (*tawhid*) and of the clear guidance which is enunciated in the divine revelation."[11]

It appears, then, that the conservatives do only too well in protecting revelation. Liberals need to reinterpret the content of revelation in order to allow science and critical scholarship more freedom, even when they challenge established interpretations. Otherwise, it is hard to see how pseudoscientific positions such as varieties of creationism will lose influence in Muslim intellectual life. Still, liberals may yet make some headway due to their common interest with conservatives: setting aside certain claims, perhaps metaphysical and supernatural propositions, as immune to science-based criticism. After all, most conservatives, living in modern times where the power of science and technology is all too obvious, readily grant science *partial* autonomy, and insist that Islamic requirements to affirm revelation by no means restrict science.[12] Liberals can agree but also try to better realize this ideal by widening the scope of science's partial autonomy.

LIBERAL IDEAS

Since Islam has traditionally centered on its sacred texts, liberal versions of Islam offer up different interpretations. They attempt to create openings for a less conservative way of life, without appearing to compromise the faith. Charles Kurzman describes three broad approaches adopted by liberals.[13] The "liberal shari'a" approach tries to convince believers that when properly understood, traditional Islamic law endorses liberal policies. Then there is the "silent shari'a" view, which says that revelation is incomplete. The sacred texts present ethical principles and fundamental doctrines, but they do not always give prescriptions that dictate the details of how Muslims should live. Where Islamic law is silent, taking a liberal direction is permissible, if this happens to benefit the Muslim community. Kurzman calls the most sophisticated approach "interpreted shari'a," which emphasizes that revelation comes to Muslims mediated through human interpretation of the sacred texts. So Muslims have to do the intellectual work to develop a general interpretive framework that can grow and adapt to changing times. Just being satisfied with the traditional interpretations favored by the ulama is not good enough. Doing this interpretive work, and even just being aware of the necessity for human interpretation, could well lead to a more liberal stand.

Most of these approaches go back at least to the early modernist Muslims of more than a century ago. Modernists such as Muhammad Abduh tried to break the straightjacket in which the ulama found themselves, trying to find more flexible ways of reading the sacred sources. In many respects, these modernists remained very traditional-minded—the Islam they envisioned liberated human reason as long as it remained within the bounds determined by revelation. Still, though deeply pious and theologically orthodox, modernists have been more open, more sophisticated, and more willing to use a Western intellectual idiom than more traditional religious scholars. Early modernists argued that many religious laws applied only to earlier times and emphasized that while the revealed laws completely determined the religious duties of people, most of the details of social life were subject to human judgment.[14] This introduced a degree of autonomy for nonreligious enterprises such as science.

Indeed, modernist-style arguments continue to be used by liberals who want to avoid confrontations with science. Muhammet Altaytaş, for example, says that "the knowledge God gives people through revelation gives us guidance not about the physical but the metaphysical (hidden) dimension of reality. For example, the Quran gives no scientific (positive) information about the creation of and the biology of humans. Its statements on such subjects carry signs about the metaphysical being of humanity, about God and the relationship between God and humans, and the meaning of life." Altaytaş argues that anything embarrassing in the Quran, such as what might appear to be scientific mistakes, obviously has to be read metaphorically.[15]

Some of the most heated debates over modern interpretations of the sacred texts take place not over science but political matters such as women's rights. Muslim feminists argue that for centuries, male religious scholars have read the prejudices of their patriarchal societies into the basic sources of Islam. Some feminists such as Fatima Mernissi even contend that many of the hadith reports that portray women as inferior have been fabricated. The sacred sources, Mernissi says, can be reclaimed by more woman-friendly interpreters.[16] Even moderate Islamists today engage in similar forms of reinterpretation. In Egypt, the well known Islamist thinker Muhammad al Ghazzaly objects to strict traditionalists who deny women leadership roles in society. Gender-conservatives find support from verses such as 4 An-Nisa 34 in the Quran, which starts with "The men are supporters of the women" and includes an instruction to "spank" or "lightly beat" disobedient women. Al Ghazzaly says such verses are only about relationships within the home, citing a tradition about the successor of the Prophet who appointed a woman as a judge in a market.[17]

Such politically modernist interpretations can help reduce some of the religious pressure on science, since reinterpretation then becomes a more acceptable notion. More systematic, less politically charged ways of liberal interpretation, however, may be more useful for science in the long run, if they consistently grant science more autonomy.

A number of Muslim scholars, including many with a Western-style academic background, propose to give precedence to the "spirit of the text" in the sacred sources over the surface meaning as seen by literal-minded and traditional interpreters. The Quran is supposed to be interested in a community centered on justice and equality before God, so upholding its spirit in a contemporary context means supporting universal notions of human rights and gender justice.[18]

Pakistani scholar Fazlur Rahman is one of the better-known modern Muslims interested in developing a new interpretive framework based on the spirit of the text. His work invokes the "Qur'anic matrix of ideas" and tries to avoid both the ossified views of the traditional ulama and the dangers of modern secularism. Arguing that there is an important distinction between the broad principles and themes presented in the Quran and those Quranic stories describing narrow responses to particular historical circumstances, he brings forth a somewhat liberalized but still deeply pious response to the sacred texts.

In connection with his concerns with revitalizing Islamic education, Rahman also expresses interest in science. Islam, for him, provides an overall cosmological and spiritual direction for science: "Although the *content* of physical or exact sciences cannot by definition be interfered with—else they will be falsified—their orientation can be given a value character."[19] Hence he is sympathetic to the aims of those who propose to Islamize science, though skeptical of the results that they have claimed to achieve. Rahman also retains a traditional view of nature. He follows the modernists in downplaying the mystical and miracle-claiming currents in Muslim tradition, but also is very conventional in stating that "Nature is the grand handiwork of the Almighty, but it does not exist just to show off His might and power. It is to serve man by meeting his vital needs."[20] So Rahman's approach to Quranic interpretation falls short of granting science full independence within its sphere, and could conceivably be harnessed for fruitless efforts to give modern science a more Muslim character. Nevertheless, this and similar claims to look to the spirit of the sacred texts rather than just their letter increase the range of what is available to Muslims.

Muslims who push liberal tendencies further than Rahman often put even more emphasis on the distinction between the sacred text and fallible human interpretations.[21] This distinction can easily be put to apologetic use, since if anything goes wrong, it is always interpretation that is at fault, never the divine word. And so conservatives as well as liberals can explain the current weakness of the Muslim world by saying a particular historical interpretation was inadequate.[22] Nevertheless, increasing awareness of the role of human interpretation generally furthers liberal political aims.

A leading Muslim thinker who emphasizes the distinction between the divine word and its human interpretation is Abdolkarim Soroush, an Iranian philosopher and religious scholar. To Soroush, religion itself is divine and immutable, but we encounter religion through human institutions. The human understanding of religion is not sacred, and nothing about human religious thought is immune to change and criticism. Traditional commentaries, bodies of law, the religious sciences, and so forth belong to this secondary level of human understanding. In this context, Soroush makes statements that could easily be made by Western religious liberals who see science and religion as separate, noncompeting aspects of life. This also has political and institutional implications:

> Religion is not identical with science, nor is it a progenitor, an arbiter, or a guide for it. Still less does it follow the objectives of science. At the same time, religion need not deny or oppose science. Everything that dons the garb of science (be it government or management) enters a similar relationship with religion. Religious management or religious science is as conceivable as religious thermodynamics or religious geometry. The truth is that politics can be mixed with religion only if a nonsacral understanding of religion is juxtaposed with a nonsacral method of administration.[23]

Soroush, in fact, consistently supports the autonomy of science, defending science not just against conservative suspicions but also against the postmodern-flavored "antipositivist" attacks that have become fashionable among many Muslim thinkers.[24]

For that matter, even postmodern views can help create space for modern knowledge, if they weaken deference to traditional readings of the sacred sources. Mohammed Arkoun is a leading academic who severely criticizes both traditionalist and Islamist thinking, instead envisioning a more liberal, intellectually open Islam.[25] And he is able to do so because he embraces those aspects of the humanities in the West that, under a postmodern label, emphasize pluralism, diversity, and the human element in interpreting all texts, including those thought to be divine. Indeed, Arkoun's view of religion and revelation owes much to sophisticated liberal approaches common among Western academic theologians. For example, Arkoun emphasizes those aspects of the Quran that suggest an oral rather than written revelation. Many modern theologians have come to associate oral discourse and religious experience with a continually vital and flexible response to a divine reality, as opposed to written scriptures that make revelation permanent but imprison it in a past context. Arkoun applies such views to Islam, praising the oral elements in Islam while criticizing traditional interpretations as serving the interests of the state and those social classes with access to the means of engaging in the interpretation of written texts.

There are many paths to a more liberal Islam and plenty of Muslim thinkers who outline a more liberal faith that is intended to be more than merely a watered-down compromise with secularism or a retreat into the private realm. Liberals usually pay more attention to immediate social and political questions than to science, but they still tend to see science as a common human enterprise, not to be appropriated for any one religion. So the possibility of more liberal expressions of Islam is not in doubt, and it seems likely that a liberal turn in Muslim societies would help science. If nothing else, a more liberal social environment would mean less pressure for scientific views to be tested according to their Islamic qualifications.

Still, this does not mean that liberal versions of Islam are easily available outside of certain intellectual subcultures. Liberal Muslim thinkers often become figures of controversy; some even suffer persecution at the hands of more conservative political and religious establishments. Fazlur Rahman, who could more accurately be described as a traditionalist who adopted a more modern intellectual style, acquired a reputation as a liberal. He was no longer able to work in Pakistan and spent the last two decades of his life as an academic in the United States. Abdolkarim Soroush is popular with younger, upper-class Iranians who dislike the rigid theocracy in Iran. But just because of that, he became subject to continual harassment and censorship. He now teaches in Western countries. And Mohammed Arkoun works in France—he almost certainly would not be able to work and publish freely in Algeria. Worse could happen. Ahmad Khalaf-Allah was an Egyptian scholar who argued that the sacred sources did not intend to convey any historical or scientific reality, that what looked like concrete claims were metaphors for an underlying spiritual and moral truth. Though radically reinterpreting the basic texts of Islam, Khalaf-Allah remained devout and never challenged the divinity or integrity of the Quran. Nevertheless, he was found to be an apostate, his marriage was annulled by the state, and he had to flee the country.

CONSERVATIVE RESPONSES

Outspokenly liberal Muslims can invite distrust or worse. Still, in many parts of the Muslim world, proposals to reform and liberalize Islam are actively debated. And though some religious leaders encourage popular outbursts of religious indignation, the conservative response to liberal proposals includes a serious intellectual element. Many Muslim thinkers who are keenly aware of the modern world and its challenge to traditional piety point out difficulties with liberal ideas. They highlight specifically religious motives for caution in reinterpreting the sacred sources.

"Conservative," in fact, can be a misleading term. Many Muslim thinkers take the view that Islam is not a private faith, that it regulates all aspects of life, and that it sets the framework for understanding all of reality—seen and unseen, natural and supernatural. They think so not because they are attached to traditional ways but because they consider Islam to provide guidance for all of life. Not just a bunch of ritual practices and moral principles, Islam is supposed to provide a comprehensive way of dealing with modern conditions. It is especially supposed to be an alternative to the secular West. God is meant to be creator and ruler, not just a pale metaphysical concept. The Quran is the revelation of the divine will, not a book of metaphors that change with every human whim.

And such views are *religiously* attractive. No doubt the Western influences that permeate life in Muslim lands today add to the urgency with which many Muslims seek a culturally more authentic form of resistance. But discomfort with liberal options does not arise only from cultural conservatism or the way liberalism is often associated with an alien West. Early modernists who introduced liberal themes into the debate among Muslims immediately received criticism. Sometimes they came under suspicion of borrowing too much from the West. But much criticism was phrased in religious terms that made no reference to a human choice between cultural alternatives. Today, a similar process continues. Conservatives certainly accuse liberals of putting up an inadequate cultural defense. But more significantly, conservatives charge liberals with going against the clear word of God.

For example, Mevlüt Uyanık analyzes Muslim modernist

thought and says that the modernists naively assumed that Western knowledge could be grafted onto Islamic culture without doing damage. Modernists mistakenly conceived of Western science as a value-free enterprise whose results could be directly transferred and even used to renew Islam. They separated fact and value and ignored the cultural aspects of knowledge creation. In effect, Uyanık argues, modernists and liberals even took their concept of religion from the West—they attempted to recast Islam in a liberal Protestant mold, removing religion and morality from the sphere of concrete realities subject to scientific investigation. This did not work; in the end, reinterpretation and modernization could only threaten to turn Islam into yet another ever-changing secular ideology.[26] Hence, for Uyanık, it is modernist failure—especially the religious superficiality of the modernist response to the West—that sets the stage for more recent ideas such as Islamizing science.

A common conservative theme is that liberals let human perceptions and earthly ideologies dictate the meaning of the divine word, when the proper religious attitude is to submit to God and let revelation guide our lives. This is not to deny the human effort to understand the sacred sources and apply them in changing circumstances. But if the human element takes the foreground, this leads to arbitrariness in religion and chaos in public life.

Consider the debate over the status of women. Feminists such as Fatima Mernissi argue that the dominant orthodox ulama have interpreted the hadith in the light of their patriarchal cultural background.[27] Mernissi's use of Muslim tradition, however, is no less tendentious. Muslims today no longer fabricate hadith literature, but in the sea of contending reports, they can select a thread that fits their sensibilities. Muslim feminists will, naturally, select according to their feminist moral orientation. Such a liberal view, however, cannot be persuasively based on religious ground common to most Muslims. Different Muslim groups will agree that the sacred texts should be read for contemporary guidance, but their subsequent disagreements suggest that their varying conceptions of what is sacred and moral are independent of the ostensible divine guidance.

To conservatives, such disagreements are religiously disturbing, over and above concerns about the unity of the *umma*. It means, at least, that the sacred sources have to be approached in a more disci-

plined way—a way that can produce consensus among acknowledged experts. And this was precisely the achievement of classical
Muslim civilization where the ulama controlled religious interpretation. The Muslim world was never short of sectarian strife, but it still
managed an impressive consensus on basic matters of faith and
practice. No one claims the ulama were perfect—many religious
scholars provided opportunistic, selective interpretations that served
the interests of the powerful. Yet there were always ulama who preserved their independence and retained popular respect. They could
criticize opportunistic interpretations and hope to correct mistakes
by referring to the substantial common ground shared by devout
Muslims. So, according to many conservatives, the methods of interpretation and bodies of commentary produced by the classical
ulama were reasonable solutions to challenges the community of
Muslims have always faced. Modern times are not especially different in this regard. The ulama tried to take a literal, plain view of
revelation as much as possible. But they also adjusted, adapted, and
developed secondary layers of doctrine and law surrounding the primary sacred sources. Any religiously authentic response to modernity, then, must use the classical tradition as its point of departure
and provide clear *religious* reasons for any proposed reinterpretation.

Liberals often aim to identify central themes, main moral objectives, or the "spirit of the text" that would guide new interpretations
applied to modern circumstances. This, too, can easily become an
excuse to let human interests shape the divine message. After all,
devout Muslims agree that revelation presents what is most sacred
and most ideally moral. If they become convinced that morality
favors a change in gender roles, they will be tempted to selectively
highlight texts that appear to undermine strict patriarchy. They might
even elevate an obscure tradition about a successor to the prophet
appointing a woman market official over Quranic verses that have
usually been read to support a subordinate public role for women.

In that case, with all the interpretive activity going on, how can
Muslims be sure that they respond to the divine will rather than to
human interests? Agreements on broad principles are not that difficult. Many moderates and even conservatives in the Muslim world
would agree with Khaled Abou El Fadl that

the specific rulings of the Qur'an came in response to particular problems that confronted the Muslim community at the time of the Prophet. The particular and specific rules set out in the Qur'an are not objectives in themselves. These rulings are contingent on particular historical circumstances that might or might not exist in the modern age. At the time these rulings were revealed, they were sought to achieve particular moral objectives such as justice, equity, equality, mercy, compassion, benevolence and so on. Therefore, it is imperative that Muslims study the moral objectives of the Qur'an and treat the specific rulings as demonstrative examples of how Muslims should attempt to realize and achieve the Qur'anic morality in their lives. Because puritans do not think of the specific rules as demonstrative examples but as objectives in themselves, they seek to implement the rules *regardless of whether their application will enhance or undermine Qur'anic principles* such as justice, equity, or mercy.[28]

Well grounded in traditional religious scholarship, Abou El Fadl demonstrates that such scholarship does not necessarily have to be a rigid application of ancient laws. But an emphasis on basic principles raises the question, just what is justice or equity? These are remarkably broad notions, and it is notoriously difficult to give them specific content that commands wide agreement. Conservative Muslims often conceive justice to be tightly connected to one's natural place as created by God. They can easily find the justice of traditional gender roles proclaimed in the Quran and further support their notion of created nature with pseudoscientific beliefs.

For that matter, what distinguishes Islam from a secular school of ethical philosophy dedicated to exploring questions about justice or equality? The Islamic character of the enterprise must come from working on just the sort of examples given in the sacred sources. In the texts, Muslims must attempt to discern a divine guidance that transcends the merely human interests of the moment. Superficial rule observers and text thumpers aside, this is just what serious conservative Muslim thinkers insist the Muslim scholarly tradition has always been about. But then, it is also no surprise if scholars tend to converge on views that tweak the "demonstrative examples" rather than do much that is radically new. Views such as those expressed by Abou El Fadl exclude bomb throwers and puritans, but they are not so liberal as to reject religious constraints on human reason or to retreat from religious regulation of social life. Politically moderate Muslims may still consider a certain degree of religious interference with scientific reasoning to be legitimate.

If some broader freedom for scientific inquiry is to emerge from any main themes or "moral objectives" of the Quran, something like Abdolkarim Soroush's separation of the spheres of science and religion should also take hold. But Soroush's views are hardly immune to religious criticism, from worries about his arbitrary choice for where to draw the boundary between the divine and human levels of religion to his specific political prescriptions.[29] Muslim debates over liberal interpretations of sacred texts always confront the religious motivation to seek divine guidance rather than human opinion. And here, conservatives, even fundamentalists, enjoy an advantage. They always claim to defer to what the text really says. It is questionable whether they do so—the texts are often ambiguous and hard to fashion into clear messages. Looking for guidance on contemporary questions will always bring in the particular perspectives of the interpreters. And so, as liberals like to point out, traditional and fundamentalist views are no less human interpretations of the sacred sources. Nevertheless, there is also something facile in the liberal position. The Quran can be remarkably opaque, but it is not entirely unclear. Traditional interpretations seem less strained than those of liberals. Furthermore, fundamentalists can at least use tradition or the mythical time of the Prophet and his Companions as a way of sanctifying their ideas. Liberals may be more sophisticated from a modern, secular point of view, but their very awareness of the human element in religion makes it more difficult for them to appeal to the more overtly supernaturalistic and faith-based aspects of their heritage. Especially in the popular arena, this remains a severe handicap.

THE WESTERN EXAMPLE

The ongoing competition between liberal and conservative religious tendencies mirrors a similar tension in Western Christianity. Christians also debate where to draw the line between science and faith;

liberal, modernist Christians also emphasize the need for continual reinterpretation of scripture and tradition. None of the main positions staked out by Muslim liberals and conservatives will be unfamiliar to an observer of recent Christian history.

There are, however, important differences between Western Christianity and Islam today. Modernity began in Europe; Western Christians have had a longer time to adapt to a powerful science and technology, modern politics, and the changing social circumstances within which their churches have had to operate. Moreover, Christians did not just react to social and intellectual change, they helped shape it. Christian theology did not passively adapt to modern times; churches were deeply involved in social movements and in constructing a new, more individualist style of religiosity. Even the evangelical Protestantism that has been very influential in the United States has been a driving force behind a more democratic, individualist ethos. Muslims, in contrast, have encountered modernity as an external imposition, and most have approached modernity as a challenge rather than as a possible expression of Muslim values. Even liberals are typically concerned with preserving faith and community rather than advancing a more modern way of being religious.

Today, one clear difference between the intellectual landscapes of Islam and Western Christianity is the greater strength and variety of liberal Christianity. This is especially true in elite circles. While ordinary churchgoers tend to be more traditionally orthodox in their beliefs, most academic theologians think their God works in subtler ways than spectacular miracles or infallible revelations. Theologians who waffle on the reality of the soul or describe God as an extremely vague "Ground of Being" are not very unusual. Indeed, there are even a few radical theologians who take a "nonrealist" view of God and the supernatural, arguing that these elements of religion do not refer to concrete realities but are symbols of our highest aspirations for a meaningful life and a humane morality.[30] It is not only some theologians who have become hard to distinguish from secular humanists. Not a few in the congregations of liberal churches and synagogues participate in their moral tradition and identify with their heritage without being greatly interested in the literal reality of the supernatural.

Nonrealist theologians are hardly representative of Western religion, but the fact that they occupy even a small part of the religious landscape is significant. Among Muslims, liberals who propose relatively tame metaphorical reinterpretations of parts of the Quran are still somewhat exotic, even controversial figures. It would be almost unthinkable for Muslim theologians to propose nontheistic ways of working within the Muslim intellectual tradition.

In fact, the status of nonbelievers can be a good indicator of the degree of liberality of a culture. Western Christians do not react warmly toward atheism—after all, they believe it is a major mistake, and it is still an open question whether human societies are better off with some common belief in a supernatural anchor for morality. Nevertheless, religious Westerners tend to treat nonbelief as a real personal option and a legitimate point of view in intellectual debates. Even fundamentalist Protestants, though they may strongly dislike religious skepticism, accommodate its presence by defining the true faith against a background of omnipresent human error and backsliding. In Muslim lands, nonbelief faces a very different cultural environment. In traditional Muslim societies nonbelief is almost incomprehensible. Since the social order is strongly coupled to shared religious convictions, radical nonbelief appears as a bizarre violation of reason. Lawrence Rosen describes this common attitude as "atheism yields chaos because it means the abandonment of reason and reason's grasp of God's articulated scheme."[31] Muslim jurists seriously discuss the death penalty for apostasy in traditional Islamic law and often concede only a limited degree of freedom for nonbelief—it is acceptable only if it keeps quiet and thereby does not disrupt the moral order of society.[32] And lately, public expression of nonbelief has become even more difficult with Islamic revivals taking place throughout Muslim lands. In the case of Turkey, David Shankland observes that "until recently, in the cities at least, it has been possible for a person in Turkey to be an atheist and not to fear for his or her life . . . there is not the slightest doubt that it is now dangerous for a man or a woman to deny openly belief in God. To do so invites condemnation from the clerics, accusations of 'provocation' from the courts and violence from those who feel that they have the right to take the law into their own hands, however firm may be the voice of quietism from moderate believers."[33] Indeed, in the past few decades, a few prominent public critics of traditional Islam, both liberal Muslims and outright nonbelievers, have been assassinated. And Turkey is the most westernized Muslim country, with aspirations to join the European Union.

So liberal Islam as a way to reconcile science and religion in Islam, though an attractive idea, faces many practical difficulties. It may be true that a more liberal religious climate would help scientific institutions and allow Muslim countries to use modern knowledge more effectively. It would probably be in the best interests of science if Islamic culture followed the Western example in religious matters. But then, many Muslims are even more concerned about the best interests of their religion. And in that case, the Western example starts to look less like a success story and more like an object lesson in what not to do.

Since Muslims became aware of the technological and economic superiority of modern Western countries, there have also been Muslim observers interested in social and cultural life in the West. Some ended up admirers, promoting westernization beyond importing technical skills and administrative techniques. Many, however, found reasons to be cautious, especially where religion was concerned. They saw a Christianity that had grown anemic, perhaps even corrupt. After all, religion was retreating from important aspects of public life. Europe was technically proficient but spiritually lost, so Muslim thinkers repeated the conventional wisdom that while the technical accomplishments of Europe should be imported, its culture was tainted with materialism and should be avoided.

The perception that the West is spiritually corrupt remains strong. Many Muslim commentators note that in Europe the churches are moribund and that as a natural consequence moral decay has set in. They present the West as a cesspit of sexual immodesty, drugs, and alcohol, permeated by a climate of greed where people pursue money at the expense of the tight-knit families and religious communities enjoyed by devout Muslims. Western lands are full of economic opportunity and so are very attractive to Muslim immigrants, but many newcomers also bring a fear that adopting Western ways would mean moral and religious corruption. And back home, Muslim intellectuals also agree that secularization would be a social disaster. While a liberal secular order has its good side—democracy, individual rights and freedoms—it depresses the civil solidarity that only religion can generate. Depending on human rationality for social order, liberal secularists privilege the individual over the community and exclude morality from public life.[34]

Indeed, according to many Muslims and even some Western thinkers, secularism is not just alien to Muslims but is riddled with violence and coercion. As John Keane puts it, in examples such as France and Turkey, "Perhaps the most strikingly contradictory, self-paralyzing feature of secularism is its theoretical and practical affinity with political despotism."[35] Plenty of moderate Muslims support putting some distance between religion and everyday politics, and admire the pluralism of modern democracies. Few want the theocracy demanded by Wahhabis and other puritans. Nevertheless, even for most liberals, the ideal is a public life that is explicitly guided by Islam and oriented toward community values.[36]

Muslim intellectuals, then, tend to judge Western religion by the resistance it has offered to the dire fate of secularization. It is clear that Western Europe has substantially secularized—in Britain, France, the Netherlands, and throughout the continent, many churches have been converted into conference centers and carpet warehouses, and few people bother to show up at Sunday services. Europeans have not turned into rationalist skeptics, but many appear to have lost interest in organized religion.[37] If liberalizing Christianity was meant to keep the faith attractive and relevant in modern times, this clearly has not succeeded. And liberal theologians appear to have capitulated to secular materialism in all important respects. They have watered down central doctrines shared by the revealed Abrahamic faiths to a degree that they are scarcely recognizable. Shabbir Akhtar, a British Muslim philosopher, admires the liberal Protestant tradition for its scholarly detachment and "candour and openness in its dealings with secularity and modernity." Yet he adds that he does not think it should be completely emulated: "On the contrary, I argue, in the manner of many Thomists within the Christian tradition, that excessive capitulation to secularism is self-defeating and that many a Protestant writer has unwittingly sold his faith down the river." Akhtar ends up insisting on a strong doctrine of revelation: the Quran must be inerrant, and there must not be any concession to contingency in the text. Christian liberals have failed to pick out the divine in the midst of the culturally conditioned. Therefore they have not been able to resist the challenges posed by secularization. Akhtar is convinced that liberal Christianity is a religious dead end.[38]

So Europe, the part of the advanced West that Muslims have been most familiar with, looks like an example of material success but religious failure. The United States is seen as a partial exception, since Americans remain a conservatively religious people in many respects. Even while deploring its imperial foreign policy, many Muslims admire how the United States appears to combine Abrahamic religiosity and modern accomplishment and to demonstrate that religious freedom need not lead to cultural secularization. Indeed, many Muslims sympathize with the cultural politics of conservative Christians in America. Moderate Islamists often approve of the Anglo-American model of church-state separation as an impartiality between sects that can leave room for general government favoring of religion.[39] Even Israel has attracted praise from Islamists because of the way Israeli identity is inextricably linked to religion, so that Israel is not secular in a Western European sense.[40] But while paying close attention to the different fortunes of Western religion, devout Muslims rarely admire *liberal* Christianity. Hence Mehmet Aydın, the Turkish theologian, ends up agreeing with earlier observers of Western Christianity:

> The spirit of modern times, according to the Muslim-Turkish intellectual who defended the position we take, did not benefit Christianity. Because it could not tolerate progress, it chose the path of abandoning its principles, or becoming corrupted, in order to make peace with its era. Therefore, when our eyes are diverted from appearances and focus on the essence, it becomes easy to see the deficiencies of modern Western civilization in the dimension of faith and morals. Our deficits in serious thought and fresh knowledge produced a "religious condition *without life*"; in the West a weak religion led to a life lacking a sufficient religious dimension.[41]

As for science, Aydın and many others do not perceive any special problem. After all, it was Christianity's specific inability to accommodate reason, and Christianity's specific organization in terms of a church and official clergy, that led to its clashes with science. The autonomy of science is a demand that emerges from unfortunate experiences in Christian history; Islam has no clerical authority to impede science. Therefore the secularist notion of autonomy, as acknowledged in liberal religious views, is unnecessary for the progress of science in an Islamic context.[42]

In the West, science and religion conflicted, cooperated, and generally muddled through to get to a point where even when they disagree today, respectable people do not make a great fuss about it. It might appear that the Muslim world could take a painless shortcut—adopt a liberal position that shies away from interfering with science. But this is not so easy. The very awareness by Muslims of how science and Christianity have developed together changes the Muslim response. Today, Islam is under reconstruction. Much is up for grabs as Muslims try to join fragments of medieval views of knowledge with modern ideas to produce an intellectual picture of the world that can command popular allegiance. It is by no means certain how an Islamic accommodation between scientific and religious institutions will be reached, or if this will resemble a Western "separate spheres" model. Many Muslims think that such a model continually demands that religion should retreat as science advances. Science becomes yet another instrument of secularization, and most devout Muslims consider secularization unacceptable.

A CLASH OF AMBITIONS

At present, conservatives have the upper hand in defining what it means to be a true Muslim. Many Muslims continue to perceive a tension between some aspects of Western science and Islamic faith. Still, the relative weakness of liberal options is just one reason for the cultural handicap faced by science. It might not even be true that increasing liberalism is the best hope for science in Muslim lands. After all, though less inclined to bring traditional doctrines into conflict with modern knowledge, liberal religion is also interested in limiting science and in proclaiming a spiritual realm beyond the natural world. Liberal Christians will not flirt with outright creationism, but they typically favor a view of evolution under divine guidance. They will not do faith healing or spirit possession, but they often have sympathy with New Age alternative healing philosophies. They favor high mysticism, not low-class miracles—unless the miracles have a more ecumenical, parapsychological flavor.[43] And though liberal theologians tend not to subordinate reason to faith in a fixed revelation, many adopt a postmodern suspicion of reason.

Moreover, among Muslims, a liberal inclination to expand the sphere of science and the desire to identify overarching themes in the Quran can clash with one another. For example, one reasonably clear and convincing Quranic theme is *tawhid*, the unity and sovereignty of God. Yet this theme of unity has caused no end of headaches for science in the Muslim world. The natural and religiously very understandable inclination of Muslims has been to interpret *tawhid* as demanding the unity of creation under God. So Muslims have been inclined to think that to understand nature properly, one must perceive the signs of divine activity in nature and come to see how the world has been designed by God. In that case, it becomes difficult to maintain a distance between science and the pervasive Muslim sense that revelation holds the key to reality.

Indeed, a fairly common feature in Islamic thought of all political colors is the tendency to put religious and moral considerations first. For many liberals as well, science must be subordinated to social needs and individual therapeutic purposes. As Mohammed Arkoun puts it, "Religions are superior to any scientific theory because they give imaginative solutions to permanent issues in human life, and they mobilize the social *imaginaire* with beliefs, mythical explanations, and rites."[44] Whether phrased in terms of counter-Enlightenment philosophies that seek certainty in bedrock ethical and religious convictions, or linked to more traditional personalist views that weigh claims according to the testimony of religiously upright authorities, Muslim attitudes toward knowledge often make the central questions those of ethics and utility for the community. Whether a claim fits comfortably into the ethical-religious worldview of Islam matters very much in deciding whether it is true. An inquirer must be morally and religiously upright to gain knowledge about more than superficial matters.

Modern science works differently, even when practiced by scientists who may be personally devout. Science is not value-free—at the least, scientific institutions have to be structured in a way that best promotes the acquisition of reliable knowledge about the world.

Honest inquiry is not easy, and the advancement of science critically depends on the intellectual ethics of its practitioners.[45] But this internal ethic of science involves a narrow commitment to actions that are instrumental for gaining knowledge. It need not be extended to other social enterprises. Moreover, the practices and methods of modern science work best in investigating a fundamentally impersonal, ethically indifferent world. They are unlike occult or religiously oriented practices that require an inquirer to enter into a proper relationship with a personal and spiritual reality. So even relatively moderate religious views can invite tension with science if they emphasize *tawhid* or otherwise ask about ethical implications when judging fact claims. Any ambitious religious philosophy will try to cast science in its own mold, and Muslims, far from breaking free of the demand that ethics should shape knowledge, tend to try to repair the breach between science and social values.

For that matter, modern science is also ambitious and routinely ignores the limitations set by philosophers. Religious liberals and, indeed, many scientists, insist that science is a modest, pragmatic undertaking that does not encroach on territory belonging to philosophers and theologians. Nonetheless, those Muslims who see modern Western science as an ambitious enterprise determined to insert itself into all questions of fact are correct. It is true that ethical prescriptions cannot be derived from biology, and that the existence of God is not a physics problem. Nevertheless, scientists are very interested in constructing a big-picture view of the world. Science is not only about collecting facts or toiling away in a narrow subdiscipline—*connecting* different disciplines with a claim to knowledge about some aspect of the world is integral to such a big picture. So it is inevitable that evolutionary biologists will try to understand altruistic behavior or that cognitive scientists will investigate moral perception. In doing so, they need not be constrained to validate traditional religious and philosophical beliefs about the nature of morality.[46] Physical cosmologists cannot but ask questions about the origin and future of the universe. Their conclusions need not respect traditional views about a creator, intelligent design, or the nature of time itself.[47]

Questions about supernatural agents, about whether reality is fundamentally personal, or about whether complexity, intelligence, and even religious experience emerge from a mindless material substrate are very interesting. And these are *scientifically* interesting questions, especially when constructing a big-picture view. So scientists investigate religiously inspired claims such as communication with the dead, intelligent design, or the healing power of intercessory prayer. Statisticians examine ideas such as "Bible codes" in ancient scriptures.[48] Historians look at how the origin stories of various religions hold up to evidence. Supernatural entities cannot be scientifically tested if science is narrowly conceived as the activity of people in white coats spending too much time in laboratories. But if science is construed broadly—as the interconnected, multidisciplinary activity of understanding how the world works—only a completely inert "God" that makes no difference in the world is invulnerable to science-based criticism.

Sometimes questions of God or revelation are said to belong to philosophers. But philosophers in advanced Western countries are aware of the ambitious nature of modern science, and many think of their work as being continuous with scientific efforts to construct the best available understanding of the world. The more traditional variety of philosophy is not extinct; fields such as the philosophy of religion are not short of metaphysicians making pronouncements from their armchairs. But this style of philosophy—insulating itself from science, even limiting contact with the religious traditions that supply the metaphysical propositions being debated—is intellectually sterile.[49] An important segment of Western philosophy has moved past first-principles-first attitudes and has joined the broadly scientific enterprise. Philosophers of physics contribute to our understanding of time, cosmology, and quantum mechanics. Cognitive neuroscientists trespass on traditionally philosophical territory, and many philosophers of mind join the debate about approaches to investigating consciousness. Philosophers of science analyze the actual practices of particular sciences in order to figure out the best ways of learning about the world, rather than laying down principles of "scientific method" from on high.

In contrast, Muslim philosophical reflections on science have been defensive, isolationist, and theological. They have been concerned with setting limits and protecting intellectual territory. In doing so, they have paralleled the most obscurantist tendencies in the Western philosophical tradition. To a certain extent, this is understandable, even hard to avoid. After all, the more ambitious, expansive version of science in Western intellectual life has made progress at the expense of supernatural views. It has become increasingly harder to defend realities that transcend nature without resorting to protective philosophical gamesmanship. And so, as Christian conservatives are quick to complain, Western intellectual culture has become deeply colored by naturalism, not just in science but in other areas as well.[50]

The Muslim adjustment to modern science cannot be just a matter of adopting more liberal views, reinterpreting sacred sources, and refraining from challenging science. The problem, as Muslim thinkers who have observed religious developments in the West are well aware, is that even when liberal religion becomes less ambitious about describing the world, science does not curb its own big-picture ambitions. In Western intellectual life, religion has continually retreated while secular forms of knowledge have gained ground. Muslim thinkers have long called for a revitalization of reason and philosophy in their tradition. They have even presented such a revival as a key to catching up with technologically advanced countries. Naturally, they desire an intellectually substantial faith as well. But they find that if they follow the Western route, an unwelcome secularization of thought looms. Like their Western counterparts, they have found it hard to steer a way in between adopting pseudoscience and bowdlerizing their religion.

A FUNDAMENTALIST ROAD TO SCIENCE?

Conservatives, even fundamentalists, have a reasonably accurate perception of the cultural difficulties involved in adopting Western ways of thinking about science. Natural science *is* part of a broader intellectual enterprise that has tended to support a big picture unacceptable to devout Muslims. And if Western intellectual life is any guide, liberal reinterpretations of religious doctrines and giving science more latitude does not solve the problem. It seems that if theology and science disagree about how the world works, it is always religion that must retreat. And even though liberal reassurances that science and faith have no reason to conflict remain the conventional wisdom, it appears that the broader, more ambitious naturalistic enterprise continually expands its intellectual territory.

In that case, the question is whether theologically conservative but also modern versions of Islam can eventually lead the Muslim world to reconciliation with science. After all, the followers of Said Nursi and similar movements produce pseudosciences mainly because they are impressed with science and acknowledge that science says a lot about the nature of our world. Moderate Muslims sometimes complain that their fundamentalist brethren, and especially many of their leaders, are unduly influenced by their background in the physical and applied sciences. This leads the fundamentalists to overlook the humanistic legacy of Islamic civilization and "values like human dignity, love, mercy and compassion" that "are not subject to quantification."[51] But if some moderates caricature fundamentalists as being overly enamored of science, perhaps there is a grain of truth in the accusation. If the cultural environment in Muslim lands will ever become more friendly toward science, this may well happen due to fundamentalists.

Fundamentalist Islam can foster a climate more conducive to science not only because it has a modern, technology-aware constituency, but also because of its very rigidity and uncompromising nature. Anthropologist Lawrence Rosen points out that Muslim culture and philosophy has lacked a strong sense of doubt:

> To doubt God was to doubt reason, and to doubt reason was to doubt the orderliness of life that God had shown possible. Whereas some Christians came to test their faith through doubt, almost all Muslims affirmed theirs by excluding doubt. . . . No comparable event [to Descartes and his radical doubt] has occurred in Arab thought, no separation of doubt from its immediate implications of unreason and unbelief. Yet one could imagine such a transformation taking place either as an unintended consequence of intensified religiosity or as a reaction to unaccountable events. . . . If much of the strength of Arab culture has come from its ability to explain new things in its own conceptual terms, then, ironically, a too ardent form of Islam—what Westerners call fundamentalism—could create so rigid a view of events that it would forge that sense of discrepancy within which the terms and implications of doubt

could take root. Something like this might have been intimated, not in the Arab world proper, but in Iran, where state-backed fundamentalism and the medical profession have clashed directly and where confidence in the claim of religion as a total explanatory scheme could erode in the face of doubt about its accuracy in describing such matters as human illness.[52]

Fundamentalism, in other words, could inadvertently create conditions more hospitable for doubt and skeptical inquiry, which are necessary for open-ended scientific investigation. For this to happen, however, fundamentalism must fail. Where fundamentalism enjoys significant political power, it adversely affects not just the cultural climate for science but also scientific institutions. Recently, this has been true even in the United States, where conservative Christian influence has done so far small but still real damage to American science.[53] Pious failure, on the other hand, can drive increasing secularity and thereby provide more room for the intellectual ambitions of modern science. It is no coincidence that Abdolkarim Soroush's liberal ideas about religion keeping its distance from science and government resonated in Iran, and these ideas may yet get a chance to be put into practice one day.

Still, failure alone is not enough. The most radical forms of political Islam have repeatedly faced political defeat and state-sponsored repression. In the few instances where radical Sunni Islamists have taken power, such as in Afghanistan and Sudan, they have not created examples other Muslims have wanted to emulate. The radicals have, in other words, failed. So in many Muslim lands, political Islam has taken on a moderate form that appears enthusiastic about popular democracy. Islamist intellectuals regularly celebrate cultural pluralism. And in today's urban, half-modernized conditions, many ways to be Muslim are available; indeed, Islamic identities are regularly commodified and expressed through patterns of consumption and media use. Islamist movements are not entirely used to pluralism; they usually have a narrowly majoritarian understanding of democracy. Still, though these movements tend to restrict religious options outside of mainstream Islam, a political Islam with any long-term chance of success has to accommodate the variety within today's Islam.

Islamists look to the past to legitimate current ideas about pluralism. And in the long history of Islam, it is easy to find acceptance of diversity within Islam and, to a lesser extent, tolerance for other monotheisms. For some, the experience of Muslim Spain has become a model for modern multicultural coexistence,[54] even if the historical reality is considerably more ambiguous. Such myths, however, illustrate a distinctly Islamic approach to cultural pluralism. Moderate Islamists typically envision pluralism as peaceful coexistence between confessional communities. In Muslim lands, religious minorities would exist as islands in a Muslim communal sea. Ali Bulaç, for example, proposes to extend the classical Muslim model by treating secular people as another quasi-autonomous community. The liberal secular state with universally applied laws, he correctly points out, is not neutral with respect to religion. It interferes with the liberty of conscience—with the ability of believers in communally oriented faiths to fully live according to their religious commitments.[55] Sociologist Ali Bayramoğlu also advocates "postmodern democracy" and cultural continuity against attempts to impose models of citizenship derived from the European Enlightenment. Postmodern democracy—an idea discussed outside the Islamic world as well as within—appears as a kind of negotiation between clusters of identity. It recognizes "group liberties" rather than requiring that citizens conform to liberal individualism.[56]

In other words, while the Muslim world is undergoing religious and political change, this change need not take a path similar to the European historical experience. As Europe became modern, communities became more fragmented. Individuals began to occupy a separable bundle of social roles, and personal identities and allegiances became focused on larger entities such as the state or the profession. Muslim thinkers feel the strain of modernization on their communities, but they are also determined to halt fragmentation at the level of confessional communities, resisting the sort of social atomization that leads to the stereotypical modern individual. Classical Islam developed in conditions of political instability. It affirmed religious solidarity but made it difficult to transfer loyalty to the state. Today, many Islamists look to develop this community orientation in a postmodern context. Their loyalties lie with the *umma*, which in many ways is a local religious community identity writ large. Muslims aspire to emerge from backwardness but to keep religion central, refusing to sacrifice community bonds to liberal individualism. So the failure of the most grandiose fundamentalist ambitions need not lead to a culture where science enjoys independence from religious concerns.

Now, it is not necessarily true that liberal societies provide the only environment for a flourishing scientific enterprise that regularly produces new knowledge. Germany before the First World War or late Russia under the tsars were not scientific lightweights; authoritarian nationalism can evidently foster scientific innovation. The Soviets did horribly in biology, where they let ideology dictate the course of research, but did reasonably well in physics, where the degree of interference was more tolerable. Nor is it true that societies that support a flourishing scientific community have a declining level of popular religious commitment. The population of the United States is remarkably religious, but the country is home to a strong scientific enterprise. The combination of religion and a community orientation, however, may be less hospitable to science. Nationalism, authoritarian or not, demands primary allegiance to the state rather than religious communities; the quest for national power and prestige can be a reliable drive for scientific and technological innovation. And the religiosity prevailing in the United States has a notably individualist character. Americans do not let their religiosity interfere with nationalist or economic aims; they handsomely support science as long as research can help produce better military capabilities and commercially exploitable knowledge.

Few people in any society will care deeply about science, let alone be intellectually engaged with it, but some societies are better at allowing science intellectual independence and exploiting technological innovation. Science is practiced within a very modern kind of professional community, therefore societies organized around religious and communal ties will likely suffer a handicap in science. Even if the naturalistic intellectual tendency of modern science could be discounted, the social environment within the scientific community discourages the kind of overt religiosity that can affect the work of science. And it is very uncertain whether Muslim cultures will develop in this more secular direction. Most devoutly Muslim intellectuals want to avoid it, and they enjoy plenty of popular support.

They might not succeed; political scientist Nuray Mert argues that Islamism is actually a force for secularization and that arguments about postmodern democracy are symptomatic of Islam becoming a cultural flavor rather than a comprehensive worldview.[57] It is possible that a modern split between the public and private realms will become more entrenched and that Islam will no longer be a significant source of legitimization of activities in the public sphere.

In that case, Islam can end up supporting a Western-style compromise between science and religion. Letting go of religion is not an option; even in intellectual circles, too much of cultural and ethical reflection is tied up with the tradition of Islam. Certainly popular commitment to old-fashioned, explicitly supernatural religion is not about to fade. Nevertheless, even in the Muslim world, it is conceivable that high-class, respectable religion will eventually settle into an evasive attitude that no longer challenges serious efforts to explain how the world works. We may yet see more Muslim theologians who specialize in moral reflection and individual existential therapy and whose vague conceptions of transcendent realities are hard to distinguish from merely symbolic expressions. In that case, as in most advanced Western countries, elite scientific and religious institutions can coexist in relative harmony.

Still, it does not seem so likely that Muslim history will follow the Western example, especially if political Islam does not end up as a clear-cut failure. Different Muslim countries may follow different trajectories, further fraying the sense of Muslim unity. Some countries may trade scientific weakness for religious and cultural stability. Or, more interestingly, the science practiced in Muslim lands may continue to develop in a more applied, technology-oriented manner, keeping more theoretical and basic sciences wrapped in a heavily Islamic packaging to make them less culturally abrasive. While modern science is an extraordinarily international enterprise, it may well be possible to sustain different emphases in different parts of the world. In any case, the future relationship of science and Islam largely depends on political developments.

NOTES

1. Jonah Blank, *Mullahs on the Mainframe: Islam and Modernity among the Daudi Bohras* (Chicago and London: University of Chicago Press, 2001).

2. Edward J. Larson and Larry Witham, "Leading Scientists Still Reject God," *Nature* 394 (1998): 313.

3. Rodney Stark and Roger Finke, *Acts of Faith: Explaining the Human Side of Religion* (Berkeley: University of California Press, 2000), pp. 52–55. See also Taner Edis, *Science and Nonbelief* (Westport, CT: Greenwood Press, 2006), chaps. 1, 7.

4. For example, Khaled Abou El Fadl, *The Great Theft: Wrestling Islam from the Extremists* (New York: HarperSanFrancisco, 2005).

5. Metin Karabaşoğlu, "Text and Community: An Analysis of the *Risale-i Nur* Movement," in *Islam at the Crossroads: On the Life and Thought of Bediuzzaman Said Nursi,* ed. Ibrahim M. Abu-Rabi' (Albany: State University of New York Press, 2003), pp. 269–70.

6. Seyyed Hossein Nasr, *A Young Muslim's Guide to the Modern World,* 2nd ed. (Chicago: KAZI Publications, 1994), p. 187.

7. Qutb's views are described in Roxanne L. Euben, *Enemy in the Mirror: Islamic Fundamentalism and the Limits of Modern Rationalism* (Princeton, NJ: Princeton University Press, 1999), pp. 67–70.

8. Much "intelligent design" literature is focused on combating this exclusion. See William A. Dembski, *The Design Revolution: Answering the Toughest Questions about Intelligent Design* (Downers Grove, IL: InterVarsity Press, 2004); William A. Dembski and James M. Kushiner, eds., *Signs of Intelligence: Understanding Intelligent Design* (Grand Rapids, MI: Brazos Press, 2001).

9. 'AbdulHamid AbuSulayman, ed., *Islamization of Knowledge: General Principles and Work Plan,* 2nd ed. (Herndon, VA: International Institute of Islamic Thought, 1989), p. 34.

10. Mevlüt Uyanık, *Bilginin İslamileştirilmesi ve Çağdaş İslam Düşüncesi* (Ankara, Turkey: Ankara Okulu Yayınları, 2001).

11. Mohammad Hashim Kamali, *Freedom of Expression in Islam,* rev. ed. (Cambridge, UK: Islamic Texts Society, 1997), p. 65.

12. Mehmet S. Aydın, *İslâm'ın Evrenselliği* (İstanbul, Turkey: Ufuk Kitapları, 2000), pp. 86–89.

13. Charles Kurzman, "Liberal Islam and Its Islamic Context," in *Liberal Islam: A Sourcebook,* ed. Charles Kurzman (New York: Oxford University Press, 1998).

14. Abdullah Alperen, *Sosyolojik Açıdan Türkiye'de İslam ve*

Modernleşme: Çağımız İslam Dünyasında Modernleşme Hareketleri ve Türkiye'deki Etkileri (Adana, Turkey: Karahan Kitabevi, 2003), p. 158. Euben, *Enemy in the Mirror*, pp. 112–13.

15. Muhammet Altaytaş, *Hangi Din?* (İstanbul, Turkey: Eylül Yayınları, 2001), pp. 76, 164.

16. Fatima Mernissi, *The Veil and the Male Elite: A Feminist Interpretation of Women's Rights in Islam*, trans. Mary Jo Lakeland (Reading, MA: Addison-Wesley, 1991).

17. Muhammad al Ghazzaly, cited in Raymond William Baker, *Islam without Fear: Egypt and the New Islamists* (Cambridge, MA: Harvard University Press, 2003), p. 101.

18. For example, Nasr Hamid Abu Zayd, as described in Farid Esack, *The Qur'an: A Short Introduction* (Oxford, UK: Oneworld Publications, 2002), pp. 143–44.

19. Fazlur Rahman, *Islam and Modernity: Transformation of an Intellectual Tradition* (Chicago and London: University of Chicago Press, 1982), p. 131.

20. Fazlur Rahman, *Major Themes of the Qur'an*, 2nd ed. (Minneapolis, MN: Bibliotheca Islamica, 1994), p. 79.

21. For example, Amina Wadud-Muhsin, "Qur'an and Woman," in Kurzman, *Liberal Islam*, p. 128.

22. Aydın, *İslâm'ın Evrenselliği*, pp. 21–22.

23. Abdolkarim Soroush, *Reason, Freedom, and Democracy in Islam: Essential Writings of Abdolkarim Soroush*, trans. and ed. Mahmoud Sadri and Ahmad Sadri (New York: Oxford University Press, 2000), p. 60.

24. Ibid., pp. 49–52.

25. Mohammed Arkoun, *Rethinking Islam: Common Questions, Uncommon Answers*, trans. and ed. Robert D. Lee (Boulder, CO: Westview Press, 1994).

26. Uyanık, *Bilginin İslamileştirilmesi ve Çağdaş İslam Düşüncesi*.

27. Mernissi, *The Veil and the Male Elite*.

28. Abou El Fadl, *The Great Theft*, pp. 156–57.

29. Some are described in John Cooper, "The Limits of the Sacred: The Epistemology of 'Abd al-Karim Soroush," in *Islam and Modernity: Muslim Intellectuals Respond*, ed. John Cooper, Ronald Nettler, and Mohamed Mahmoud (London and New York: I. B. Tauris, 1998).

30. Don Cupitt, *Is Nothing Sacred? The Non-realist Philosophy of Religion* (New York: Fordham University Press, 2002).

31. Lawrence Rosen, *The Culture of Islam: Changing Aspects of Contemporary Muslim Life* (Chicago: University of Chicago Press, 2002), p. 122.

32. Kamali, *Freedom of Expression in Islam*, pp. 93, 193.

33. David Shankland, *Islam and Society in Turkey* (Huntingdon, UK: Eothen Press, 1999), p. 170. My observations are much the same.

34. Rachid Al-Gannouchi, "Secularism in the Arab Maghreb," in *Islam and Secularism in the Middle East*, ed. Azzam Tamimi and John L. Esposito (New York: New York University Press, 2000).

35. John Keane, "The Limits of Secularism," in Tamimi and Esposito, *Islam and Secularism in the Middle East*, p. 34.

36. Baker, *Islam without Fear*, pp. 116–21. Abdou Filali-Ansari, "Can Modern Rationality Shape a New Religiosity? Mohamed Abed Jabri and the Paradox of Islam and Modernity," in Cooper, Nettler, and Mahmoud, *Islam and Modernity*, pp. 164–65.

37. Steve Bruce, *Religion in the Modern World: From Cathedrals to Cults* (Oxford: Oxford University Press, 1996). Steve Bruce, *God Is Dead: Secularization in the West* (Oxford, UK: Blackwell Publishers, 2002).

38. Shabbir Akhtar, *A Faith for All Seasons: Islam and the Challenge of the Modern World* (Chicago: Ivan R. Dee, 1990). Quotations from pp. 12, 13.

39. Feisal Abdul Rauf, *What's Right with Islam: A New Vision for Muslims and the West* (New York: HarperSanFrancisco, 2004). Yalçın Akdoğan, *AK Parti ve Muhafazakâr Demokrasi* (İstanbul, Turkey: Alfa Yayınları, 2004), pp. 78–80. Aydın, *İslâm'ın Evrenselliği*, p. 171.

40. Rıfat N. Bali, *Musa'nın Evlatları, Cumhuriyet'in Yurttaşları* (İstanbul, Turkey: İletişim Yayınları, 2001), pp. 294–96.

41. Aydın, *İslâm'ın Evrenselliği*, p. 61.

42. Ibid., p. 86. See also Azzam Tamimi, "The Origins of Arab Secularism," pp. 16, 26, and S. Parvez Mansoor, "Desacralising Secularism," pp. 90–91, in Tamimi and Esposito, *Islam and Secularism in the Middle East*.

43. For examples of liberal theologians enamored of parapsychology, see David Ray Griffin, *Parapsychology, Philosophy, and Spirituality: A Postmodern Exploration* (Albany: State University of New York Press, 1997); Michael Stoeber and Hugo Meynell, eds., *Critical Reflections on the Paranormal* (Albany: State University of New York Press, 1996).

44. Mohammed Arkoun, "Rethinking Islam Today," in Kurzman, *Liberal Islam*, p. 217.

45. Patrick Grim, "Scientific and Other Values," in *Philosophy of Science and the Occult*, 2nd ed. (Albany: State University of New York Press, 1990). Susan Haack, *Defending Science—Within Reason: Between Scientism and Cynicism* (Amherst, NY: Prometheus Books, 2003).

46. Taner Edis, *The Ghost in the Universe: God in Light of Modern Science* (Amherst, NY: Prometheus Books, 2002), chap. 9.

47. Taner Edis, "Origin of the Universe and Unbelief," in *The New Encyclopedia of Unbelief*, ed. Tom Flynn (Amherst, NY: Prometheus Books, 2007); Leonard Susskind, *The Cosmic Landscape: String Theory and the Illusion of Intelligent Design* (New York and Boston: Little, Brown, 2006).

48. Mark Perakh, *Unintelligent Design* (Amherst, NY: Prometheus Books, 2004), chap. 14.

49. Purely philosophical atheists can be as bad as theists in this regard; for example, see Michael Martin and Ricki Monnier, eds., *The Impossibility of God* (Amherst, NY: Prometheus Books, 2003). See criticism in the introduction to Kai Nielsen, *Atheism and Philosophy* (Amherst, NY: Prometheus Books, 2005).

50. Phillip E. Johnson, *Reason in the Balance: The Case against Naturalism in Science, Law & Education* (Downers Grove, IL: InterVarsity Press, 1995).

51. Abou El Fadl, *The Great Theft*, p. 99.

52. Rosen, *The Culture of Islam*, pp. 127–28.

53. Chris Mooney, *The Republican War on Science* (New York: Basic Books, 2005).

54. Iftikhar H. Malik, *Islam and Modernity: Muslims in Europe and the United States* (London: Pluto Press, 2004), chaps. 2, 3.

55. Ali Bulaç, "The Medina Document," in Kurzman, *Liberal Islam*.

56. Ali Bayramoğlu, *Türkiye'de Islami Hareket: Sosyolojik Bir Bakış (1994–2000)* (İstanbul: Patika Yayıncılık, 2001). See also Neera Chandhoke, *Beyond Secularism: The Rights of Religious Minorities* (New Delhi, India: Oxford University Press, 1999).

57. Nuray Mert, *İslâm ve Demokrasi: Bir Kurt Masalı* (İstanbul, Turkey: İz Yayıncılık, 1998).

CHAPTER 7

SCIENCE AT ARM'S LENGTH

THE PROSPECTS FOR SCIENCE

It is now centuries since Muslim elites were forced to realize that Europe's wealth and power had far surpassed Islamic civilization. Muslims have long been trying to adapt the new forms of knowledge that appear to be an integral part of Western success. Many generations have grown up learning that Islam is a scientific religion, that the faithful should seek knowledge even in China.

And yet, the Muslim world continues to lag in science. To correct this situation, many Muslims look to the past, thinking that they need to revive a golden age when Islamic science was strong and vigorous. But such myths only obscure the important differences between modern science and medieval intellectual pursuits. Today, devout Muslims tend to embrace technology but keep science at arm's length. Culturally, a scientific outlook has been hard to absorb, therefore many Muslims wrap science in protective layers of pseudoscience. Large numbers of the faithful are convinced that the Quran contains miraculous hints of modern discoveries. Muslims, even reasonably well-educated Muslims, overwhelmingly reject Darwinian evolution. After all, theories such as evolution do not sit comfortably with the common Muslim perception that our world is obviously designed by a higher intelligence. And most important, Muslims tend to view natural science as a pragmatic, nontheoretical, fact-collecting activity that exists in glorious harmony with literal-minded faith. Among more sophisticated Muslim thinkers, many who approach science from a social scientific or philosophical perspective do no better, getting lost in postmodern labyrinths and fantasies of Islamizing science.

Now, I do not want to suggest that the relationship between science and Islam is one of ceaseless conflict. Most scholars and scientists from a Muslim background work within the mainstream of modern intellectual life. More than a few of them think of themselves as faithful Muslims, identifying with Islamic civilization and adopting a more liberal interpretation of their religion. Nevertheless, Muslim lands have been very hospitable to a fascinating set of pseudoscientific ideas. Moreover, the popularity of ideas on the fringes of science regularly spills over into Muslim intellectual circles. As devout Muslim thinkers get more ambitious, trying to describe the world in distinctly Muslim terms, they also depart farther from mainstream science. So I think it is fair to say that there is a serious mismatch between the views of the universe and the intellectual habits associated with most varieties of Islam and the current state of science. On close examination, the illusion of harmony is not very convincing.

One reason for this, I suspect, is that although Muslim societies have begun to modernize, their cultural ideals continue to endorse a strong sense of community. Instead of individuals functioning in a network of weak, overlapping associations and allegiances, devout Muslims typically prefer a community of the faithful organized around strong personal ties. Today's versions of Islam continue to do well in providing adherents with a firm sense of identity and in nurturing the solidarity that comes from affirming a group's self-conception. They do less well in providing avenues to gain prestige from innovation and criticism. This problem is usually exacerbated by a lack of resources to dedicate to research and education. As a result, Muslim countries often have difficulty fostering an intellectual environment that allows much more besides political cheerleading and the text-driven scholarship of the ulama.

The many overt conflicts between a modern scientific picture of the world and traditional Muslim views also make it difficult to achieve harmony between science and Islam. But such conflicts could be ignored, or perhaps reinterpreted away. The communal orientation of most forms of Islam intensify the conflict, making it harder for science to gain autonomy from religion. Popular debates involving science are often really debates over what kind of modernity Muslims should construct for themselves. And in these debates, traditional Muslim culture has few resources to legitimate a scientific enterprise that may cast doubt on the claims of revealed religion.

I would like this to change. I am, after all, an Enlightenment rationalist. I grew up immersed in the Turkish secularist tradition, where our admiration for modern countries was always mixed with a degree of resentment toward our more traditionally minded compatriots for holding us back. The habits of thought that characterize a Turkish westernizer remain deeply ingrained in me. For example, recently a news item caught my eye, describing plans for a Malaysian astronaut to join a Russian mission to space in 2007. Speakers at a conference of scientists and religious scholars expressed hope that the Malaysian astronaut will be an inspiring example to other Muslim countries. That was not, however, their only concern. Saiyad Nizamuddin Ahmad, an Islamic studies professor in the American University of Sharjah in the United Arab Emirates, also discussed the challenges faced by a Muslim astronaut trying to pray in space when zero gravity and the difficulty of facing Mecca can cause complications. According to the news story, he observed that "when you're in a zero-gravity environment, you're floating around and as soon as you go into rukuk (a prayer position), that motion will project itself forward, and maybe you'll do a somersault or go into some other direction. So you're going to have to be held down or something." And then there are difficulties involving the performance of ablutions and ensuring adherence to Islamic dietary laws.[1] I found a little more in a Turkish newspaper online, describing how the assistant director of the Malaysian Space Agency announced that dealing with such concerns was as important as being able to send an astronaut into space, since they showed that being Muslim was no barrier to space travel.[2] My first reaction was to think what an absurd preoccupation this was for a country so intent on not being left out of modern technological achievements. After all, Westerners seem to manage without being sidetracked by minutiae of religious observations.

Indeed, in some ways, the story about the prospective Malaysian astronaut is not a bad illustration of the relationship between modern science, technology, and Islam. It is not any Muslim-developed technology that will bring a Malaysian Muslim into space. It is not even borrowed technology; a Malaysian will just hitch a ride with the Russians. None of the news reports identified any scientific work to be done by the Muslim astronaut. And so far the distinctive Muslim contribution to the whole enterprise is a public discussion of religious ritual. As is too often the case, cultural defense takes central stage—efforts to maintain the illusion of harmony overshadow the scientific and technological backwardness of Muslim countries.

So what can be done? My westernizing instincts keep drawing me toward the solution favored by Turkish secularists: make religion a matter of private conscience rather than public policy. Let science operate without religious constraints. And many others who give thought to the problems of Islam and the modern world also keep coming back to liberal and secularist views. For example, in one of my rounds of browsing through Istanbul bookstores, I came upon a short book called *Türklam*, which argued for an ultraliberal Turkish variety of Islam. The practice of Türklam, apparently, involves letting go of all rules and required rituals, adopting an individual sense of ethics, and downplaying heaven and hell. It reduces all supernatural beliefs to a very minor level, with the exception of belief in God.[3] Something like this Türklam would presumably invite much less conflict with modern science. And among the secularized elite in Turkey, such views can be reasonably popular. But this is a small segment of the population; moreover, it is a segment that is losing its status as an undisputed elite. Political and economic power are no longer closely tied to the trappings of Western culture.

In the end, I do not think that more secular approaches to Islam are viable alternatives. The Muslim world will not secularize in the foreseeable future. While I also do not expect that most Muslim countries will choose a close marriage between religion and government, it seems clear that public life will be partly regulated by appeals to Islam. Ordinary Muslims will continue to perceive the world in thoroughly supernatural terms. God, the prophets, and the holy book are in no danger of going out of fashion. In any case, it no longer appears so obvious that westernization and secularization are inevitable on the road to modernity. That has come to be seen as a mistaken idea, neither practicable nor particularly desirable.

A more traditional way to depart from the Islam of the ulama has been Sufism—emphasizing divine love and spiritual devotion rather than rules and observations. Sufism has allowed many Muslim thinkers to look beyond ritual obligations. I doubt, however, that the Sufi current in Islam can lend science much breathing space. Annemarie Schimmel quotes Maulana Jalaluddin Rumi, perhaps the best-known Sufi mystic, reflecting about Muhammad splitting the moon:

> The astronomer who believes in this miracle
>   should laugh at his own profession as well as at sun and moon,
> As everyone who has attended the school of Ahmad the *ummi*
>   may ridicule knowledge and art.

She comments that "in this verse, Maulana Rumi combines two miraculous aspects of the Prophet: the Splitting of the Moon, which shows the futility of man's scientific approach to nature, and the fact that the Prophet was *ummi*, 'illiterate.'"[4] Muslims traditionally believe that Muhammad was illiterate, which is more proof that the Quran is no mere human document. And today, Sufis continue to emphasize miracles and other signs that the world cannot be grasped by reason, that the way to truth lies in surrendering to the divine. The most noticeable influence of Sufism on Muslim views about science and religion is the way some modern Muslims look to alleged psychic phenomena to support their beliefs.

In today's climate of religious experimentation, there is every reason to think that modern varieties of Sufism will flourish. The mystical tradition will adapt, providing an alternative sense of community and a different emphasis within Muslim supernatural beliefs. There is much less reason to expect that Sufism will significantly change Muslim views of modern science.

The West Is the Best?

Exploring science and religion in Islam inevitably requires comparing Muslim views to views prevailing in more technologically advanced parts of the world. After all, Western countries, together with a few other highly modern nations such as Japan, clearly do a good job in creating and making use of scientific knowledge. There are good reasons why I prefer to do my teaching and research in American institutions rather than returning to Turkey. In the United States I enjoy superior resources, but even more important, I find a better intellectual climate.

I have to admit, however, that westernizers such as myself often get carried away when comparing Muslim lands with the West. Although I had spent a few summers visiting relatives when growing up, I had my first adult acquaintance with life in the United States when I started my graduate studies. And during my first couple of years in graduate school, when I visited Turkey on break, I tended to behave like a stereotypical westernizing Turk who brought up Western practices as the best way to solve problems. If Turkey suffered from soul-crushing bureaucratic procedures and government inertia, well, Westerners conducted their business a lot more efficiently and with a lot less pain. If the Turkish education system demanded too much rote learning and deference to authority, Western ways allowed more individual creativity and criticism. None of these observations were necessarily wrong, though I drew them with a very broad brush. But I must have irritated no few of my friends by starting every other sentence with "in America . . ." and going on to describe what I thought was a clearly superior way of organizing modern life.

So I should make it clear that the West is not necessarily the best. There is a mismatch between Islam and modern science, but this does not mean that the advanced Western countries provide the perfect environment for science or that Western cultures have completely adjusted to modern scientific knowledge. Indeed, I do not think that the mismatch is due to much that is unique to Islam. Any viewpoint centered on strong supernatural commitments, particularly conservative Abrahamic monotheisms, will likely have an uneasy relationship with modern science.

The United States is a good example, harboring fervid worship of the latest technology and ancient scripture alike. Malaysian worries about prayer in space are not so strange, considering that the American space program was primarily motivated by nationalism. In the context of the Cold War against godless communism, it was not that difficult to find religious rhetoric linked to the space race. Furthermore, if popular pseudoscience is symptomatic of cultural discomfort with science, it is notable that American Protestant creationists remain inspirations to their colleagues worldwide. The high-tech, intensely innovative environment of Silicon Valley is notorious for its hospitality to all varieties of New Age enthusiasms. Here, too, Rumi is popular—not because his poetry translates exceptionally well, but because mystical sentiment appears to have a therapeutic effect on stressed-out professionals.

More interestingly, secular developments in the West can also hurt the scientific enterprise. In the Muslim world, science suffers because it is an unavoidably elite activity in conditions where religious populism is an important support for social cohesion. Western lands also harbor anti-intellectual forms of populism, but in the long run, this has affected Western science less. Again, this may be due in part to differences between Islamic and Western attitudes toward community. In the advanced capitalist West, social critics have to worry more about the difficulty in sustaining human community under the conditions of Western modernity. Although the comparatively individualistic nature of Western societies lessens the ability of community-sustaining myths to interfere with science, it can also create problems for scientific institutions. For example, in the extremely individualistic United States, we tend to think that since the free market rewards technical innovation, scientific ingenuity should automatically flourish. But even though science and technology are closely connected, their connection is only evident in the long term. Basic science does not immediately lead to a technological advantage in the marketplace. If nothing else, science is inherently *public*—it cannot be extensively patented, classified, or otherwise controlled without disrupting the free and critical exchange of ideas vital for the advancement of knowledge. The scientific enterprise demands a degree of stability and institutional memory—it cannot be abandoned to the anarchic tendencies of the market.

So when I argue that Islamic civilization has not been especially hospitable to modern science, I do not want to suggest that the advanced Western countries are dominated by a truly scientific culture. Especially with fundamentalism becoming more visible in the United States, writers worrying about a looming decline of American power have begun to point to the strong populist antiscience tendencies within American culture.[5] Even the US scientific establishment appears to be losing its edge as it comes under pressure from corporate and religious interests.[6] Resurgent fundamentalism, however, is not the only source of cultural challenges to science. Discomfort with science also runs deep in religiously and intellectually more sophisticated circles. In 1994 Vaclav Havel, the playwright who became president of the newly liberated Czech Republic, gave a famous speech in which he endorsed scientifically dubious ideas concerning "the Anthropic Cosmological Principle" and "the Gaia Hypothesis." He did not pick out these somewhat New Age notions at random. Havel and many other intellectuals think that the world as described by modern science lacks the essential ingredient of meaning. Science, the arbiter of truth in a technological civilization, can make us lose sight of a transcendent spiritual reality. Havel declares that

> the relationship to the world that the modern science fostered and shaped now appears to have exhausted its potential. It is increasingly clear that, strangely, the relationship is missing something. It fails to connect with the most intrinsic nature of reality and with natural human experience. It is now more of a source of disintegration and doubt than a source of integration and meaning. It produces what amounts to a state of schizophrenia: Man as an observer is becoming completely alienated from himself as a being.
>
> Classical modern science described only the surface of things, a single dimension of reality. And the more dogmatically science treated it as the only dimension, as the very essence of reality, the more misleading it became. Today, for instance, we may know immeasurably more about the universe than our ancestors did, and yet, it increasingly seems they knew something more essential about it than we do, something that escapes us. The same thing is true of nature and of ourselves. The more thoroughly all our organs and their functions, their internal structure, and the bio-

chemical reactions that take place within them are described, the more we seem to fail to grasp the spirit, purpose, and meaning of the system that they create together and that we experience as our unique "self."[7]

I remain an Enlightenment rationalist; I think that sophisticated Havel-style complaints about science are no less mistaken than those made by more conservative religious figures. Nevertheless, I do not want to set this discomfort with science aside, noting only that Muslim responses to science have powerful parallels in the Western world. Yes, the idea that there is some humanly significant meaning written into the fabric of the universe is very likely mistaken. Still, both Muslim and Western critiques of modern science are also rooted in some serious practical and cultural difficulties presented by science. To begin with, many of our modern-day problems cannot be solved by a quick technological fix. Many of these, such as environmental degradation, are themselves the result of how we have constructed technological civilization.

There are also less urgent but perhaps even more intractable problems. Human nature seems much more attuned to religious ways of thinking than to modern science. It is no surprise that many people from very different cultures feel that some things are missing in the universe as described by modern science—just those things that give life meaning and help build a moral community. And just reinterpreting the old stories is not good enough, since an intellectually ambitious scientific enterprise that adopts a full-blown naturalism undermines all myths that help construct a moral perception of the universe. Hence, I suspect that all civilizations that sustain a broader range of human concerns than those of a narrowly focused scientific community must keep science at arm's length. All cultures must try to use science for their own ends while containing the threat science poses to the socially meaningful myths that frame their ways of life.

From this perspective, it is not so easy to pronounce the West a model of success while Islam lags behind. Muslims have been less able to harness science for their use, which is certainly a handicap. But also, compared to the West that was once Christendom, Islam has done better in containing the culturally corrosive aspects of science. So

Islam's response to modernity incorporates some advantages in cultural reproduction as well as the obvious handicaps. I am not sure which civilization will prove more successful in the long term.

ENLIGHTENMENT'S END

Turkish secularists have usually believed in progress. The modern world advances, and one has to try to move along or be left behind. When we object to some traditional practice, such as women veiling themselves, we are liable to exclaim that it is incredible that people still do such things in this day and age. The path of progress has not always been clear—it could be toward socialism, democratic capitalism, or perhaps something else—but we have typically thought that there was a way forward, away from the practices of mullahs or dervishes.

Lately, secularism and the ideals of progress derived from the European Enlightenment have become harder to defend. They never took root among the Turkish population, beyond a small elite. Today's secularists have been reduced to looking beyond the ordinary political means of debate and persuasion. Some believe that the military should prevent popular Islamism from completely taking over the state. Others hope that Turkey will eventually join the European Union, irrevocably committing the country to the secular, liberal democratic standards of Europe. Secular elites hope that somehow they will retain their privileged position, even if much of the Turkish public continues to reject the Enlightenment political culture that the secularists present as the only legitimate modern option.

Again, my personal sympathies are with Enlightenment ideals. My interests and my way of life are inseparable from a liberal democracy, secular government, and a high degree of intellectual autonomy for the scientific community and elite intellectual institutions in general. But I can no longer be confident that my position represents progress toward a universally acceptable goal. Nowadays I tend to agree with John Gray that there is no one way of life demanded by reason and that trying to negotiate a peaceful coexistence between incommensurable ways of life is a more realistic goal.[8] I have not abandoned my interests, and I remain convinced that the scientific form of rationality is the best way of understanding our world. But I cannot claim that my Enlightenment rationalism is a universal way of life that should compel the allegiance of every rational person.

What, then, of Muslim secularists, dissidents, and reformers? When a well-known critic such as Ayaan Hirsi Ali, for example, writes about the suffering of women under traditional Islam, I still respond, even as I worry that such legitimate concerns may be hijacked by Western conservatives intent on their own culture wars. Acknowledging that varieties of Islam can be compelling ways of life does not mean that I think ethical critiques of Islam are futile. I would like the secular forms of life that I prefer to become more available to Muslims. I am not, however, so sure about appeals to progress. Deploring the condition of Muslim women, Ali says that Muslim culture is behind the times, and that Muslim progress demands increasing individualism and westernization.[9] I certainly would not mind if an individualistic trend were to take hold, though I doubt that devout Muslims will choose such a path themselves. But I also think that Enlightenment rationalists have to acknowledge that Enlightenment values are not universal. Liberal, secular societies are not the only way for reasonable people to live together—liberalism might not even be the best way to peacefully manage conflict between different communal cultures. Science, I think, would flourish best if the influence of conservative Islam were to recede. But I do not want to pretend that scientific accomplishment comes without significant social and cultural costs. A committed Muslim might reasonably decide that these costs are too high.

So, in the end, I have to concede a lot to postmodern views of life in our late modern times. Coming from the westernizing tradition, I perhaps should have concluded my discussion of science and Islam with a ringing exhortation in favor of science and reason, in the best style of the Enlightenment. My personal interests still incline me in this direction, but I also find that I am rather ambivalent.

Yet there is little satisfaction in falling back upon a superficial cultural relativism, giving all different cultures equal standing. Science, after all, does seem to converge upon the best available descriptions of our world. Although Enlightenment ambitions for a universal morality and politics seem dubious, science is the one enterprise where Enlightenment universalism is a spectacular success. And that is a problem, since even if we abandon dreams of a universal way of life, not every way of life can sustain science. Not every culture can generate and use genuine knowledge effectively. It might have been best if Muslims were able to set their own agenda, independent of Western modernity. But progress in science and engineering is very real. Due in no small measure to technological backwardness, Muslims today always have to react to Western developments.

So perhaps a better way to describe the relationship between science and religion in Islam today would be as a search for balance. Muslims are looking for a balance between moral clarity and critical inquiry, between social stability and technological power. The uneasy relationship between science and Islam today—the strength of pseudoscientific notions, the priority of cultural defense—comes about as Muslims negotiate these tradeoffs. If the Islamic world reaches any sort of equilibrium, it is likely to be different from the Enlightenment ideal or any Western model. I hope that Muslims will achieve a balance that allows more scope for genuine inquiry but still preserves the generosity of spirit that Muslim cultures at their best have been able to encourage.

Meanwhile, the Muslim experience with science is also relevant to the international scientific community, though it is largely based in the more secular West. The internal ethic of science cultivates a regard for criticism and the pursuit of even inconvenient truths. But as any robust social enterprise should, science also inspires allegiance to itself. Scientists care deeply about the status and general health of scientific institutions. These two tendencies—valuing intellectual truth and caring for the institutional interests of science—do not always reinforce each other. Evolutionary science, for example, can challenge socially important beliefs, thereby eroding support for scientific institutions. It then becomes tempting to think that any friction between science and religion is due to misunderstandings and that a deeper harmony prevails otherwise.

So values encouraged by the scientific enterprise can come into conflict, particularly if, as I think is the case, there are no spiritual realities that can anchor hopes such as those expressed by Vaclav Havel. The world as understood by today's science is so counterintuitive, so radically unanthropomorphic that close ties to religion and social morality can only constrict the scientific imagination. But scientists cannot insulate themselves from the societies they live in. So in the scientifically advanced West, we have our own illusions of harmony, our own myths that help us strike a balance. We have not eliminated the tension between science and socially significant myths. Eventually, we may achieve a balance that requires fewer illusions. But we cannot expect that everyone will call this progress.

NOTES

1. "Muslim Nations Urged on Space Exploration," *New York Times* online, April 25, 2006. Quotation from "Muslim Countries Urged to Reach for the Stars," Yahoo News online, April 26, 2006, based on an AFP report.

2. "Malezyalı astronot uzayda nasıl namaz kılacak," *Hürriyet* online, April 28, 2006.

3. Erdem Alptuna, *Türklam: Yeni Bir Yaşam Biçimi ve Felsefesi* (Ankara, Turkey: Arkadaş Yayınevi, 2005).

4. Annemarie Schimmel, *And Muhammad Is His Messenger: The Veneration of the Prophet in Islamic Piety* (Chapel Hill: University of North Carolina Press, 1985), p. 71.

5. For example, Kevin P. Phillips, *American Theocracy: The Peril and Politics of Radical Religion, Oil, and Borrowed Money in the 21st Century* (New York: Viking, 2006).

6. Chris Mooney, *The Republican War on Science* (New York: Basic Books, 2005).

7. Vaclav Havel, "The Need for Transcendence in the Postmodern World," http://www.worldtrans.org/whole/havelspeech.html (accessed December 4, 2006).

8. John Gray, *Two Faces of Liberalism* (New York: New Press, 2000).

9. Ayaan Hirsi Ali, *The Caged Virgin: An Emancipation Proclamation for Women and Islam* (New York: Free Press, 2006).

INDEX

253